The Lantern of History

Essays in Honour of
Jeremy Black

The Lantern of History
Essays in Honour of
Jeremy Black

Edited by Ric Berman and
William Gibson

The Old Stables Press
2020

Copyright © The Old Stables Press

The right of the editors and contributors to be identified as the authors of
this work has been asserted in accordance with the Copyright, Design and
Patents Act, 1988

First published 2020 in the United Kingdom
The Old Stables Press, Goring Heath, Oxfordshire, RG8 7RT
theoldstablespress@gmail.com

British Library Cataloguing in Publication Data
A CIP catalogue record for this book is available from the British Library

Library of Congress Cataloguing in Publication Data
Berman, Ric & Gibson, William
The Lantern of History: Essays in Honour of Jeremy Black

ISBN 978-0-9957568-4-7

Europe – History – Modern
UK – History - Modern

I grope my way through a dense fog of ignorance and no lantern of history goes before me to direct my path

— William of Malmesbury, *Gesta Pontificum*

Table of Contents

Contributors

Nigel Aston, formerly Reader in History, University of Leicester.

Jonathan Barry, Professor of History, University of Exeter.

Ric Berman, a former doctoral student of Jeremy Black and most recently author of *The Foundations of Modern Freemasonry* (2014) and *Espionage, Diplomacy & the Lodge: Charles Delafaye and The Secret Department of the Post Office* (2018)

Bruce Coleman, Senior Lecturer in History, University of Exeter.

William Gibson, Professor of Ecclesiastical History, Oxford Brookes University.

Bob Harris, Harry Pitt Fellow, Professor, and Tutor in Modern History, Worcester College, Oxford.

Colin Haydon, formerly Reader in History at the University of Winchester and a contemporary of Jeremy Black at Oxford.

Paul Lay, editor of *History Today* and author of *Providence Lost: The Rise and Fall of Cromwell's Protectorate* (2019).

Jeffrey Lee Meriwether, a former doctoral student of Jeremy Black and Associate Dean and Professor of History, Roger Williams University, Bristol, Rhode Island, USA.

Murray Pittock, Bradley Professor of Literature at the University of Glasgow and Pro-Vice-Principal at the University.

Andrew Roberts, a writer, historian and Visiting Professor at the War Studies Department, King's College, London.

Sir Steve Smith, Vice-Chancellor, University of Exeter.

Daniel Szechi, Professor of Early Modern History, University of Manchester.

Foreword

Sir Steve Smith, Vice-Chancellor of the University of Exeter

It is a great pleasure to have been asked to write the foreword to this celebration of the work of Professor Jeremy Black –one of the University of Exeter's most distinguished and successful academics. I have been Vice-Chancellor of Exeter for nearly eighteen years, and during this time I have witnessed History at Exeter go from strength to strength. Today, it is one of very best History departments in the country with an outstanding reputation for excellence nationally and internationally. Jeremy has played a significant role in this achievement and I would like to take this opportunity to thank him for his contribution and dedication.

Jeremy is one of the UK's most well-known and prolific historians, having published extensively across a broad range of issues as well as historical periods. He has authored over 100 books on topics ranging from his works on eighteenth-century Britain and military history through to the Holocaust, and even a book on James Bond. His commitment to public service was reflected in his work on the design of the Millennium postage stamps, for which he was awarded an MBE in 2000.

Throughout his academic career, Jeremy has been keen to bring his research to a wider audience, rejecting any kind of ivory tower view of History. The historical profession has unquestionably changed radically since his career began in the 1980s, and in many respects Jeremy has been a trailblazer. For instance, his distinguished works of military history brought attention back to a field that had started to fall out of fashion. This did not deter him but spurred him on to produce some path-breaking work. His original take on non-Western history demonstrated his willingness to look beyond the range of accepted historical narratives and find fresh perspectives.

More recently, Jeremy has engaged actively with debates about decolonising the curriculum in his characteristically questioning and sceptical manner. And needless to say, many students have benefited from Jeremy's inspiring, enthusiastic and challenging voice.

In 2015, Jeremy published a much-anticipated history of the University of Exeter. I for one was intrigued to see what he might find in the archives, and whilst the book was commissioned by the University, I decided early on that it had to be Jeremy's history, and not an 'official' one. And that is just what it was. Little did we know that our University history would be quite so exciting!

In my role as Vice-Chancellor, Jeremy's advice has been invaluable to me over the years. Personally, it is his honest counsel that I have appreciated more than anything. The University of Exeter is very proud of Jeremy's achievements and of his contribution to the University over many years.

Professor Sir Steve Smith
Vice Chancellor
University of Exeter

Jeremy Black

William Gibson

This book celebrates the work of Jeremy Black in the form of essays from some of his friends and colleagues. Jeremy has written over two hundred books, and we could have obtained at least as many pieces from the people who would have been willing to contribute essays. So this collection is highly selective, and seeks to represent only a fraction of the aspects of Jeremy's professional life, and of the friends who would want to celebrate his work.

We have also consciously not published this collection with an established academic press for two reasons: first, we did not want to have a narrow theme imposed on the contributors, which publishers tend to do with *festschrifts*; and secondly we didn't want the book to languish in a bookseller's catalogue for £100. By using The Old Stables Press, an enterprise formed by one of Jeremy's school fellows and former doctoral students, we have been able to invite contributors to write what they want and what we hope will interest Jeremy, and it also means that this volume will be available through Amazon and other outlets in paperback relatively inexpensively.

Jeremy's webpage describes him thus:

> He is a prolific lecturer and writer, the author of over 100 books. Many concern aspects of eighteenth century British, European and American political, diplomatic and military history but he has also published on the history of the press, cartography, warfare, culture and on the nature and uses of history itself.

I am not sure that this entirely captures Jeremy's work.

© David Smith

Andrew Roberts, in the December 2008 issue of *Standpoint* magazine, referred to him as:

> Jeremy Black, the Professor of History at the University of Exeter, ought to be a National Treasure, but instead is hardly known outside a few cognoscenti of history-writing… The sheer quality of his output, especially in the field of 18th-century studies, ought to have marked him out as one of our great historians, yet he is curiously neglected, possibly because of his quiet Toryism, innate modesty and horror of providing TV-friendly soundbites… Black is equally at ease with post-1500 military history, 18th-century UK and European history, international relations, cartographic history and newspaper history. He can also do *pointilliste* monographs when required, as *The Collapse of the Anglo-French Alliance 1727-31* (1987) proves. Black's sense of humour might count against him in some po-faced history circles. *The Politics of James Bond* (2000) might indicate a light heartedness not considered appropriate in a profession that all too often takes itself extremely seriously.

The article was accompanied by a cartoon by David Smith.

Andrew Roberts addressed the issue that we cannot ignore: quantity. Jeremy is a man of quantity, and this is one of the things for which he will be remembered. But, as Jeremy himself says, the issue of quantity is irrelevant, the real question is about quality: are his books any good? Here, there is no doubt that Jeremy's work is superb and of enduring worth.

Jeremy has recently written of his decision <u>not</u> to write some specific books: a history of projectiles in warfare ('not interested'), a history of the War of Spanish Succession ('nothing new to say') and a history of sex ('beyond me, but my excuse was that only a woman or a homosexual male would be sufficiently politically correct'). He conceded that he lost enthusiasm for a book on the world in the eighteenth century because of the scale of the secondary reading involved. And he chose not to write a book on the War of the Polish Succession because he said 'it would only interest a crowd in a telephone kiosk'. When interviewed for the post at the University of Exeter, Jeremy was asked the fatuous question: what are your plans for the next five years. His response was that he had none because he might be knocked down in the street by a bus. 'That was how I conducted my life' he commented, 'there is no point in leaving unfinished works while striving for transient would-be perfection. Write good books, to time and agreed length. Leave the 'perfect', definitive work to unfinished dreamers, or should I say poseurs.'

And the 'good' work has been pretty impressive. As Ciro Paoletti wrote:

> I'm always amazed by the wideness of [Jeremy's] culture and by [his] unique ability in digesting and resuming so clearly and so well all these different aspects, allowing every reader to properly understand them: Masterful!

John Bew has recently written of Jeremy's *Military Strategy a Global History*:

> Jeremy Black is one of Britain's foremost historians and a world leader in the subject of military strategy. He has expanded his purview to the global story of strategy in a bold and imaginative study.

Is there a 'Black thesis'? —Certainly in the field of diplomatic and foreign policy in the eighteenth century Jeremy's work has revolutionised our view of how Britain saw and dealt with the world, and the world saw Britain. But there are other 'Black theses', among them: that maps can represent how we view the past; that military history has been unduly narrow and should be a much more capacious and contextualised field; that contemporary history has a legitimate role to play in historical and political debates (Jeremy is after all the author of *A History of Britain: 1945 to Brexit* (2017), *War Since 1990* (2009), *Altered States: America Since the 1960s* (2006), and *Britain Since the Seventies* (2004)), that counterfactual history has its place and function (see for example Jeremy's *What if? Counterfactualism and the Problem of History* (2008)) and that leading figures, of whom he had been a biographer [including Pitt the Elder, George III, George II and Walpole], deserved significant re-evaluation.

In his work, Jeremy has not shied away from controversy, indeed some of his work has been deliberately provocative. Phillip Larkin and Henry de Montherlant claimed that 'happiness writes white'; Jeremy might have equally asserted that conformity writes white in history. His books on slavery, the Holocaust, universities and Britain's recent history do not avoid tough questions, nor do they duck interpretations which may not be fashionable but are replete with logic and good judgement. This is because they are rooted in the primary sources.

They reflect the past as it was, not how people today might want it to have been. In the current climate in higher education such courage is rare; fashion in academic 'discourse' is a powerful force and too few academics have stood against its gravitational pull. But in this, as in much of Jeremy's work, independence of thought and spirit have been guiding principles; and these are principles that have stood Jeremy, and the discipline of history, in good stead.

Perhaps the most remarkable thing about Jeremy's output, something that people who don't know Jeremy can't quite believe, is that he doesn't use a computer. Hand-written, his manuscripts travel to Durham, where Wendy Duery, his long-standing secretary, types them and formats them for publishers. In some respects, publishers and readers might breathe a sigh of relief that he does not type. One can only imagine his output if he did.

Those of us on Jeremy's email circulation list know of the extent of his range of speaking engagements. He often speaks at a couple of dozen events a year, from lectures in schools, local history associations and societies, literary and history festivals, to academic conferences and seminars; and he does this across Britain and the world.

Much of this is poorly paid, or not paid at all, and travel arrangements and hospitality are sometimes rudimentary. His willingness to take on these activities is indicative of Jeremy's sense of a wider duty to the historical profession and to the general public.

Quantity is also a factor in some of Jeremy's personal characteristics. He has a memory of prodigious extent and perfect recall. He has used it well: there can be no historian who has used and deployed such a wide array of archives and repositories. Are there any major European collections of manuscripts that Jeremy has not mined? He reads astonishingly widely, it is very rare that his friends have read books which he has not. As Anthony Seldon wrote of Jeremy, he is 'peerless in the History world for [his] breadth of scholarship'.

His lectures, given without notes, are a thing of legend. Not since A. J. P. Taylor has a historian demonstrated Jeremy's mastery of the art of lecturing without notes and always focusing on the issue at hand. To do this requires not just a capacious and superbly-functioning memory, but the self-possession and confidence to think on one's feet and formulate ideas with precision and clarity. Patrick Deane said of Jeremy he has:

> a skill in inducting your audience from attentive civilians to a familiarity at least with the loopholes and parapets of front-line scholarship, along the way to delivering your message in a manner which is seamless and inclusive...

Quantity is also an aspect of Jeremy's friendships. To quote John Gambold's words about Charles Wesley: he is 'a man made for friendship'. Jeremy embodies the eighteenth-century ideal of sociability, and he is keen to share his hospitality and home. Those who have attended one of Jeremy's parties in London or Exeter will know of his kindness and generosity. His students, both undergraduate and graduate students, speak extraordinarily highly of his capacity as a teacher and the welcome they have received from him in Exeter and elsewhere. On his retirement, one colleague wrote of Jeremy:

> Working with ... you makes me realise that there is a level above the humdrum, managerial, target-driven, work-load monitored, quality-assured, grant-captured, battery-farmed academic life whose attention is always focused on incremental improvements in the median. Knowing that some colleagues work towards (and achieve) more absolute standards of scholarship helps put the rest of it in its proper perspective.

From the very back of a lecture theatre, the bookshelf, on the page, or from other far distance, Jeremy might appear a formidable, even a forbidding, character. But this view cannot be sustained when one has seen him any closer. He is essentially a kind and generous man.

Sometimes blunt, always honest, he is occasionally intolerant of foolishness, but no more so than the rest of us.

He is also a force of nature of prodigious energy, willpower and determination. These characteristics can appear intimidating, but they are tempered by forbearance and tolerance. Jeremy is also great fun. He has an impish sense of humour and it if difficult to spend much time with him without laughing and enjoying yourself.

As Colin Haydon indicates in his recollections of Jeremy, there are those who envy his talents and achievements, such is academic –and other walks of– life. Henry Kissinger (or was it, Wallace Sayre?) claimed that 'academic politics are so vicious because the stakes are so small.' And recognition of Jeremy by academia, at least in Britain, has been marked by a pettiness and spite that is alien to the man himself. It can only be a reproach to the British Academy that Jeremy is not a fellow.

Jeremy's open Conservatism undoubtedly plays a part, but this is shocking; it seems unlikely that most of the great historians of the past –Gibbon, Stubbs, Acton, Macaulay- would have been sufficiently liberal or progressive to be elected to the British Academy today. It is dispiriting to find a national academy that utterly lacks the confidence to include men of greater talents with whom its officers might differ. Until that changes, the British Academy can only remain a modern Blefuscu. And Jeremy refuses to 'trim' his views. His problems in publishing *Imperial Legacies* were in part due to an unwillingness to accommodate the political correctness of a publisher; and his *History of the British Isles* found a new publisher because he 'could stimulate a zeal for Irish nationalism.'

It would be an omission in an introduction to this *festschrift* not to refer to Sarah, who has silently aided this project and supplied the frontispiece. Of course, Sarah has been Jeremy's partner and anchor throughout their life together. Her profound contribution to Jeremy's success should be acknowledged as should those of Tim and Pippa in framing Jeremy's professional life in a happy home. Without that security and fastness, Jeremy's work would undoubtedly have been diminished.

On first meeting Jeremy Black: Oxford 1978-80

Colin Haydon

I remember my first meeting, in 1978, with Jeremy almost to the second, certainly to the minute. I was reading a bound collection of eighteenth-century newspapers in the south-east corner of the Bodleian's Upper Reading Room, overlooking Hertford College, when Jeremy, noticing the distinctive volume, descended on me, and, wrapping an arm around my shoulders, asked, perhaps demanded, what I was researching. Given the place, the image of Lewis Carroll's monstrous crow came to mind. But, as I discovered, the crow had remarkable plumage.

How rare, indeed exotic, that plumage was I quickly heard from friends who had studied at Cambridge contemporaneously with Jeremy. They spoke of the starred First; the sparring, displaying a range of unlikely knowledge, with visiting speakers; the interest in so many periods. And trickles came from Jeremy himself: the surprise of his interviewers at Queens' at the extent of his reading; his contempt for stock questions and approaches ('Why not study the *pacification* of the Catalans?').

The same merits were displayed at Oxford graduate seminars. At one, an unwary speaker underestimated how much Jeremy knew about subjects related to the paper and his ability to make 'telling' comments on the paper itself. He retreated, gored.

Jeremy's capacity for work was tremendous, first in evidence, naturally, in the Bodleian and the Public Record Office. Then he worked in other archives, where he not only sought to uncover material for his thesis but also aimed to 'degut' collections, noting information that might prove useful for future projects. I became accustomed to mapping these visits from shreds of conversation and chance remarks. Jeremy's accountant of many years tells me that he likewise enjoys reconstructing Jeremy's travels from his receipts – now global travels, of course.

At Oxford, those who watched Jeremy at work commented on his ferocious concentration and the amazing speed at which books and manuscripts were mined for nuggets of value. One leading academic, meeting Jeremy on a Bodleian staircase, once asked why he wasn't working: enough said.

The breadth of Jeremy's historical conversation and thinking was especially refreshing when one was focusing on one's own, necessarily narrow, research. Jeremy evinced not the slightest personal interest in religion (though there were occasional swipes at enthusiastic excesses).

Yet he acknowledged its importance *per se* in eighteenth-century England —although that was frequently minimized by 1960s -and- '70s historians, who envisaged faith as a spume on fundamental economic and social developments or simply discounted religious commitment. His stance resulted from his appreciation of the huge number of religious works which poured from the English press under the Hanoverians -an almost casual anticipation of the research of Bob Tennant and other scholars in recent years.

It showed an open mind, and his determination to ground analysis on evidence. For, above all (and his own efforts bolstered the conviction), Jeremy maintained that the production of accurate history was best achieved by the sustained, gruelling investigation of surviving primary sources.

Although stressing the need for sound, pertinent methodologies, he was sceptical of -sometimes contemptuous about— certain fashionable or voguish extravagancies, ignoring historical contexts (the unthinking deployment of Clifford Geertz's Balinese cockfighting elicited something between a dismissive chuckle and a growl). Yet he liked probing, thought-provoking comparisons, between, for instance, the political crises provoked by the illnesses of Henry VI and George III. The range of his reading permitted him to assess the validity of a comparison properly.

I was also impressed by the clarity and precision of Jeremy's thinking. For example, how, through exhaustive and exhausting consideration of surviving records, it might be possible to ascertain accurately the real military capabilities of eighteenth-century states; and hence assess the wisdom, sensible or undue caution, or folly of a ruler's foreign policy. How healthy such mental efforts seem, in retrospect, when compared to the sloth of those, who, having imbibed loud-sounding theories, retreat to the examination of historians and historiography and choose to eschew locating and wrestling with the problematical, sometimes near-intractable, sources themselves. But, as Gibbon observed, 'precepts are easily obeyed which indulge ... the natural inclinations of their votaries'.

Jeremy's election to a Harmsworth Senior Scholarship at Merton was a fitting recognition of his abilities and promise. While at Merton, he regularly held parties at which one met interesting people and future scholars of great distinction -Robert Gildea, Ronald Hutton, Jon Parry (visiting from Cambridge) among them.

With hindsight, these seem like the forerunners of the many parties which Jeremy has hosted in London -at The Athenaeum, The Travellers Club, and many other locations- and at his home in Exeter. Sadly, there are some disagreeable memories of the period at Merton too -notably another research student snarling that Jeremy had secured the Scholarship only 'because of his contacts'. That too now appears a precursor -a precursor of the unhealthy jealousy which Jeremy's extraordinary talents and energy have sometimes unleashed during his career.

I was also somewhat awed by Jeremy's understanding of how the academic world worked: too often I was left feeling like a Sussex rustic ('They watch the stars from silent folds') encountering metropolitan sophistication. He knew the type of individual particular Oxford or Cambridge Colleges favoured; a good topic for high-table conversation (the bells of Heidelberg and Oxford); who would secure a fellowship (one -seemingly improbable– bull's-eye was especially impressive). His conversation could be alarming too. As university cuts deepened, he announced that we might well not obtain academic posts (and, one wondered, if he could not, who could?).

Before he left Oxford for Durham, I went for a walk with Jeremy around Christ Church meadow. By Merton's wall, he generously said that he would always be happy to publish something jointly with me. We have, in fact, never done that: given his stupor-mundi speed of writing, I feared my dismay, if not mortification, was likely to result from the attempt. But it was a kind offer, recalled after nearly forty years with appreciation.

Along with the monstrous crow, recalling our first meeting summons another literary memory. For Hertford's predecessor on its site was Magdalen Hall, one of the settings for J. Meade Falkner's short novel *The Lost Stradivarius*, a novel displaying some of the characteristics of M. R. James's supernatural stories.

In one of the Hall's rooms, the principal character sees the ghost of an eighteenth-century scholar (and much else) and experiences 'the profound self-abasement or mental annihilation caused by the near conception of a being of a superior order'. I suspect now that that probably summarizes a proper response to first meeting Jeremy. One might add that the novel's ghost seems to manifest 'some malign and wicked influence'. Jeremy's influence respecting historical scholarship, however, is very different.

His works are invigorating, incisive, challenging, and quite breath-taking in the scope of the subject matter, the chronological span, and the geographical range.

Enduring Much, Achieving More

Paul Lay

On 7 October 2010, Jeremy Black held a party in central London, attended by his many friends and colleagues, to celebrate the launch of his 100th book. A decade on, he has written many more, making him easily the most published living historian, one for whom the word 'prolific' is entirely inadequate.

His centenary of books was reached with *Britain, 1851-2010: A Nation Transformed*, which offers a rigorous account of the many changes Britain underwent, and endured, from the Great Exhibition to the earliest consequences of the economic crisis of 2008, which may or may not have contributed to the political crises that have held the nation captive over the last decade. The final chapter of this thoughtful, reflective study is called 'Contesting the Past', a vigorous challenge to our cultural amnesia, so evident in the final days before the General Election of 2019, amid a climate in which feeling trumps thought and a willingness to conform to the pieties of the day offers easier professional advantages than courage, honesty and historical method.

Black has often focused on what is now routinely dismissed a 'great man' or, as Diarmaid MacCulloch prefers, 'Big Beast' history, exemplified by Black's 1985 debut, *British Foreign Policy in the Age of Walpole*, born of his Oxford doctoral research. It also signified his deep, lifelong immersion in the history of the turbulent, compelling eighteenth century. It fed into one of his major achievements, the biography of George III in the Yale English Monarchs Series, which won acclaim for its insight and wide range of sources (Black has recently published a biography of the same monarch in the Penguin Monarchs series). Black has a deep affinity for cultural history, too, evident in *A Subject for Taste: Culture in Eighteenth-Century England*, which reflects his deep interest in aesthetics: Black lectures regularly on opera, for example, placing and explaining often ludicrous plots within their historical context. On a more prosaic level, though no less valuable, Black's textbook, *Eighteenth-Century Britain, 1688-1783*, has few peers for that period, and many undergraduates have benefitted from its clarity and instruction.

There are few members of *History Today's* advisory board who are as active as Black, a scholar committed to the ideals of public history and a firm belief that a liberal democracy, if it is to prosper, needs an engaged public sphere in which the past is present in discussion and debate. It is no surprise, given his record of engagement that, in 2001, he was awarded an MBE for the advice he gave to the Post Office on their range of historic stamps with which to mark the millennium. His efforts deserve greater recognition.

His prodigious output as a writer combines with his love of reading, nurtured first at Edgware Public Library, near his childhood home. It was not uncommon for him, he claims, to drop the occasional borrowed tome and drop it in the bath; a reason that he later gave up marking essays when bathing. A love of military strategy and in particular the map, found an outlet in Avalon-Hill wargames, concentrating on the Eastern Front during the Second World War, and on the Western Front in the First.

Black's family was hard-working and socially mobile, high achievers, even: his sister is a leading agent in the entertainment industry, and his brother is a property developer. Raising his own children led to one of his most engaging works (though Black calls it one of his 'lollipop' projects): *The Politics of James Bond*, in which he trawled Ian Fleming's novels and the subsequent films in order to better understand the febrile, paranoid politics of the Cold War, especially from the perspective of the West. His children, then teenagers, found pleasure in Bond, while for Black, typically they became work, objects of study and elucidation: so much so that the tax man allowed the books and videos to be claimed as tax-deductible expenses. Few opportunities to claim expenses elude him.

His benign, encouraging influence on his now high-achieving children, reflects his relationship with his own gently argumentative father, who encouraged his precocious son's love of the past, accompanying him to historical sites in Europe. Argument – history is an 'endless argument' said Leopold von Ranke, the father of the modern discipline – was grist to the mill of the young Black, who developed a passion for debating, still the best way to develop the dialectical skills of the questioning, open-minded historian that he became and embodies. He represented his school, the illustrious Haberdashers' Aske's, in debates, the perfect pursuit, Black claims, for a competitive but bookish rather than sporty adolescent, who was 'noisy but gawky'. Sceptical of ideologies of all kinds, Black still has what he thinks of as a 'debater's view of history', instinctively looking for alternative views, evidence that challenges the conventional wisdom. 'Humane scepticism' is his creed.

By the age of eleven, he was giving talks to the class – and has not stopped since. His teacher, the 'somewhat terrifying' Mr Carrington, even got him to mark his fellow pupils' essays – an entire set on the Crusades. No wonder Cambridge came as a disappointment by comparison.

His fondest memory of school, a harbinger of later professional interests, was a project on the Congress of Vienna. His teacher asked if anyone knew anything about the event and, typically, Black put his hand up and was assigned the role of Talleyrand, no less, the only non-voting delegate. The boys embarked on their own negotiations, the details of which were recorded in a diary. At the end, pupils were asked to compose an essay which would relate how their treaty compared to the original one. Despite his passive role, Black was, inevitably, able to influence the treaty negotiations; keeping Prussia out of the Rhineland, for example. Having sorted out the peace after the Napoleonic Wars, they moved on to the Treaty of Versailles, mirroring the original with their lack of success. Black was head of the Italian delegation; as the only skilled cartographer among the students, he managed to rectify the Libyan-Egyptian frontier along a line of longitude that gave Libya the Suez Canal.

His love of maps, a lifelong passion, meant that Black, who also enjoyed field work, considered geography as a potential subject at university, but he didn't think that his maths would be up to it: 'Inter-quartile ranges turned me off', he said. Geopolitics and historical geography, however, remain key interests. A polymath, Black was of that generation of students – he cites Ronald Hutton and the late Roy Porter among contemporaries – for whom the omnivorous acquisition of knowledge – any knowledge –was part of their very being. There is no point, Black has insisted, in limiting one's specialism to one field; the curse of the modern PhD.

Black was, like that other fine product of Haberdashers' Aske's, Simon Schama, an undergraduate at Queens' College Cambridge –

where he gained a starred first – and recalls fondly his Director of Studies, Jonathan Riley-Smith, the distinguished medievalist and a world authority on the Crusades.

Always highly literate, widely read in the canonic literature, Black considered transferring from History to English as undergraduate. Black might have been lost to History in other ways, too. Offered a job by the Bank of England in the Cambridge 'milk round', he was tempted by the security and certainty such a position offered. The Bank was even willing to defer a place for him so that he could complete a doctorate in three years. Black had no particular plan at the time but ended up at Oxford as a research graduate.

His deep knowledge of the eighteenth century set him on his path. Eighteen months after beginning his research, he was one of six candidates interviewed for a post at Durham in early-modern European History. Black believed his prospects were all but zero, but if he scraped an interview, he would at least gain a trip to Newcastle, with expenses covered, where he could examine newspapers from the time of Walpole.

The youngest and least-qualified candidate, Black was able to answer some difficult questions on Edmund Burke's views on foreign policy – on which he had published an article – as well as on French foreign policy. His omnivorous knowledge gathering paid off: 'a little bit about lots of subjects' rather than a lot about one. The interview committee wanted a lecturer who could range far and wide. No one does that better than Black.

Black is instinctively and unashamedly a Tory Historian, opposed to determinism and the inevitable, with no time for Whiggish teleology. Never one to accept the status quo, existing interpretations on their head, to hope that archival work will throw new light, and to provide support for a view of life that sees people and events as able to have an impact alongside the great forces that others focus on.

For seven months he taught at Aberlour House – 'an extraordinary place above the Spey that would have provided wonderful copy for Evelyn Waugh'. His first sight of the headmaster was of a man in waders, with a full-bore shotgun and two wet dogs, who announced himself: 'Toby Coghill. Sorry I'm late. I've been shooting ducks on the Spey'. At this isolated prep school which was a feeder for the austere establishment of Gordonstoun – a Calvary for Prince Charles – he cultivated an engaging style of instruction long before he held any university post.

Black's incisive, sometimes reckless, challenges proffered in comment pieces irritate more sensitive souls, though he contends that 'I don't set out to irritate people, or try to show that I am better than everybody else … but I clearly do irritate people by thinking for myself.' Black is very aware of how his extraordinary output is received, conscious that, among some historians, it is regarded as counter-productive; that he simply 'turns out one damn book after another'. It may come as a surprise that he was a relatively late starter as an author. He was thirty, well progressed on an academic career, before he published his debut.

From then on, he made no secret of his early ambition to have authored forty books by the time he turned forty. By the age of fifty, by then Professor of History at Exeter, he had stepped on the accelerator, and had some sixty books to his credit. It is a pedal that must have been replaced many times.

Has anyone, apart from the author, read all of Black's books? They are, he insists, like all histories, no more than interim reports, which inform and build upon one another, an ecology of learning and erudition. There can be no 'master narrative', according to Black, no definitive statement or last word on any historical matter.

Black regards himself – and is – a maverick, not least because of his location on the political right. TV history, though he does not oppose it fundamentally, is often, he judges, too simple and one-dimensional to make sense of great figures and complex events. It is worth reminding ourselves that Black was a global historian *avant la lettre*: military history, a persistent interest, tends, he thinks, to still focus too much on Europe and the West, privileges state-versus-state conflicts, is obsessive about weaponry and is reluctant to see naval and land conflict as dependent on one another. Take, for example, the growing emphasis in his recent work on military and world history. An accomplished linguist in the main European languages, Black, like so many western historians, has embraced other's translations of Arabic and Chinese sources.

Foreign policy, he insists, cannot be understood in isolation from domestic policy, or vice versa. As distant parts of the globe engage with each other more and more, Black feels it is increasingly urgent that people in the West know more and more about cultures other than their own. Most warfare in the modern world has not directly involved western powers, he points out, despite popular perceptions – or rather, misperceptions. Mutual misunderstanding, as we see the re-emergence of civilisation states, is a luxury we cannot afford.

Black is an inveterate traveller: he has lectured in most states of the USA and is a regular visitor to Japan. Ultimately, though, he is a man of the archives, never happier than when in the British Library. One gets the sense that he is still very much in love with London, his home city; though he protests that he cannot afford to live in the capital – unless, that is, one of his books becomes a bestseller.

Why is he so outrageously prolific? Insecurity is a factor 'I get depressed about my own abilities', which may come as a surprise to those who come into contact with Black's imposing presence, though this, too, may be an act of compensation.

He does concede that he is very bright, an intellect he flourishes in his theatrical lectures and talks. The money from advances and royalties is nice, too.

When it comes to writing, he is a Stakhanovite – not, perhaps, the most appropriate term for a man of his politics. There is never enough time for a man such as Black. If you take the London train to Exeter or back (Black doesn't drive), you may well see him correcting proofs, scribbling down notes, or scrawling his expenses. Yet he has a love/hate relationship with the act of writing: it makes him exhausted – hardly surprising given his remorseless output – and leaves his body 'incredibly tense'.

New technology, though kept at arms' length for some time, has now been embraced, though one can be grateful that such a brave and contentious figure spurns social media. His friends and colleagues are privileged to belong to the circle of his correspondents, who receive with regularity his emails outlining robust thoughts on academia's plight, a steady flow of reviews and memories of his fascinating and highly productive past. Just occasionally his self-doubts, anxieties and insecurities emerge, to reveal more fully the human face.

Only a few periods are beyond his ken. When a bookshop in Texas displayed a selection of his *oeuvre*, he had to point out that a volume on Ancient Sumerian Poetry was the work of another Jeremy Black.

While thinking of Jeremy, I was researching a figure who, for some reason resonated as I collected thoughts on my friend and colleague. That figure is Daniel O'Neill: Irish exile, Royalist plotter and architect of the Industrial Revolution. A man of courage, principle and remarkable self-belief, who fought for many years in a hostile environment, to emerge redeemed as his enemies scattered.

When Cromwell's army landed in Ireland on 15 August 1649, there was relatively little opposition to his conquest. James Butler, Marquess of Ormond, had been savagely defeated at the Battle of Rathmines just two weeks before. The vanquished royalist leader was forced by 'cruel necessity' to combine with the principal player in Ulster and long-time exile, Owen Roe O'Neill. Daniel O'Neill, nephew of Owen Roe, was sent to conclude the new negotiations. He met his uncle at Ballykelly, twelve miles east of Derry, and found him surprisingly keen to cement the alliance, which was still undrafted, not least to relieve Drogheda from Cromwell's grim vice.

Owen Roe's apparent enthusiasm was tempered by physical ailment: a 'defluxion' in his knee, which meant he was reduced to travelling by litter. While he travelled precariously and in starts, Owen Roe advised Ormond, sensibly, to avoid direct engagement with Cromwell's forces. He did so in vain.

Daniel O'Neill – who was related to the earls of Tyrone, 'the shadow of a great name' – stood out among his generation. His father having recklessly managed the family's estates in Ireland, O'Neill, as a ward of the crown, was raised a Protestant in England, after which he served under Lord Vere among the English troops in the traditional military school of the States General. He became familiar with the politics of the Palatine, serving on missions to the titular Queen of Bohemia, Elizabeth, Charles I's sister, even being allowed to greet the Elector's brother Prince Rupert on his return to the territory. He had surprising reach and influence for a young, inexperienced Irishman with little more than a great name.

'They alone did their duty' was written of O'Neill and two fellow officers, following a rear-guard skirmish against the Scots under Leslie during the Second Bishops' War. He was for a while thought killed, but he had in fact been captured and treated 'handsomely' by the commander. O'Neill was set free on the king's wishes during preliminary peace talks.

He was to become an incorrigible plotter in the Stuarts' cause, long after the king's trial and execution, though his relationship with Royalism was curiously complicated. Archbishop Laud had supported the young man in his desire to reclaim his Irish lands, and 'restore to this gentleman that which is lost without his own fault'. The Earl of Strafford, Charles I's lord deputy in Ireland, took a different view: O'Neill was a 'traitor, bred no other, Egg and Bird as they say'. The loathing was mutual: O'Neill attended Strafford's trial, losing Charles I's long-term trust, though never forsaking his utter loyalty to the Crown.

His devotion to the Stuarts was total, despite the serial difficulties, despair and demoralization he would face as he sought to advance their cause. O'Neill, who had been implicated in the Second Army Plot to protect the king from parliamentary radicals, had escaped the Tower in 1642 in comic-book style. Wearing women's clothing, he had tied his bed sheets together and clambered out of his cell. Quick-witted and charming, according to Edward Hyde he was 'ingenious and reasonable in all things – in subtlety and understanding much superior to the whole nation of the old Irish'.

When all hope of Royalism in the three kingdoms was extinguished at the Battle of Worcester on 3 September 1651, O'Neill's existence became one of constant movement. It was he who passed information between Charles II, his sister Mary, Princess of Orange and Hyde, the exiled king's secretary. The young king knew nothing of his father's dislike for him: 'The king hath a good opinion of him', claimed Hyde. Three times he made it to England during Cromwell's rule, where the proximity of death breathed new life into him. He produced accurate and perceptive reports on the political situation there, noting, for example, that it was

Thomas Harrison rather than Cromwell who had sought the expulsion of the Rump.

His rapid rise at the exiled court in The Hague was aided no doubt by his much commented upon flattery and charm; Hyde had noticed that O'Neill was 'honest and kind to the Marquis of Ormond and me'. O'Neill, in turn, had wisely identified the pair of Old Royalists as the most able and hard-headed of the king's supporters.

He accepted the kind hand of providence at the Restoration: Daniel O'Neill, from the time he left the Tower of his own volition, disguised as a woman, had endured much and was to achieve more. The bravest and most brilliant of Charles's Royalist agents had fought for the king's cause for more than a decade. There were no questions over his loyalty. Though he did not enter the Lords – as an O'Neill, he was aristocrat enough – he gathered sinecures almost at will: he had interests in mining, an activity that would be the bedrock of Britain's Industrial Revolution; he gained a monopoly on the country's gunpowder manufacture and distribution; he became the warden of St James's Park and the commissioner for building in London. All helped to make him one of the richest men in the restored realm of a monarch he had served at considerable hardship and danger for so long and in such difficult circumstances, enjoying the fruits provided by a God satisfied with what he saw. O'Neill died in Whitehall, close to the centre of English political power, where a king had been killed, where a new regime of uncertain foundation and full of contradictions had lost the will of God, and where a king was restored, on 24 October 1664. Revolutions are sometimes the turning of a wheel to a realm restored rather than an empty rupture with the past.

'Always Look Up! Context, Complexity, and Passion in History Education'

Jeffrey Lee Meriwether

'Whenever you observe these buildings, you must remember to look up. Shops come and go, but as an historical marker, the first floor and above tell you the story.' I interjected that in Britain, the first floor is the equivalent of the second in the United States. But that mattered less than the fact that my students were now peering upward, already noting the flower boxes and knickknacks on the sills. We were in London, engaged in experiential learning and inquiring what made the British capital a 'great city'. Jeremy Black graciously agreed to speak to my students in return for a fee, 'lunch, and a good chat'. Once he had noted the building, Jeremy began to discuss the neighbourhood, in this case just off Piccadilly. He offered up the history, its impact, and current use. My students took notes and asked each other how to spell Piccadilly. More importantly, they thought about context.

In his approach to history, Jeremy Black consistently reminds us about the importance of context and the complexities of understanding. There is no straight forward, but there is clarity when greater understanding and appreciation are achieved. I learned that as a PhD student at Exeter, and I continue to do so with each conversation I have with Jeremy. In his *A Brief History of Britain 1851-2010: A Nation Transformed* (2010), Jeremy writes, 'I think it important to be frank about the difficulties of covering the past, about the choices made in what is covered, and how it is treated and organised, and about the degree to which others will take different approaches'.[1] This point is that which he made to my students: look up, expand your gaze; there is much more to history than meets the eye. History education is under pressure in the United States, with the liberal arts more generally losing enrolments to the technical and scientific subjects, notably engineering, architecture, and marine sciences. While seemingly undervalued, history is at the core of the liberal arts and is therefore human centred in its importance to education.

---

[1] Jeremy Black, *A Brief History of Britain 1851-2010: A Nation Transformed* (London: Constable & Robinson, Ltd., 2010), ix.

'History is both what happened and how we see it.'[2] Jeremy argues the manner in which history is remembered, and considered, ultimately can shape the way societies see themselves, the manner in which they mythologize themselves, and the actions they take in consequence. We know this in the moment, with fake news reinforcing confirmation bias, as the ugly, difficult truth challenging national myths is dismissed, leaving an opportunity for growth and progress wasted. When the students see flower boxes outside first floor windows, do they imagine the space is a business, a flat, or a space up for rent? The interrogation begins with looking *above* the ground floor, but there is more to it. Jeremy's students have been learning that for four decades. I am honoured to be one of them.

***

My first assignment for Jeremy required me to write up what was effectively an outline of an outline. I was new to the University, only just arrived in England, and had yet to be advanced to PhD candidacy. I handwrote the document and submitted it. Jeremy returned it promptly (via another student, Robert Johnson, now at Oxford), informing me that the process was worth neither my time, nor his if I was going to operate in this manner. I was embarrassed and angry, but also impressed with the fact that Jeremy was serious about the project we were to undertake. A history education mattered too much; tracking history's development was a deliberate act and would not suffer laziness.[3]

Such sentiment is standard fare in the field. On its ethics page, the Royal Historical Society sets membership expectations, stressing integrity in source citation, bias self-awareness, and openness about conflicts of interest. 'Since ethical standards are not constant, there is a need to eschew anachronistic value judgments when

---

[2] Ibid., 307.

[3] Another stand-out interaction with Jeremy came when on my way to a GP appointment. I received in the post a chapter I had submitted to Jeremy, who promptly read and returned it. I sat in the car park and opened the envelope, only to reveal a document covered in red ink and indignation. I could not spell in British English fashion, Jeremy stridently pointed out. Moreover, my scholarship was such that I was on the cusp of failing the whole endeavor. My GP later told me my blood pressure was elevated. He asked me if I ever exercise, if I smoke and drink, and if my diet was high in fat. In short, Jeremy Black put me on the map for high blood pressure. Thankfully, the effect was temporary. Another lesson learned.

investigating and describing the past.' With history's prevalence in popular culture, its themes dominating entertainment, including print, film, and television, the RHS argues that history's ethical treatment is more important than ever. Wider access provides more varied opportunities to do history justice *and* undermine its credibility.[4]

Greater popular access to the field was enabled by History.com, first appearing on cable television in 1995 (then as The History Channel). Early in my teaching career my students raved about the productions, some arguing it motivated them to pursue history undergraduate education. As a graduate student, I spent many hours watching the channel, as opposed to studying. Over the years, History.com developed more varied programming, and is known currently for its *Pawn Stars*, *Swamp People*, and *Ancient Aliens* productions. History.com also devotes pages to education in the shape of History Classroom. Here educators may access videos detailing city neighbourhoods, vignettes of World War II experiences, and study guides supporting America's past.[5] Writing for educationworld.com, Jason Tomaszewski encouraged teachers to engage History.com's educational resources exclusively, arguing it is worth their time to 'leave the network's shows alone'.[6]

Moreover, the majority of critics target History.com's wide-ranging programming as a sign of losing the plot, with the channel given over to low-brow entertainment. Even *The Bible* (2013), a topic with its own text and a mountain of historical scholarship undergirding it, literally chooses the path of lesser evil. As *The Guardian's* Alan Yuhas writes, 'the Bible doesn't work without its many strong women, but the [television] series keeps them on the margins. These decisions are aimed at making the show more immediately familiar to the conservative, American Christians, who apparently can't handle actors who don't look like them'. The series broke television viewing records, and Rachel Ray suggested it

---

[4] 'RHS Statement on Ethics', Royal Historical Society (12 January 2015), https://royalhistsoc.org/rhs-statement-ethics/ [accessed 8 August 2019].
[5] 'History Classroom', History, https://www.history.com/classroom [accessed 8 August 2019].
[6] Jason Tomaszewski, 'Site Review: History.com', Education World (2011), https://www.educationworld.com/a_curr/site-reviews/history.shtml [accessed 8 August 2019].

might have aired on the Disney Channel for all its sentimentality and over dramatization.[7] Complaint-board.com has a page dedicated to History, with viewers arguing the channel should dedicate itself to the history discipline, as opposed to the search for antiques (or 'garbage') or catching alligators.[8]

In truth, History, a cable channel viewers may watch only if purchasing a subscription package that includes it, is not the only place for the public to consume the past. Yet, as with all 24-hour programming and website access, there is ample opportunity to learn history by way of History.com. In his *Using History* (2005), Jeremy contends that academic historians ('part of a largely self-referential academic culture') have little interaction with the *popular* understandings of history, understandings ever further informed by current trends. Moreover, governments and political action are often informed by history, also through the lens of current events and themes. In the chapter 'Confronting the Past', Jeremy considers public apologies for former wrongs. He writes, 'The pressure for apology can well lead to a disproportionate account of the past.'[9] It becomes the classic case of history vs. memory, with contemporary, popular conceptions of the past legitimizing potentially under-informed, yet largely accepted understandings.

There is also the 'feel-good' effect of augmenting one's credibility by way of establishing a link to a cherished historical event. In the public mind, the effect is immediate and acute. *U-571* (directed by Jonathan Mostow, 2000), tells the story of an American effort to capture the Enigma machine in 1942. Absented from the story is the Polish analysis of an early Enigma device in the late 1920s, followed by code breaking several years later. It also left to the film

---

[7] Alan Yuhas, 'History Channel's The Bible Series is Worse Than Reality TV', *The Guardian* (25 March 2013),
https://www.theguardian.com/commentisfree/2013/mar/25/history-channel-the-bible-series-is-reality-tv [accessed 8 August 2019]; Rachel Ray, 'The Bible, final episode, History Channel, Review', *The Telegraph* (1 April 2013),
https://www.telegraph.co.uk/culture/tvandradio/tv-and-radio-reviews/9961605/The-Bible-final-episode-History-Channel-review.html [accessed 8 August 2019].
[8] 'The History Channel', Complaint Board,
https://www.complaintboard.com/the-history-channel-13129.html [accessed 8 August 2019].
[9] Jeremy Black, *Using History* (London: Hodder Education, 2005), ix, 91.

credits any mention of Royal Navy successes capturing Enigma devices in the years before the real American action in 1944 (then fictionalized back to 1942 in the film). Screenwriter David Ayer told BBC Radio 4's *The Film Programme* spinning this American tale was a mistake he would not repeat.[10]

In his review, journalist Roger Ebert labelled *U-571* 'a clever wind-up toy of a movie', the type of film that is effective, 'at least on a dumb action level'. His film autopsy, one in which he removes all the organs, is finished off with a nod to the history. Facts vs. Entertainment: the British win-'they pretty much did everything in real life that the Americans do in this movie.'[11] *The Guardian* made it clear in its headline: '*U-571*: You Give Historical Films a Bad Name'.[12] Academics seized on this production as well. Writing for the Society of Military History, U-Boat historian Tim Mulligan underscored Jeremy's point about public historical understanding as indicative of a society's current world view: 'This paradoxical blend of bad history and mass appeal may concern today's historical profession, but future historians may well be indebted to Mostow for his snapshot of American values and attitudes toward World War II at the turn of the millennium. If not, they will at least be in his debt for a good laugh and a renewed appreciation of *Das Boot*'.[13]

U-571 appeared on the heels of Tom Brokaw's *The Greatest Generation* (1998) and *The Greatest Generation Speaks* (1999), two books that fixed the righteousness of the American effort in the Second World War -and the Cold War- and applied a veneer of the sacred struggle to the new American myth taking shape after 9/11.[14] These albums of historical memory reshaped the American experience of the three middle decades of the twentieth century,

---

[10] 'U-571', Fandom, https://david-ayer.fandom.com/wiki/U-571 [accessed 24 November 2019].

[11] Roger Ebert, 'U-571', rogerebert.com (21 April 2000), https://www.rogerebert.com/reviews/u-571-2000 [accessed 21 August 2019].

[12] Alex von Tunzelmann, 'U-571: You Give Historical Films a Bad Name', Reel History (26 February 2009), https://www.theguardian.com/film/2009/feb/25/u-571-reel-history [accessed 21 August 2019].

[13] Tim Mulligan, 'Film Review: U-571', https://www.smh-hq.org/gazette/u571.html [accessed 21 August 2019].

[14] Tom Brokaw, *The Greatest Generation* (New York: Random House, 1998); Tom Brokaw, *The Greatest Generation Speaks: Letters and Reflections* (New York: Random House, 1999).

leaving no room for doubt in the popular mind. This reshaping was itself a part of a return to what Jeremy describes as an 'attractive, in the sense of both positive and readable, account of the national past' in the decades following World War II. The Vietnam experience challenged these readings, but the Reagan years reasserted their attraction.[15]

There is little entertainment value in critical analysis, at least in popular history consumption. Educators know the value of close reading and reflection in their classroom assignments, but as Elizabeth Elliott stresses in 'Why Read *Why Learn History*', easily obtained information from the Internet does not equate to students operating as 'responsible consumers of digital information'. Writing for *Perspectives*, Elliott's review of Sam Wineburg's *Why Learn History (When It's Already on Your Phone)* (2018) interrogates the daily grind of information delivery / student perusal of web sources / conclusions drawn.

The challenge, according to Wineburg's research, is that educators also sometimes find difficulty distinguishing between corrupted, misleading information, and sources of integrity.[16] It is the discernment of context that Black demands: 'we should expect more'. More specifically, when considering critiques (and critics) of the Brexit debate, Jeremy looks specifically at the setting of Brexit into the larger context of British imperial history. If historians justify their positions primarily by 'authorising by profession', as opposed to a solid grasp of context, intention, and nuance within the period in question, they are giving credence a pass-a luxury they never would allow their students.[17]

---

[15] Black, *Using History*, 177.

[16] Elizabeth Elliott, 'Why Read *Why Learn History* (When It's Already Summarized in This Article)?', *Perspectives on History* (20 August 2018), https://www.historians.org/publications-and-directories/perspectives-on-history/september-2018/why-read-emwhy-learn-history/em-(when-its-already-summarized-in-this-article) [accessed 27 August 2019]; see also Sam Wineburg, *Why Learn History (When It's Already on Your Phone)* (Chicago: University of Chicago Press, 2018).

[17] Jeremy Black, 'Academics Should Look in the Mirror Before Smearing Their Rivals', *The Article* (19 August 2019), https://www.thearticle.com/academics-should-look-in-the-mirror-before-smearing-their-rivals [accessed 27 August 2019].

Peter N. Stearns' 'Why Study History?' (American Historical Association website, 1998) answers the question, with references to enriching our own lives, moral understanding, and citizenship. He also stresses the developed skill of assessing interpretations in conflict. All of these elements are essential to practicing history, but the fact that a passage from Stearns' now 21-year-old piece is the primary content on the AHA site *currently* flies in the face of history's commitment to ongoing, contemporary research and thinking.[18]

More helpful is Paul B. Sturtevant's analysis of humanities, and particularly history-related paths followed by university graduates. The facts are encouraging: a history degree prepares a student for a vast array of careers (with almost half the graduates focusing on business, education, or legal) across the wage range, all of which require the types of skills teachable in history.[19]

Therefore, and as we know, studying history and learning how to think historically are fundamental to living as active citizens of the world. The value intrinsic to a history education, and specifically study-abroad experience, goes to the heart of training in the liberal arts. Additionally, learning to value the histories of other societies is enhanced by a student's understanding of their own past. Jeremy contends that Americans would do well to develop an appreciation of the struggle in which they engaged for sovereignty in North America. While Americans' myths tend to dismiss British troops and control as anachronistic and undemocratic, they also undervalue British strength, and therefore American fortitude, in the final victory in 1783.

In the same way Americans' historical touchstones lie centuries apart (Plymouth → Declaration of Independence → Civil War →

---

[18] Peter N. Stearns, 'Why Study History?', American Historical Association (1998), https://www.historians.org/about-aha-and-membership/aha-history-and-archives/historical-archives/why-study-history-(1998) [accessed 27 August 2019]; 'Why Study History?', American Historical Association, https://www.historians.org/teaching-and-learning/why-study-history [accessed 27 August 2019].

[19] Peter B. Sturtevant, 'History is Not A Useless Major: Fighting Myths With Data', *Perspectives* (1 April 2017), https://www.historians.org/publications-and-directories/perspectives-on-history/april-2017/history-is-not-a-useless-major-fighting-myths-with-data [accessed 27 August 2019].

World War II), so do the events of the republic's birth story miss out the essential details that truly bring the events to life, and provide a clear understanding of what actually occurred. Without the nuance, the path to victory is rather sparse (Lexington Green → Declaration → Yorktown).

The fact that the struggling would-be republic also had to develop skills for managing foreign affairs and sustainability are overlooked (has not the United States always been exceptional?).[20]

Not overlooked is the positive impact studying abroad can have on the student experience, especially that of undergraduates just stepping away from the shelter of family life. In 'More is Better: The Impact of Study Abroad Program Duration', Mary M. Dwyer considers the experience, time abroad, and longevity of impact study abroad programs have had upon students over a half century. More *is* better when it comes to time spent in country, language immersion, cultural and historical awareness, and perhaps most importantly, a love of learning.[21] Full-year experiences are by far the most valuable, but experiential gems can be found in the medium- and short-term programs as well. When Jeremy encourages students to look up, he is providing a short cut to wider learning, for 'look up' becomes synonymous with 'look beyond' and consider what meets the eye, and the context in which it is presented.

Such an approach is the one he takes in many of his monographs, explaining up front that his will not be the standard chronological analysis, but instead a thematic interrogation that considers people, ideas, and culture through and over time. Timelessness becomes the undertone, in the same way that a current shop front does not define the aged building.

---

[20] Jeremy Black, 'The Geopolitics of the American Revolution', Lecture, Foreign Policy Research Institute (Philadelphia, 31 March 2016), https://www.youtube.com/watch?v=WXQUxhzAcaU [accessed 29 August 2019].
[21] Mary M. Dwyer, 'More is Better: The Impact of Study Abroad Program Duration', *Frontiers: The International Journal of Study Abroad,* vol. 10 (Fall 2004), 153, 155-158, https://www.iesabroad.org/system/files/More%20is%20better%20%28Dwyer%2 C%202004%29.pdf [accessed 1 September 2019].

Such awareness as cultivated in studying abroad is the product of higher student engagement resulting from the intense academic effect of cultural engagement. Isaiah O'Rear, Richard L. Sutton, and Donald L. Rubin maintain as much when considering the impact of study abroad experiences upon graduation rates in American public university systems.

With 250,000 students studying abroad each year, many opportunities are in place, still with ample room for growth. O'Rear, et al.'s research suggests studying abroad has a profoundly positive impact upon graduating on time, thereby positing that it should become part and parcel of the undergraduate degree path. That global awareness and higher-order thinking are also by-products of a study abroad education speaks to the benefit history students can realise.[22]

Studying abroad in Paris can deliver on this realisation. When Baron Georges-Eugène Haussmann oversaw the transformation of the city in the mid-19th century, he facilitated an organised, highly centralised building process that saw city blocks mirroring each other rise around Paris's central core. This architectural effect has contributed to the city's reputation for beauty and stylistic grandeur. It has even augmented the shock some visitors experience when they discover that Paris, for all its glorious façades and grand boulevards, is a working city with crime, homelessness, and road construction (some call it Paris Syndrome).[23] For the historian, whole blocks of similar-looking buildings can boggle the mind—where did it begin? Yet, these buildings also tend to have the architects' names, as well as dates of construction conveniently

---

[22] Isaiah O'Rear, Richard L. Sutton, and Donald L. Rubin, 'The Effect of Study Abroad on College Completion in a State University System', Georgia Learning Outcomes of Students Studying Abroad Research Initiative (2012), 4-5, 9, http://glossari.uga.edu/wp-content/uploads/downloads/2012/01/GLOSSARI-Grad-Rate-Logistic-Regressions-040111.pdf [accessed 1 September 2019].

[23] Chelsea Fagan, 'Paris Syndrome: A First-Class Problem for a First-Class Vacation', *The Atlantic* (18 October 2011), https://www.theatlantic.com/health/archive/2011/10/paris-syndrome-a-first-class-problem-for-a-first-class-vacation/246743/ [accessed 3 October 2019]; Gavin Fernando, 'Is Paris Syndrome Really as Crazy as it Sounds?', news.com.au (2 October 2017), https://www.news.com.au/travel/world-travel/europe/is-paris-syndrome-really-as-crazy-as-it-sounds/news-story/efc292aa54a542cfb78d2e90dc6767f5 [accessed 3 October 2019].

chiselled just above the ground floor. One simply has to look up! Suddenly, the city takes on a visible, easily accessible chronology that students can begin to map.

Paris's buildings also display other clues. At 60, Boulevard Saint-Michel (on the border of the 5th and 6th arrondissements) lies the Musée de Minéralogie Mines Paris Tech - the mineralogy museum and mining school. The institution dates from the 18th century; the building appears as so many others in Paris: grand, buff in colour, massive. While Jeremy encourages historians to look upward upon a building façade, one need only approach the museum and stare straight ahead to be transported back both to January 1918 and August 1944.

The German *Luftstreitkräfte* attacked during the final year of the Great War, and the battle for Paris raged in the late summer of 1944. This spot also marks the final combat of Jean Montvallier-Boulogne, who died on 25 August, the day the German garrison surrendered. Writing on the Invisible Works website, one passer-by recorded the first interaction with the address: 'I spotted what looked like a [sic] large-calibre bullet holes in a wall around a window and a big layer of history peeled off right in front of me.... I just stood there staring at it in temporal disarray while the others walked on unaware.... [Y]ou can almost take it apart with your eyes.' The site is impressive, and disturbing: evidence of violence in what appears a modern, sophisticated street. It is especially pleasant and calm on a Sunday morning. Imagining Montvallier-Boulogne in that space, with the building façade suggestive of his fate, bursts that bubble. He died a few blocks away at the School of Medicine.[24]

Taking students to this location, down this street, and through this neighbourhood provides an opportunity for onsite, experiential learning not always available in study abroad experiences. It is often the challenge for the historian to aid students in imagining themselves in another era. Impressive buildings and statues rarely lend themselves to telling stories of the past if left floating free of context and analysis. In Paris, there are impressive buildings

---

[24] Hidden Histories: Traces-Boulevard Saint-Michel, Paris, https://www.invisibleworks.co.uk/traces-boulevard-saint-michel-paris/ [accessed 3 October 2019]; http://mapage.noos.fr/liberation_de_paris/episodesenat.htm [accessed 3 October 2019].

everywhere, so many that they tend to drown out sounds from history. If you have seen one impressive building, well you have seen them all. With that approach, the learning ceases. The buildings still function, with modern automobiles out front and modern fashions passing along the pavement. Façades vary, but the movement of the city is something we understand. As such, when examined with a cursory eye, Paris appears similar to other cities (one of the challenges of teaching in Paris is aiding students in ceasing to compare it with New York City).

The shell holes at 60, Boulevard Saint-Michel are a violent, but useful gift for the historian. Their power helps transform the student experience, suddenly equating street scapes with battle fronts. If there is combat damage at the museum of mineralogy, is it just a few doors down at no. 64, or perhaps over the road at no. 95, the Comédie Saint-Michel? This search for clues, along with course reading materials detailing the battle for Paris, places the student at the heart of the historical event and amongst the discussion. With the context established, the complexities may be examined.

In his *The Age of Total War*, Jeremy considers the concepts of totality and modernity and the nature of their relationship. They do not always complement each other. He asks, in fact, 'how far, in the context of an industrial system and a bellicose socio-political system, is the very existence of a multiplier constitutive of total war, rather than causing it as a separate state?' It is relative, as we might imagine, according to Jeremy. The concept of total war 'can also be contested in both specifics and in more general terms.... This relates to the possibility that total war is a continuous phenomenon across time, the forms of which change in particular environments.'[25] For the students engaged in their experiential learning in Paris, the city of Jean Montvallier-Boulogne, Baron Haussmann, Bonaparte, and even Clovis exist simultaneously, setting Paris as a phenomenon continuous across time. Everything is relative; the challenge is to teach students how to see it, recognize it on their own, and contextualize its elements. For Jeremy, the variables are every bit as important as the chronology. They are the chronology.

---

[25] Jeremy Black, *The Age of Total War: 1860-1945* (Lanham: Rowman & Littlefield, 2006), 2-3.

This is the art of thinking historically, and it is important now more than ever (yet even that conclusion is relative to the author's own understanding!). Disagreements and fallings out are part and parcel of the academy, ever much so as in life. History educators must make this fact clear to their students, while continuing to stress respect for the discipline. Teaching them to 'look up' is teaching them critical thinking-something fundamental to living in the world. Jeremy faces this issue head on in his 'Academics Should Look in the Mirror Before Smearing Their Rivals' (*The Article* August 2019). Among the topics of empire, identity, and Brexit, he takes up the differences between scholarship and polemics, and the danger of conflating the two. Foregrounded are the contradictory reasonings of Richard Drayton and Nigel Biggar in the Brexit debate. Research and empirical evidence matter to the history conversation, and for Jeremy, 'authorisation by profession'-arguing 'I'm an historian, so I know best'-is no way to engage in a well-informed conversation.[26] What matters less is the title of 'historian'. What matters so much more is respect for facts and a reasoned handling of archival material.

Jeremy's critique in the above article is one episode in a longer history of examining the discipline's place in the world. While considering authorisation by profession in the Drayton/Biggar analysis, he interrogates the other side of the equation in his *Using History*. Scholarly research and argument are laudable, but 'more fractured, complex discussions, are not usually welcome to the community at large. Instead, in the West, works by academics that enjoyed a widespread and favourable public response were generally those that presented an attractive, in the sense of both positive and readable account of the national past...' Even if the work is written by scholars, in the popular market, according to Black, a tight adherence to scholarly approach is commonly absent.[27]

Once again, it is the dilemma of making history accessible squared against maintaining public interest. Hopefully, teaching students to think historically in Paris will help develop their historical curiosity. Yet, for the historian, it is also about knowing one's audience. At

---

[26] Jeremy Black, 'Academics Should Look in the Mirror Before Smearing Their Rivals', *The Article* (19 August 2019), https://www.thearticle.com/academics-should-look-in-the-mirror-before-smearing-their-rivals [accessed 10 October 2019].
[27] Black, *Using History*, 176-177.

Changingminds.org ('the largest site in the world on all aspects of how we change what others think, believe, feel and do'), the advice encourages the information presenter to consider the audience's education level, affiliations, likely attention span, and even psychological profiles. One should also respect one's audience while working to earn its respect.[28] *Forbes* echoes this advice.[29] In Paris, it is difficult to make Haussmann's neighbourhoods come alive. So, how do historical educators who engage in living history or re-enacting handle the challenges of educating through impression?

From worst to best (or perhaps worst to not quite as bad), Nazi reenactors carry the heaviest burden of convincing, and more specifically, legitimizing. Is it *really* about an interest in military culture, uniforms, and tactics? In *The Atlantic*, Joshua Green argues it can never be solely about bravado, buckles, and boots. The overarching evil that was the Holocaust, and Nazi imperial expansion generally, are either forgotten or minimized, both of which do a disservice to humanity and history.[30] Confederate (American Civil War) reenactors fare better, with Civil War events routinely drawing incredibly large crowds. For Americans and others, these re-enactments offer a glimpse into a pivotal point in American history. Perhaps the racial element-that is: slavery and other egregious human rights abuses connected to the era-is more easily glossed over, as the argument that there is no United States without the Civil War is highly preferable to the heinous American history of racism.

One is noble, and therefore palatable; the other is highly regrettable, uncomfortable, and hopefully forgettable to the onlooker watching re-enacted battles. Finally, British reenactors are

---

[28] Changingminds.org, https://changingminds.org/ [accessed 31 October 2019]; 'Know Your Audience', changingminds.org, http://changingminds.org/techniques/speaking/preparing_presentation/know_audience [accessed 31 October 2019].

[29] Dean Brenner, 'Communicating Respect: Know Your Audience', *Forbes* (16 May 2018), https://www.forbes.com/sites/forbescoachescouncil/2018/05/16/communicating-respect-know-your-audience/#a58e3ea40675 [accessed 31 October 2019].

[30] Joshua Green, 'What's Wrong With Nazi Reenacting', *The Atlantic* (13 October 2010), https://www.theatlantic.com/politics/archive/2010/10/whats-wrong-with-nazi-reenacting/64489/ [accessed 31 October 2019].

well received and warmly hated, especially in New England. Many British army reenactors will report they are in it for the material culture (predictably the uniforms), and they might even argue they boost the record and reputation of American colonial troops by offering up a powerful foe duly smote (see Jeremy's point above). Moreover, 1783 was such a long time ago, whereas 1865 still feels a bit like just last week.

On home ground, these red-coated, off-side reenactors find a willing audience to affirm their beliefs. British troops in Canada are always most welcome and openly applauded when taking the field. Would it were the same in Lexington, Massachusetts. Soldiers in His Majesty's 10th Regiment of Foot[31] already know their audience when in front of a friendly crowd. It is everyone else who requires convincing when the reenactors begin to speak. The crowd knows its role as well: boo, hiss, and reject. Moreover, to onlookers ignorant of the complexities of historical fact, a discussion about tax burdens carried by colonial British subjects and their fellows in Britain leads quickly to glazed expressions and a quick exit from the conversation.

Alternatively, agreeing that Britain was wrong enhances the viewer's experience, affirming what they are already sure to be true. It is not historical, but it is excellent for positive interaction with the public.[32] Yet, history loses in the process. Jeremy notes in *Using History* that while 'academic history continues to focus on empirically grounded scholarship....[i]t offers the objectivity sought in popular history, but, frequently, this scholarship also reveals a complexity and an understanding of past values that does not match modern popular concerns, nor the presentist habit of seeing the past like the present.'[33] Reenactors are at the centre of public history, where public consumption and interest matter as much as scholarship. Without the public, there is no 10th Regiment of Foot.

More recently, public history and public concern have collided over the monuments issue. In April 2015, in front of Leander Starr Jameson Hall at the University of Cape Town, university officials

---

[31] The regiment has been in operation since 1968. See its website: tenthfoot.org.
[32] See Black's discussion of the past as spectacle vs. the past as complex, *A Brief History of Britain*, 324-325.
[33] Black, *Using History*, 178.

removed a statue of Cecil John Rhodes.[34] He served as Prime Minister of the Cape Colony in the early 1890s and is perhaps best known for his Rhodes scholarship programme. Scholars and the general public are also aware that Rhodes is famous, or perhaps infamous, for his efforts to expand the British Empire and encourage the growth of British culture across the globe. When students demanded the removal of Rhodes' statue in March 2015, it was the latter activities to which they objected, and the colonisation of South African education in the nineteenth and twentieth centuries.

The resulting #RhodesMustFall (RMF) movement sought out more robust, deeply ingrained colonial-era systems, as noted by Zethu Matebeni. The Rhodes statue disappeared, but '[i]t is really about the everyday psychic manipulation that enforces one's complicity in glorifying and celebrating statues of colonial conquerors and perpetrators as heroes.'

As Matebeni explained, monuments provide further affirmation of history, and more firmly legitimate the actions of parties responsible for erecting the commemorative art pieces.[35] The American Historical Association concurs, maintaining American memorials highlighting 'the Confederacy were intended, in part, to obscure the terrorism required to overthrow Reconstruction, and to intimidate African Americans politically and isolate them from the mainstream of public life.... To remove such monuments is neither to "change" history nor "erase" it. What changes with such removals is what American communities decide is worthy of civic honor.'[36]

The debate made its way to Rhodes's alma mater, Oriel College, Oxford, in May 2015. As with Cape Town, Oxford students

---

[34] 'Rhodes Statue Removed in Cape Town as Crowd Celebrates', BBC (9 April 2015), https://www.bbc.com/news/world-africa-32236922 [accessed 4 November 2019].

[35] Heinrich Böll Foundation, '#RhodesJustFall-It Was Never Just About the Statue', interview with Zethu Matebeni [19 February 2018], https://za.boell.org/en/2018/02/19/rhodesmustfall-it-was-never-just-about-statue [accessed 4 November 2019].

[36] AHA Statement on Confederate Monuments [August 2017], https://www.historians.org/news-and-advocacy/aha-advocacy/aha-statement-on-confederate-monuments [accessed 4 November 2019].

focused their physical protest upon their Rhodes statue, but similarly also channelled their ideological energy toward the decolonisation of the Oxford curriculum. Abdul Kayum Ahmed describes as much in his *The Rise of Fallism: #RhodesMustFall and the Movement to Decolonize the University* (2019, doctoral dissertation), detailing student efforts to 'de-link' from the traditional epistemologies and foreground the 'black pain' experience and associated histories and understandings. Ahmed argues Oxford University is a blessing and a curse, offering a valuable educational experience that both liberates and oppresses.[37] In January 2016, *The Daily Telegraph* newspaper reported students at the Oxford Union voted narrowly to support the removal of the Rhodes statue from the Oriel College façade, part of a larger curricular decolonisation effort that developed in the wake of the initial statue protest the preceding May. The Oxford Union discussion centred upon Rhodes as benefactor vs. Rhodes as racist, and the consequential impact upon an Oxford curriculum that privileges white students, faculty, and culture-all to the detriment of people of colour.[38]

Speaking against Rhodes' removal at the Oxford Union debate was Nigel Biggar, Regius Professor of Moral and Pastoral Theology at the University. He interrogated the notion of tearing down monuments, noting that '[i]f we insist on our heroes being pure, then we aren't going to have any.'[39] Biggar also praised Jeremy's new book, *Imperial Legacies* (2019), and Jeremy defended Biggar in the RMF conversation.[40] At the Oxford Union, Biggar pointed to

---

[37] Abdul Kayem Ahmed, *The Rise of Fallism: #RhodesMustFall and the Movement to Decolonize the University*, abstract, doctoral dissertation, Columbia University (2019), https://academiccommons.columbia.edu/doi/10.7916/d8-n7n3-e372 [accessed5 November 2019].

[38] Javier Espinoza, 'Oxford Union Backs Motion to Remove Cecil Rhodes Statue', *The Telegraph* (20 January 2016),
https://www.telegraph.co.uk/education/educationnews/12109394/Oxford-Union-backs-motion-to-remove-Cecil-Rhodes-statue.html [accessed 5 November 2019]; André Rhoden-Paul, 'Oxford Uni Must Decolonise its Campus and Curriculum, Say Students', *The Guardian* (18 June 2015),
https://www.theguardian.com/education/2015/jun/18/oxford-uni-must-decolonise-its-campus-and-curriculum-say-students [accessed 5 November 2019].

[39] Espinoza, 'Oxford Union Backs Motion to Remove Cecil Rhodes Statue'.

[40] Jeremy Black, *Imperial Legacies: The British Empire Around the World* (New York: Encounter Books, 2019); Black, 'Academics Should Look in the Mirror Before Smearing Their Rivals'.

Churchill and Lincoln as the next possible targets for deconstruction, the undergirding theme being it is possible to identify negative qualities across the spectrum of otherwise-lauded historical figures. In *Using History*, Jeremy refers to the judgement of past people and events informed by 'modern popular concerns...and the related pressure for a new public history that wears its heart clearly on its sleeve.'[41] Zethu Matebeni disagrees, maintaining the Rhodes statue in Cape Town, and more broadly the University of Cape Town educational structure, were simply the key components of an 'assumption and expectation to assimilate to white standards and white values of excellence.'[42]

Jeremy details the process of decolonisation-the end of empire-in his *A Brief History of Britain*, pointing to Indian independence (1947) as the fulcrum upon which popular support for empire began to wane. The Suez crisis a decade later put paid to imperial dreams, with public opinion changing and effectively moving on from long-established tangible elements of international standing. Jeremy writes, '[t]he balance between the generations was also important, with the young not experiencing the sense of discontinuity felt by their elders. This difference constitutes an instructive contrast between the historical memory and imagination of the generations.'[43] It might also engage that notion of presentism Jeremy references when considering the manner in which current generations interrogate ideas and values from another age. In defiance of what at least some in the crowd demanded toward progress at Oxford, the University, citing 'overwhelming' support, decided to maintain Rhodes's presence at Oriel College. Oriel argued the statue represented 'the complexity of history and the legacies of colonialism.' The elephant standing confidently in the room, Rhodes further confirmed the College's commitment to its mission, which, according to its website, is to 'provide an enriching environment dedicated to...education.... [S]tudents are encouraged to see themselves as having joined a community with a shared purpose.'[44]

---

[41] Black, *Using History*, 178.

[42] Heinrich Böll Foundation, '#RhodesJustFall-It Was Never Just About the Statue'.

[43] Black, *A Brief History of Britain*, 226-227, 231-232.

[44] Oriel College, Who We Are and What We Do, https://www.oriel.ox.ac.uk/who-we-are-and-what-we-do [accessed 6 November 2019].

One of the valuable aspects of the statue debate, and more generally the history of power, race, and culture in the West, is the opportunity it provides to consider historical memory, historical fact, and the particular needs of communities as they interact with the past at any given moment, and in any given context. Jeremy suggests as much when considering the popular consumption of British history fed by presentist appetites for affirmation: 'Indeed, the grasping of the past in the image of the present represents an unwillingness to think historically that is an important indication of a desire for simplicity that says much about current popular culture. In particular, there is a desire to emote about the past, which is an obvious result of being asked to empathize with figures from history.'[45] Here Jeremy is reminding the reader of the importance of thinking, research, reason, and debate. His arguments are also a reminder of the importance of history in our lives and its interplay with our daily existence. His *Imperial Legacies* further suggests modern castigation of the British Empire is closely linked to modern confrontation of American foreign policy. In the case of the University of Cape Town students' RMF efforts to confront their history, Rhodes did indeed fall, with a student confirming 'We finally got the white man to sit down and listen to us'. The University embraced the effort as it stressed '[t]his is exactly how a university should work and we believe is an example to the country in dealing with heritage issues'.[46] Zethu Matebeni argued the *invisible* statues were next on the list: the less obvious, but no-less oppressive cultural traits of the imperial past.[47]

At Oriel, however, Rhodes remains (although a plaque was removed), but now present is an enhanced understanding of the significance symbols carry as identifiers of time, place, and values. Their longevity increases the public's access to the symbols'

---

[45] Black, *A Brief History of Britain*, 324-325. One must note the reception of Black's *Imperial Legacies*. It has its supporters (Nigel Biggar, Andrew Roberts, Neil Ferguson), while the publisher lauds the book as a 'vigorous assault on political correctness', https://www.encounterbooks.com/books/imperial-legacies/. The work also has its detractors, Kim Wagner, 'Imperial Legacies by Jeremy Black Review-Whitewash for Britain's Atrocities', *The Guardian* (10 August 2019), https://www.theguardian.com/books/2019/aug/10/imperial-legacies-jeremy-black-review-empire-multiculturalism [accessed 7 November 2019].

[46] 'Rhodes Statue Removed in Cape Town as Crowd Celebrates',

[47] Heinrich Böll Foundation, '#RhodesJustFall-It Was Never Just About the Statue'.

celebrity and notoriety. Oriel acknowledges as much and invites deeper thinking about Rhodes' life and legacy. Yet, for #RhodesMustFall supporters, this gesture lands very short of its intention.[48]

In the United States, the monument debate is further shaped by Donald Trump's 2016 election victory. Making America Great Again equated, to some, with waving the flag of racism, inviting Americans to rally around the colours. One rally in particular stands out in the statues conversation: on 12 August 2017, thousands gathered in Charlottesville, Virginia, centred on the planned removal of a monument honouring General Robert E. Lee. A statue of Stonewall Jackson was also on activists' removal agenda. White nationalists and counter-protesters clashed, resulting in the death of one person and over thirty injured. Two police officers also died when their helicopter crashed during a crowd-control operation.[49] In the wake of the deadly confrontation, Lee and Jackson have yet to fall, with the court citing a state statute preventing the act. In response to the ruling, someone defaced the Lee statue, spray painting 1619 across the plinth.[50]

---

[48] David Matthews, 'Oxford College Agrees to Remove Cecil Rhodes Plaque', *THE* (18 December 2015), https://www.timeshighereducation.com/news/oxford-college-agrees-remove-cecil-rhodes-plaque#survey-answer [accessed 7 November 2019]; Cecil John Rhodes (1853-1902), https://www.oriel.ox.ac.uk/cecil-john-rhodes-1853-1902 [accessed 7 November 2019].

[49] Marianna Sotomayor, Phil McCausland, and Ariana Brockington, 'Charlottesville White Nationalist Rally Violence Prompts State of Emergency', *NBC News* (12 August 2017), https://www.nbcnews.com/news/us-news/torch-wielding-white-supremacists-march-university-virginia-n792021 [accessed 7 November 2019]; Benjamin Hart and Chas Danner, '3 Dead and Dozens Injured After Violent White-Nationalist Rally in Virginia', *Intelligencer* (13 August 2017), http://nymag.com/intelligencer/2017/08/state-of-emergency-in-va-after-white-nationalist-rally.html [accessed 7 November 2019].

[50] Shannon Van Sant, 'Judge Blocks Removal of Confederate Statue that Sparked Charlottesville Protest', NPR (14 September 2019), https://www.npr.org/2019/09/14/760876494/judge-blocks-removal-of-confederate-statue-that-sparked-charlottesville-protest [accessed 7 November 2019]; Jenn Brice, 'Lee Statue Found Defaced After Judge Rules Civil War Monuments Will Remain', *The Cavalier Daily* (17 September 2019), https://www.cavalierdaily.com/article/2019/09/lee-statue-found-defaced-after-judge-rules-civil-war-monuments-will-remain-standing [accessed 7 November 2019].

Another response has found greater success in Richmond, Virginia, where Kehinde Wiley's sculpture 'Rumors of War' will take its permanent place in front of the Virginia Museum of Fine Arts in December 2019. In describing his interaction with the Civil War statues adorning the city's Monument Avenue, Wiley recalled '[w]hat does that feel like, physically, to walk a public space and to have your state, your country, your nation say, "This is what we stand by." No. We want more. We demand more'. Wiley's new work presents an equestrian design featuring a young African-American man astride a horse, in a position traditionally reserved for white military leaders. The artist challenges ingrained readings of race and state violence, while simultaneously representing inclusivity.[51]

Rather than tearing down monuments, Wiley responds with his own, in the nature of dialogue. The longer view of this development, and the tragic events of August 2017 require, as the American Historical Association maintains, 'not only attention to historical facts, including the circumstances under which monuments were built and spaces named, but also an understanding of what history is and why it matters to public culture.'[52]

Attention to fact and an appreciation of why history matters: stated another way, this is historical complexity at work. When Jeremy introduces the historiography of military history or the practiced treatment of the American past, his intention centres upon complexity and its value as a subject of interrogation. The chronology is there; it is the *why* that is fundamental to deeper historical understanding, and therefore education.[53]

***

---

[51] Mark Kennedy, 'New Statue by Kehinde Wiley Is in the Richmond Confederate Style. But It's Unlike Any Other', *The Virginia Pilot* (28 September 2019), https://www.pilotonline.com/entertainment/arts/vp-nw-kehinde-wiley-new-sculpture-20190928-bh7abktspfbz3abshke3guf5ny-story.html [accessed 7 November 2019]; 'Richmond is Getting a New Statue; and It's in Direct Respond to Confederate Monuments', WTKR (21 June 2019), https://wtkr.com/2019/06/21/richmond-is-getting-a-new-statue-and-its-in-direct-response-to-confederate-monuments/ [accessed 7 November 2019].

[52] AHA Statement on Confederate Monuments.

[53] Jeremy Black, *War: A Short History* (London: Continuum, 2009), 2-3; Jeremy Black, *Altered States: America Since the Sixties* (London: Reaktion Books Ltd., 2006), 8.

Is the academy safe or in peril in Jeremy's hands? No historian is safe, because history matters too much to be reduced to personality politics or self-aggrandizement. Sir Simon Schama might well appreciate this after being taken to task by Jeremy for historical comparisons that, according to Jeremy, were overblown, unnecessary, and plain sloppy. More than once has he compared such activity to the scholarly fumblings of undergraduates.

It is the assessments of Schama and Sir Richard Evans that Jeremy interrogates in his 'Richard Evans, Simon Schama and the Plight of the Historical Profession' (*The Article*, 2019). Specifically, Jeremy considers the historians' comments regarding the Brexit debate.

While he scans the current state of the profession, Jeremy also takes issue with the boilerplate use of language and comparisons to make an intellectual point. 'For a scholar, there are also interesting questions to consider in the form of the weakness of diachronic comparisons-those across time.' It is the easy path to stressing a conclusion, with a layby pause 'to simplify episodes, to decontextualise them, and to rob them of internal development'.[54]

In the interest of full disclosure, I find Schama's *The Power of Art* (2006)[55] to be incredibly useful in the classroom. It is attractive, dramatic, and highly engaging for American history undergraduates. In short, it helps make history *accessible*. Moreover, Evans is lauded and respected, because he is an excellent historian. Perhaps more to the point here, he agrees with Jeremy on the discipline's value: history 'introduces us very quickly to societies that are separated from us by time.... [Y]ou have whole different sets of assumptions, different ways of doing things, different beliefs.... That...enlarges our sense of what it means to be human; it gives us a whole range of new aspects of what humanity is...both positive and negative.'[56]

---

[54] Jeremy Black, 'Richard Evans, Simon Schama and the Plight of the Historical Profession', *The Article* (8 September 2019), https://www.thearticle.com/richard-evans-simon-schama-and-the-plight-of-the-historical-profession [accessed 17 November 2019]; Black, 'Academics Should Look in the Mirror Before Smearing Their Rivals'.

[55] Simon Schama, *Simon Schama's The Power of Art* (BBC Home Entertainment, 2006), DVD.

[56] Richard Evans, 'The Importance of History', Gresham College, https://www.youtube.com/watch?v=x0ggGRy7dIA [accessed 21 November 2019].

Already appreciated is history as fundamental to greater understanding. Yet, who has not engaged in a bit of hyperbole when seeking to help others appreciate links between the past and the present? Referencing Mussolini (as Schama did), or Weimar Germany (Evans' gaffe, according to Jeremy) provide another doorway into a deeper awareness of the complexities of the here now/back then dialogue. It also goes to the debate on public history, and therefore public *access* to history. Most of us want to keep it honest, and most of us understand it is the texture, the complexity that keep it vibrant. And, in the case of Brexit, debate is very, very vibrant.

Ultimately, Jeremy's is a 'tough-love' approach calling us to task, when appropriate, and always in defence of the discipline (with heavy emphasis on the tough and the love). As he writes in review of David Abulafia's *The Boundless Sea: A Human History of the Oceans* (2019), the author 'handles issues such as climate and current in a subtle fashion, one in which the very use of what is termed possibilism makes for a much better engagement with how different cultures have responded to such factors…. [Abulafia] has to offer assessments that draws [*sic*] on an appreciation of complexity in causation.'[57] Once again, complexity is the rule for historical appreciation and understanding.

Context, complexity, and a passion for history. Jeremy has never swayed from driving those points home. One will discover this dedication only a few minutes into most conversations with him. I am grateful for all he has taught me, from the evil of the split infinitive, to the value of history in my life. The next time I go round his house, I shall be sure to stop by his pigeonhole and collect his post. I know there will be a nice cup of tea (or hopefully coffee) waiting on the other end. And a biscuit!

---

[57] David Abulafia, *The Boundless Sea: A Human History of the Oceans* (London: Allen Lane, 2019); Jeremy Black, 'A Flawed Masterpiece That Will Dominate the Field', *The Critic* (14 November 2019), https://thecritic.co.uk/a-flawed-masterpiece-that-will-dominate-the-field/ [accessed 21 November 2019].

'A Provincial Enlightener': Andrew Hooke of Bristol, Whig writer and newspaper proprietor in the reign of George II

Jonathan Barry

Despite the astonishing breadth of his historical interests and writings, Jeremy Black has continued to publish ground-breaking studies on the intersection between politics, foreign policy and the press in Hanoverian England, especially during the reign of George II, and the understandings of religion, trade, history and geography which underpinned the cultural politics of this period. It therefore seems appropriate to offer here an essay on an understudied Whig writer, Andrew Hooke (c.1688-1753), who published on history, geography and political economy, as well as running, from 1742 to 1749, a newspaper whose avowed aim was to educate his fellow Bristolians in a proper understanding of politics and foreign policy to reinforce their loyalty to the Hanoverian regime against the threat of Jacobitism. In 1987, Black characterised Hooke, with typical acuity, as a 'provincial enlightener',[1] but this is the first attempt to see Hooke's life and writings in the round. It establishes the basic details of his life before considering his aims and achievements as a newspaper proprietor and author.

Hooke's native Bristol was one of England's major provincial cities, with an extensive electorate (freemen and freeholders) leading to hotly disputed contests between Whigs and Tories throughout the first half of the century, culminating in the by-election of 1739 where Edward Southwell triumphed for the Tories, giving them both seats until 1754. By contrast the self-perpetuating city Corporation had become increasingly Whig, with Presbyterians sitting alongside moderate Anglicans, and during the 1730s they supported a range of measures designed both to improve Bristol's amenities and display an enlightened Whig politeness, such as the equestrian statue of William III in Queen Square or the opening of the Infirmary, followed, as we shall see, by the new Exchange and other street improvements. However, the late 1730s also saw Bristol at the forefront of the new evangelical movement, led by George Whitefield (from nearby Gloucester) and the Wesley brothers. This dismayed many in the Anglican elite, including

---

[1] Jeremy Black, *The English Press in the Eighteenth century* (London, 1987), p. 33.

Bristol's bishop, Joseph Butler, and his chaplain, the Bristol clergyman Josiah Tucker, who feared Methodism's appeal to popular zeal and associated it (unfairly) with popery and Jacobitism (which they also feared as a lurking sentiment among Bristol's Tories).[2] It was therefore of great concern to the Whig corporation, including its Recorder (the future Sir) Michael Foster (1689-1763)[3] not only that their opponents were proving successful electorally, but that they also controlled Bristol's only weekly newspaper, produced by brothers Samuel and Felix Farley. Samuel, a Quaker, increasingly left the Bristol press to Felix, an early convert to Wesleyan Methodism, who was one of John Wesley's major publishers throughout the 1740s. He was opposed by the *Gloucester Journal*, for which Tucker was a regular contributor, but until 1742 Bristol itself lacked a rival paper to support the Whig establishment both nationally and locally against Farley's blend of country, Tory and evangelical views.[4] Like Foster and Tucker, Hooke was to step forward to defend Whig values.

Life

Andrew Hooke was the son of Joseph Hooke (1656-99), a Bristol brewer, and his wife Mary, daughter of the sugar maker Godfrey van Ittern, who had married at St James, Bristol, on 16 October 1684.[5] Joseph was the third son of the wealthy Bristol brewer

---

[2] Jonathan Barry, 'Provincial town culture 1640-1780: urbane or civic?' in Joan H. Pittock and Andrew Wear (ed.), *Interpretation and Cultural History* (Basingstoke, 1991), pp. 198-234; id., 'Cultural patronage and the Anglican crisis: Bristol c.1689-1775', in J. D. Walsh et al., ed., *The Church of England c.1689-c.1833* (Cambridge, 1993), pp. 191-208; id., 'Bristol as a "Reformation city" c.1640-1780', in N. Tyacke, ed., *England's Long Reformation* (London, 1997), pp. 261-84. Steve Poole and Nicholas Rogers, *Bristol from Below: Law, Authority and Protest in a Georgian City* (Woodbridge, 2017) brings together the work of two outstanding scholars of Bristol's Hanoverian political culture. For Tucker see G. Shelton, *Dean Tucker and Eighteenth-Century Economic and Political Thought* (London and Basingstoke, 1981), pp. 21-36.

[3] J. Latimer, *Annals of Bristol in the Eighteenth Century* (n.p., 1893), pp. 192, 197, 224, 341; Bristol Archives (hereafter BA) 14754/1; N. G. Jones, 'Sir Michael Foster' at https://doi.org/10.1093/ref:odnb/9964. Shelton, *Dean Tucker*, pp. 37-41 notes that Tucker's anti-Jacobite publications were sponsored initially by Foster.

[4] Jonathan Barry, 'The press and the politics of culture in Bristol, 1660-1775' in Jeremy Black and Jeremy Gregory (ed.), *Culture, Politics and Society in Britain 1660-1800* (Manchester, 1991), pp. 49-81; Jonathan Barry, *Methodism and the Press in Bristol 1737-1775* (Wesley Historical Society, Bristol Branch, bulletin 64, 1992).

[5] E. Ralph (ed.), *Marriage Bonds for the Diocese of Bristol, 1637–1700* (BGAS Records

Andrew Hooke (1616-88) and was freed on 1 January 1681 as his father's son and apprentice.[6] His elder brother Robert died in 1681,[7] and his other brothers never married so Joseph inherited his father's brewing business, based in Lewin's Mead where the family lived, as well as the extensive properties to the east of Bristol on Ashley Hill which Andrew Hooke senior had bought from the Winter family, and where he had built a country residence, Ashley Court.[8] The exact date of our Andrew's birth is not known but he was reported as age sixty-five when he died in 1753, so he was presumably born around 1688.[9] He was his father's eldest son and in the 1696 Marriage Tax listing he was living in Lewins Mead with his father (taxed at the higher £600 rate) and mother, two younger brothers (Joseph and Humphrey) and two servants, as well as three bachelor uncles or cousins.[10]

His mother's father, Godfrey van Ittern, was a sugar maker from Hamburg who had moved to London by the early 1660s and was naturalised in 1667, shortly after which he moved to Bristol to provide the technical expertise for the sugarhouse established by the Bristol merchant Thomas Ellis in Whitson Court and continued by Joseph Hooke's brother-in-law Michael Pope (a Presbyterian, whose son and namesake was minister of Lewin's Mead Presbyterian chapel 1705-18).[11] Ellis was a founder and ruling elder of the Broadmead Baptist congregation, which included a 'sister Vanittern', but Godfrey, presumably born a Lutheran, conformed to the Anglican church, serving as churchwarden of St James in 1677 (as Joseph Hooke did in 1694), and bequeathed money in 1686 both to the parish poor and foran Anglican funeral sermon.[12]

---

series 1, 1952), p.158; R. Price, *Marriages at St James Church Bristol 1559-1753* (Bristol, 2014).

[6] G. D. Squibb (ed.), *The Visitation of Somerset and the City of Bristol 1672* (Harleian Society, N.S. 11, 1992), p. 33; BA 04359 (3).

[7] The National Archives (hereafter TNA) PROB 11/366/418.

[8] TNA PROB 11/391/195, will made 27 May 1687, proved 16 May 1688.

[9] H. R. Plomer, *Dictionary of the Printers and Booksellers Who Were at Work in England, Scotland and Ireland 1726-75* (Oxford, 1969), p.130.

[10] E. Ralph and M. Williams (eds), *The Inhabitants of Bristol in 1696* (Bristol Record Society, XXV, 1968), p. 53.

[11] I. V. Hall, 'Whitson Court sugar house, Bristol 1665-1824' *TBGAS* 65 (1944) 1-97 at 1-4, 22-3, 32-6, 57-9.

[12] TNA PROB 11/384/325 made 14 June 1686 and proved 14 September 1686; W. Barrett, *The History and Antiquities of the City of Bristol* (Bristol, 1789), pp. 395, 398.

Like both Andrew (senior) and Joseph Hooke, Godfrey died a wealthy man, leaving several thousand pounds to his children in legacies. The family's German background and partnership with Protestant nonconformists must have shaped Andrew's Whig beliefs and his commitment to that 'forward policy' of support for Protestantism across Europe which distinguished Whigs from Tories.

Andrew's father Joseph died in 1699, after which the young Andrew succeeded his father and grandfather as a parish feoffee for St James (first recorded as such in 1701).[13] However, Andrew did not follow the family business or reside in the city, but rather lived as a gentleman at Ashley, becoming a Justice of the Peace for Gloucestershire. Indeed, he may have moved away for a period, if he is the Andrew Hooke of Bridgwater gentleman who was licensed to marry Mary Grevill of the same parish spinster at Bridgwater, Charlton or Chedzoy on 17 January 1709-10.[14] Andrew Hook or Hoock 'gent' obtained the freedom of Bristol as Joseph's son on 12 August 1713 (just before that year's election). His first public act occurred the following year, when a loyal address from the 'Protestant dissenters of the city of Bristol' was presented to George I by 'Andrew Hooke esquire', introduced by Thomas, Earl of Wharton.[15] The next year the Independent minister John Catcott dedicated his *Sermon First Preached at Bristol on His Majesty's Inauguration* (London for J. Penn, 1715) to 'Andrew Hooke esquire of the city of Bristol' as one of the lovers of the country who have 'for four years past been stemming the tide of those who have used I hope their last offices to enslave us to France and Rome'. He values Hooke's friendship, praising him as 'so correct a judge of men's writings' and welcoming his concern for the preservation of the honour and safety of the royal family, the continuation of 'our constitutional and religious rights and privileges', the suppression of a 'malignant prosecuting spirit' and the 'universal reformation of

---

[13] BA P/StJ/VCD/1/2/4 19 July 1701, P/StJ/D/23/3 10 February 1718, BA PSt J/d/14/6a-b documents of 1-2 April 1736 where described as 'of London esquire', P/StJ/D/23/4 13 June 1740 and /5 and /6 ditto in 1745, P/StJ/VCD/5/1/1 1743; PSt J/d/14/7a-b 29-30 June 1743 and 18 a-b.

[14] A. J. Jewers, *Marriage Allegation Bonds of Bath and Wells* (Exeter, 1909), p.209. TNA C8/653/36 is a case regarding Bridgwater property where defendants include Andrew Hooke.

[15] BA 04359 (5); *London Gazette* 5270, 19 October 1714.

manners'. In 1722 (the first election when Whig voters are recorded) Hooke voted as a St James freeholder for the Whig ticket of Earle and Elton.

Little is known of his activity over the next twenty years. He had become a J.P. for Gloucestershire by 1719, when he was one of the justices who sent a suspected 'popish priest' seized at Bristol to Gloucester for trial.[16] He was clearly outspending his income, as he began gradually to mortgage or sell off parts of the family estate, and there are also various law suits.[17] The Ashley estate included two substantial houses, which have sometimes been confused.[18] One, the future Ashley Manor House, described as being by Grove Mill (later known as Hooke's Mill) was bequeathed by Andrew Hooke senior in 1688 for their lives to members of the Pope family, but when they had all died it was to pass to Joseph Hooke or his heirs, and so to Andrew.[19] It was occupied by Foster when he became Bristol's recorder, suggesting he must have known Hooke well.[20] The second property, where Andrew Hooke senior himself had lived, is the future Ashley Court. Hooke sold this property, with about 200 acres of land, in 1731 to George Bridges, a distiller, for £9600.[21] His son William Bridges had the house enlarged and refronted in the late 1730s; it was demolished in the 1870s.[22]

By the mid-1730s Andrew appears to have run through his inheritance and moved to London, but then he adopted a new strategy to re-establish himself in Bristol, offering his services to the

---

[16] BA 09701(14), letter of 28 December 1719.

[17] BA 4964 is a series of documents from 1720 to 1751 re Hooke's Ashley estate ending with its sale. For various Chancery cases between 1718 and 1732 see TNA C11/1714/21, C11/613/3, C11/500/23, C11/93/17 and C11/2619/34.

[18] Notably by Roger Leech, *The Town House in Medieval and Early Modern Bristol* (Swindon, 2014), pp.110-11, 255, 385-6.

[19] See BA 4964(5); J. Pritchard, 'Bristol archaeological notes for 1908', *TBGAS* 31 (1908), pp. 304-8.

[20] Latimer, *Annals*, pp. 92, 197, 224, 341; BA 14754/1; N. G. Jones, 'Sir Michael Foster (1689-1763)' at https://doi.org/10.1093/ref:odnb/9964.

[21] http://maps.bristol.gov.uk/knowyourplace/images/her_pc/1688.jpg; BA 4964 (19 and 25).

[22] BA 4964 and 34901/1 1776 April 20, the latter involving Bridges' heir, Joseph Beck's wife; J. Evans, *Chronological Outline of the History of Bristol* (Bristol, 1829), footnote on p.219; O. Ward, 'Glass Mill, Ashley Vale, 1528-1898', *Regional Historian*, 10 (2003), pp. 11-17; Bristol and Region Archaeological Services unpublished report 1840/2007.

Whig-dominated Corporation. In January 1738 he submitted a series of plans for financing the building of a new Council House and Exchange 'humbly offered to the mayor and magistrates of the city for consideration'. After calculations respecting the purchase of existing houses, building the Council House and Exchange and 'making 2 new streets and building dwelling houses contiguous thereto', amounting to a total cost of £22,000, he then outlines five suggested schemes to raise finances, with detailed annual calculations for sixty years regarding ways to raise £22,000 on annuities at both seven and ten percent.[23] Proposals to build a new Exchange dated back to 1717, with an enabling act passed in 1722 and some properties purchased in 1732, but on each occasion the plan had lapsed, due to the level of borrowing required.[24] Although Hooke's specific financing proposals were not adopted and the Council House, only built in 1704, was not rebuilt, the purchase of the surrounding properties commenced in 1739, eventually costing over £19,000, with Hooke leading in arranging the process.[25] The foundation stone of the new Exchange was laid on 10 March 1741 and John Wood's new building, which apparently cost about £50,000, was opened on 21 September 1743.[26]

On 29 March 1740 Andrew and Mary Hooke took apprentice John Davis, a cordwainer's son, to be educated as a scrivener but on 26 February 1741 Davis was transferred to John Farnell merchant.[27] By early 1742, with his work on the Exchange scheme completed, Hooke was apparently in Newgate prison for debt,[28] but on 3 April

---

[23] Library of Institute and Faculty of Actuaries in London – MS RKN 14403.

[24] Latimer, *Annals*, pp, 118-19, 180.

[25] See BA 00448/23 and 00445/2 for Hooke's signatures on 1739 documents re properties for the market area.

[26] Latimer, *Annals*, pp, 58-9, 226, 247.

[27] BA 04353 (5-6).

[28] Latimer, *Annals*, pp. 51-2; *London Gazette* 8225 24 May 1743 lists 'Andrew Hooke esq.' among those prisoners for debt in Bristol Newgate taking advantage of the act for relief of debtors. *Oracle* 12 June 1742 contains an account of a correspondent being told by Hooke's wife, who was running the new St Michael's coffeehouse Magdalen Lane, that 'her husband, being under confinement, has lately for the support of his family engaged in a weekly paper called the Oracle'. But he was clearly not confined in Newgate until May 1743 since *Bristol Oracle and Country Intelligencer* 22 January 1743 reports that printing work is taken in for the author at the Printing Office in Shannon Court or St Michael's coffeehouse or at London coffeehouse in Corn Street 'where he may be spoke with every day between hours of 12 and 2'. BA F/AC/Box 50 corporation vouchers for 1742-3 include a bill from Hooke for work

1742 he launched his new venture, a weekly newspaper, the *Oracle or Bristol Weekly Miscellany*, backed by subscriptions.[29] In his last issue in 1749 he acknowledged the favour of the town especially those gentlemen whose 'original encouragement' and 'annual subscriptions' supported the paper, as well as occasional customers and advertisers. He lamented his 'fatal experience' of the difficulty of supporting two newspapers in Bristol, especially blaming a 'foreign paper': 'swimming against the stream is a laborious and disagreeable exercise but the most melancholy idea of it arises from the certain knowledge that a man makes no way and has only his own labour for his pains ... let a man's courage and resolution and vigour be however so great, he must at last cede to fate or sink under the operation'. If 'gentlemen of fortune' established another paper, he would 'cheerfully contribute my mite', subscribing for three sets for seven years altogether and other assistance from time to time as needed but it 'will require more stock and credit than I am or perhaps ever can be master of'. He signed off as the 'humble servant of my fellow citizens in all useful public undertakings'.[30]

Hooke was constantly seeking ways to increase his paper's circulation, not just in Bristol but across the country, and to save costs. This included, from January 1743, an ingenious process of alternating titles for his paper (initially *Bristol Oracle and Country Intelligencer* or *Advertiser*, then from April 1745 *Bristol Oracle* and *Oracle and Country Advertiser*) intended to render each a fortnightly publication rather than a weekly one subject to the normal Stamp Duty.[31] In both this and in using the postal system to circulate his

---

to the front of the late Surgeons' Hall 'now fitting up for a dwelling house for him'. *Bristol Oracle and Country Advertiser* 4 June 1743 Hooke denounced Farley for printing comments on his period in Newgate, denouncing him and his 'reverend hirelings' and predicting that the scandal would recoil on them.

[29] BA 40442/168 is an advertisement of 15 March 1742 for the new weekly paper. The first issue is 'printed for the Society' and the second issue contains letters 'from our chambers' from 'your well-wishers and subscribers' (presumably lawyers) T.H., S.P. and N.W. (*Oracle* 10 April 1742).

[30] *Bristol Oracle* 16 September 1749.

[31] He also issued unstamped pieces on the victory at Dettingen and, when Farley 'exceedingly griev'd to see his labours to propagate sedition and disaffection among the populace for half an age overturned' had Hooke's hawkers arrested, justified his actions by saying the Town Clerk had confirmed that a publication needed two separate pieces of news to require a stamp (*Bristol Oracle and Country Advertiser* 16 July 1743).

newspapers to buyers across the country he probably relied on connivance from the Whig officials who managed Bristol's stamp duty collection and post office,[32] but by 1749 he faced the threat of government prosecution for not paying the proper advertising duty.[33] Naturally his rival Felix Farley, who boasted the much greater sales of his newspaper in Bristol, was keen to denounce Hooke's various schemes, though Farley also used alternating titles between 1743 and August 1746.[34]

Hooke's newspaper also faced rivals in capturing the 'anti-Farley' market. The *Gloucester Journal* was already well-established with a Bristol bookseller as its local agent. A rival paper, the *Bristol, Bath and Somerset Journal*, was also begun in 1742 by a Bristol vintner, Richard Winpenny, assisted by the poet, clergyman and schoolmaster Emanuel Collins, and its few surviving issues indicate a more populist publication than Hooke's, satirising Farley and his fellow Methodists. This paper lasted until at least 1746 and possibly until May 1747 when Winpenny announced he was giving up printing to run a tavern, and the next month he passed over his printing apprentice to Edward Ward, who late in 1747, probably using Winpenny's premises and equipment, began to publish the *Bristol Mercury*, a single-sheet paper costing only one penny, of which only one issue (20 September 1748) survives. Although this had probably lapsed by early 1749, Ward took advantage of the imminent end of Hooke's paper in September 1749 to start his *Bristol Weekly Intelligencer*, which ran until 1760.[35] Like Hooke, neither Winpenny nor Ward were trained printers and were probably encouraged by the Corporation to enter the market against Farley (Winpenny was used as a scrivener by the Corporation from 1740-6, while Ward, who had been a haberdasher and maltster before 1747, later became Clerk of the

---

[32] *Bristol Oracle and Country Intelligencer* 14 May 1743 claimed he had free use of the mails provided by Ralph Allen of Bath.

[33] See TNA E134/22Geo 2/Hil2 1748-9 for depositions taken by commission on behalf of His Majesty vs Andrew Hooke regarding usage and custom among printers and publishers of newspapers in Bristol as regards charges for inserting adverts and E 134/22Geo2/Mich8 The Attorney-General v. Andrew Hook and 22 Geo. 2/Hil2.

[34] For a bitter attack by Hooke on Farley's 'puffs' and 'sauciness', claims to 'innumerable impressions' and geographical blunders, predicting his rapid decline into madness see *Bristol Oracle* 14 November 1747.

[35] *Bristol Weekly Intelligencer* 23 September 1749 Ward refers to a 'fellow citizen to whom we sincerely wish well' declining publication.

Market), perhaps reckoning that Hooke's highbrow papers could not appeal to the full range of Bristolians,[36] but this did not help Hooke turn a profit.

In response, Hooke sought to build a larger 'intelligence' service around his newspaper. The St Michael's coffeehouse his wife had run while he was confined was succeeded by one next to the Exchange, both offering customers access to the newspapers from which he compiled his paper, in particular his translations of the continental papers (showing his knowledge of French, Dutch and German).[37] Hooke stressed that, unlike other provincial editors (such as Farley), he did not obtain his continental news indirectly via the London press's summaries of such papers, but directly, so increasing the speed and accuracy of his reports on the military, political and financial developments on the continent. But he also ran an 'intelligence office' alongside the paper, advertising jobs and services.[38] Furthermore, he offered courses of lectures in enlightened topics such as the use of globes to subscribers, possibly the same group as supported the paper itself. Initially he appears to have relied on other jobbing printers to produce his papers, but gradually he and Mary employed their own staff and offered other printing services. He also advertised in October 1747 that he intended to publish a monthly supplement, the 'Bristol Magazine', from April 1748, for a sixpenny subscription, with subscribers paying 2s 6d in advance. In addition to his historical memoirs of Bristol (discussed below), this would contain shipping and trading information, political papers and a historical chronicle of European events, with moral, philosophical and poetical essays and occasional dissertations on geography, history and politics.[39]

Following the closure of the newspaper in 1749, Hooke continued both his coffeehouse and his printing office in Shannon Court.[40] A written note on the back of a copy of his *Essay on National Debt*

---

[36] *Bristol Oracle and Country Intelligencer* 21 July 1744 boasts that his paper appeals to the 'superior class of mankind'.

[37] Ibid, *Oracle* 12 June 1742.

[38] Ibid, 6 April 1745.

[39] *Bristol Oracle* 3 October 1747; *Oracle and Country Advertiser* 2 January 1748 and *Bristol Oracle* 9 January 1748 (by which time the start date had slipped to May; it is unclear if the magazine ever appeared).

[40] See his advertisement in *Bristol Weekly Intelligencer* 25 August 1750.

(published in January 1750), records 'Yesterday at a general meeting of the subscribers to the academical lectures at Hooke's coffeehouse it was agreed and ordered that a course of six lectures on Mr Locke's Essay ... be given successively ... in every week till the whole be ended'.[41] However the printing office had moved by December 1751 (when Emanuel Collins opened a school there) and in July 1752 Hooke advertised the lease of the coffeehouse for sale, stating that he was forced by ill health to reside in the country.[42] He died the following February, with Farley's paper carrying a surprisingly generous death notice: 'Thursday last died Justice Hook, so called, a gentleman well-beloved and respected. He had an annuity of fifty pounds per annum allowed him from the Corporation and Merchants Hall of the city for his singular services in forming an excellent scheme for purchasing the lands for building the Exchange and establishing the markets of this city'.[43]

The annuities in question (thirty pounds from the Corporation and twenty pounds from the Society of Merchant Venturers) had been paid following a petition from Hooke in August 1749, but two years earlier Hooke had submitted a much more elaborate printed petition offering a new scheme to pay off the debt on the Exchange. Claiming that 'I was the original projector of the Exchange and Market', he noted that his 1737-8 proposal had been 'not a romantick and imaginary but a practicable scheme' for carrying out the project without 'one shilling's expense to the chamber', but they had followed another method, so robbing him of the fruit of his labours and invention. Now he offered to pay off £40,000 of the debt within six months by an annuity of £1600 p.a. for ninety-nine years rent to the annuitants and survivors, which he claimed would only cost £35,460, so earning the Corporation £4540. Hooke also requested the liberty to inspect any of the public books belonging to the city under the direction of the mayor.[44] In 1751 he proposed another building scheme to the Merchant Venturers, who owned much of Clifton, offering to establish a Cold Bath and other

---

[41] *Bristol Journal* 20 January 1750; Bodleian Library, Oxford, shelfmark G116 Jur.

[42] *Bristol Weekly Intelligencer* 28 December 1751 and 25 July 1752.

[43] *Felix Farley's Bristol Journal* 3 February 1753. Both Samuel and Felix Farley also died in 1753, with Felix's widow Elizabeth carrying on this paper.

[44] BA, 02417 fo. 21, F/AC/Box 59 (1747), M/BCC/CCP/1/12 Common Council Proceedings (1745-54), February 1747 and August 1749, SMV/2/1/1/7 16 October 1749.

conveniences for the good of the city, expending £1000 on premises, in return for an altered lease, which the Society approved with a fifty pound fine, but this was apparently not implemented.[45]

Following his death, his widow Mary continued his printing business, producing handbills for the Jacob's Well Theatre and keeping a coffeehouse nearby.[46] In 1757 she petitioned the public for support, describing her husband as 'for many years' a J.P. for Gloucestershire but 'reduced to indigent circumstances by misfortunes from a very considerable estate'. His annuities had ended at his death, so that for four years his widow and two daughters had been left unprovided, printing playbills for the 'late theatre' and keeping their coffeehouse, but now the theatre was shut up (it was only open for a summer season) so they sought donations.[47] She continued her businesses there, however, until the theatre finally closed for good in 1766 with the opening of the new theatre (later known as the Theatre Royal) in King Street, when she moved her printing office to the Maiden Tavern in nearby Baldwin Street, operating there until at least 1772.[48] In January 1767 she sought to rent a small house with garden near town.[49] Mary Hooke was buried at St James, Bristol on 13 August 1774. Her will, as Mary Hooke widow of Clifton, made 'being low in decline of life', was proved by her daughter Mary Hooke spinster on 21 October 1774, together with the other daughter Hester Hooke 'the only next of kin of said deceased'. It shows that, despite reduced circumstances, the widow still lived in some comfort.[50]

---

[45] BA, SMV/2/1/1/7 18 July 1751.

[46] BA 45883/7-8. Her playbills between 1754 and 1761 are described as 'printed by M. Hooke on St Augustine's Back', but from 1762 as from 'near the Theatre' or 'near Jacob's Well'.

[47] *Felix Farley's Bristol Journal* 13 August 1757.

[48] Bodleian GA Glos B4a, fo. 293; BA 8978(3), 45883/7-8 and 49534/11; *Felix Farley's Bristol Journal* 12 September 1767 and 16 July 1768.

[49] *Felix Farley's Bristol Journal* 24 January 1767.

[50] TNA PROB 11/1001/354. She leaves £400 in cash to Hester and £300 to Mary, as well as giving Mary £500 lent to the Bristol Bridge at rate of 4%. Hester receives '3 large pictures, a man and two women', and Mary 'all the other pictures' and 'all my letter press and types and everything thereunto belonging', plus 'all the furniture of my best parlour viz two sconce glasses, 8 leather bottom chairs, 3 large mahogany tables'.

Writings

Hooke published all his works in a few years between 1747 and 1751, and they can all be considered as extensions of his newspaper, expanding on its aims to educate the public in Whig truths and support George II and his Pelham administration. [51] Hooke broke with the standard press practices in presenting the news (primarily of European developments, such as the course of the War of Austrian Succession, though he also boasted contacts across the American colonies) in order to give his readers a correct understanding of events from a Whig perspective, This involved experimenting with various techniques, such as: abandoning the traditional presentation of the news in segments according the various postal deliveries, in favour of a single summary of the week's events; the provision of 'geographical notes' about places and people in the news; and essays offering perspectives on the news, including several on Russia which stressed its geographical and economic position and hence its long-term interests within the European system of powers.[52] While celebrating victories (such as Dettingen) and fully supporting the need for Britain to lead a coalition to contain the pretensions to universal monarchy of the Bourbons of France and Spain, Hooke counselled against oppositionist patriots who neglected the complex realities of warfare and diplomacy. He also sought to denigrate such oppositionists by associating them with Jacobitism and sedition, accusing them of hidden motives for questioning the policies and achievements of George II's government.[53] His readers were being given the intellectual resources to read and debate the news in an enlightened fashion.[54]

---

[51] *Oracle and Country Advertiser* 28 September 1745 has a front-page essay 'A Calm Address to all Parties in Religion' where Hooke argues that, leaving religion aside, the Jacobite rebellion was a profound threat to the 'civil interest and commerce' of Britain, as it would undo all the gains since 1689 and make Britain a puppet of France.
[52] *Oracle* 3 April 1742, 10 July-14 August 1742; *Bristol Oracle* 21 March 1747, 2 September 1749.
[53] In an essay on the 'selfish and egocentric tendencies of men' he observed that 'this humour keeps up Jacobitism' and was the only cause of opposition to His Majesty and the administration (*Oracle and Country Advertiser* 20 May 1749).
[54] For example, *Oracle and Country Advertiser* 1 January 1746 commenced a 'Short Review of the Affairs of Europe in 1745', 'better to open' the views of 'the intelligent reader' to future events.

His only publication to have attracted either contemporary or later scholarly attention[55] is his *Essay on the National Debt and National Capital*, which was published in two impressions in 1750,[56] with a second edition with additions the following year.[57] This presented a series of calculations of what we would now call the Gross Domestic Product to prove that the level of national debt was not, as government critics claimed, unsustainable, but rather perfectly manageable, adding, in line with his proposals for Bristol's corporation debts, a scheme for paying off the national debt via annuities.[58]

Its scope is therefore much greater than that of his first publication, *A Dialogue between a Member of Parliament and one of his Electors concerning the Window Tax* (1747), which is primarily a practical guide to the workings of that tax, written as a dialogue between 'Sir John' and an 'elector'.[59] However, they share both an underlying

---

[55] E.g. Robert Wallace, *Characteristics of the Political State of Great Britain* (London, 1758), pp. 123-4; V. de Mezague, *General View of England* (London, 1766), pp. 33, 115; Thomas Mortimer, *The Elements of Commerce* (London, 1774) vol. 1, pp. 423-7, 431-2 (urging Dr Price to use Hooke's tables); John Brand, *The Alteration of the Constitution of the House of Commons* (London, 1793), p. 70, citing praise for it by Sir John Sinclair and Malachi Postlethwayte. The fullest modern discussion is in B.H. Mitra-Kahn, 'Redefining the Economy' (unpublished PhD thesis in Economics, City University, London, 2011), pp. 135-42.

[56] Both impressions (ESTC N008694 and T033387) are 'London: printed for W. Owen publisher at Homer's Head, near Temple Bar; and sold by B. Hickey and J. Palmer booksellers and stationers in Bristol', but there are titlepage differences in the typeface, layout and spelling. *Bristol Journal* 20 January 1750 advertises it as just published at one shilling. *London Evening Post* 13 February 1750 advertises it with a notice that 'whoever pyrates it will be prosecuted' and 'to prevent impositions on the public no copies will be warranted genuine and correct but such as are signed with the author's own hand A. Hooke'.

[57] London: printed for W. Owen, publisher, at Homer's Head near Temple-Bar. MDCCLI. The dedication to Pelham is identical except that the date is changed from Bristol 6 December 1749 to January 1 1751. Subsequent quotations are from this edition. *Bristol Weekly Intelligencer* 6 April 1751 advertises it at 1s 6d.

[58] Hooke, *Essay*, pp. 53-61.

[59] London: printed for B. Hickey and J. Palmer, booksellers and stationers in Nicholas Street, Bristol; and sold by most other booksellers in town and country; as also by the author at his office in Shannon-Court and at his coffeehouse in Exchange Alley, 1747. (Price six-pence) (ESTC T182191). It is advertised in *Oracle and Country Advertiser* 11 April 1747. A 2nd edition (not recorded in ESTC) is advertised in *Bristol Oracle* from 19 July 1748.

political aim, namely to justify the financial policies of the Pelham administration, and a common method, namely political arithmetic. The *Dialogue* concludes with 'an estimate of the probable annual produce of the duties both in England and Scotland' which is based on estimates by 'your best political arithmeticians' of the numbers of houses in England and Scotland, the likely rates of exemption in both countries (fifty percent in the poorer Scotland, twenty five percent in England) and an (unexplained) average of sixteen windows per house, to give £510,000, with £60,000 in costs, leaving a net sum of £450,000.[60] The 'elector' voices the opinion that this is 'a noble fund for the government's service' and 'the most equitable and least burthensome that could have been thought on', praising the minister responsible (Pelham) as 'a gentleman of great honour and humanity'.[61] In his preface 'to the reader' Hooke characteristically asserts that if lawyers disagree with his interpretation, he 'preserves his modesty by assigning the reasons of his opinion and appealing to the publick judgement; and, if it should be his unhappy fate to be reproach'd with heresy, by your orthodox canonical lawyers … he thinks he runs no risqué of fire and faggot in a *Protestant* country, where free-thinking, and a right of private judgment, must always subsist on the basis of the Reformation'. Disagreements in opinion, 'since error is inseparable from humanity', should be dealt with in 'fair debate (either in publick or private)', treating 'the author with candour, good nature and lenity, becoming a scholar and a gentleman'.

A similar tone is struck in An *Essay on the National Debt*, dedicated to Pelham: the conclusion to the preface in 1751 adds a long list of the achievements of the Pelham administration: 'such masterstrokes of policy, executed under almost unsurmountable difficulties and in spite of the united efforts of all the branches of the House of *Bourbon* are overlook'd in the Pelhams which, in *British* story, would have done honour to the celebrated memories of a *Cecil* and a *Walsingham*'.[62] The dedication explains its purposes: to prove that 'commerce is the genuine source of wealth and power' through the gradual advance in British wealth since Elizabeth so that 'the annual

---

[60] Hooke, *Dialogue*, pp. 43-7.

[61] Ibid, p. 45.

[62] Hooke, *Essay*, p. xii. Hooke had written a letter of 6 folios to Henry Pelham 6 August 1748 suggesting the scheme to raise revenue to pay off the national debt (Univ. of Nottingham Special Collections, papers of Henry Pelham: NeC 318/1-3).

superlucration or increment of the capital stock over and above the expences of the people surpasses, at this day, the revenues of the French king, and doubles the produce of the mines of Peru and Mexico'. Hence, a British King 'reigning in the hearts of his subjects, at the head of Britain's Parliament and wise ministry is the richest and most potent prince in Europe' with 'great national abilities', if fully asserted by his ministers, 'to render His Majesty the terror of tyrants, the arbiter of Europe and a most powerful protector of the rights and liberties of mankind'. Through Hooke's 'new and arduous … critico-political survey of the internal state of Great Britain', the 'leaders of the Opposition may, to their mortification, see their grand mystery of iniquity revealed', by disproving their 'daring denunciations of a national bankruptcy'. Hence 'the unhappy deluded population may, to their great consolation, see, that the grand battery, or *dernier ressort*, of the disaffected, introduced with so much pomp and parade to deceive and intimidate the credulous and inattentive, when unmasked, proves a mere harmless apparatus devoid of every direful consequence; and that the source of all the fears and clamours, artfully raised and industriously propagated on the subject, is only the produce of phantom and chimaera, and has no real foundation in reason and nature'.

The 'introductory preface' to the second edition extends this. Explaining that the pamphlet is an expansion of the 'first sketches … hastily drawn in July 1749' and published 'in three successive *Bristol Oracles*' to oppose those 'weekly writers against the administration', he reports that some of his readers thought it 'might be a public service to give it a more diffusive circulation' in a small pamphlet with London publication, where it sold out of its first edition in a very few weeks.[63] Before issuing a revised edition, he 'determined to wait the public judgment', including critical responses, especially as he was conscious that he lacked key evidence of the 'mint account of the coinage in the last four reigns' and would have been happy to revise or retract his case 'as a sincere lover of truth'.[64] Instead, the response came in an attack by James Ralph in his opposition paper *The Remembrancer* (issue 120, 24

---

[63] Ibid, pp. i-ii. The original essays 'Of the National Debt' had occupied 10 and a half columns in *Oracle and Country Advertiser* of 15 and 29 July 1749 and *Bristol Oracle* 22 July 1749.

[64] Ibid, p. ii.

March 1750). But, to Hooke's delight, Ralph's attempted discrediting of his argument provided exactly the coinage information he was lacking, in a way which, Hooke claimed, confirmed his own arguments, 'so that what was before a matter of belief and opinion only, is now become a matter of confidence and assurance, upon the highest evidence the nature of the thing is capable of'.[65] As he explains 'arguments grounded on historical facts, and by proper mediums drawn out into just and coherent consequences, will discover remote truths, with as much certainty in the *moral* as in the *natural* world: so that Political Arithmetic is not barely a speculative amusement, as 'tis generally esteemed, but, when rightly apply'd has a better claim to be rank'd among the sciences than many other branches of literature thus dignify'd'.[66] He develops this claim later in the pamphlet, comparing what he has done first to 'political chemistry' in analysing 'this complicated subject' and 'fairly resolving' it 'into its original principles, with an honest intention to reveal it to the public in its natural, simple, and naked form, abstracted from all mystery and disguises'.[67] Then he claims to have given his reader a 'specimen of the *new philosophy*, as applicable to politico-arithmetical subjects … We have built no castles in the air, upon mere hypothetical foundations, by making our own data, like the *Cartesian* philosophers, who reason right, indeed, but upon wrong principles: No! our scheme is perfectly *Newtonian*: our first principles are a few plain historical facts, well established, and our conclusions from them, clear, natural and, we hope, just.'[68]

It is beyond the scope of this essay to detail Hooke's methods in calculating the level of the 'national stock', which draws largely on data from Petty and Davenant (with ample criticism of both) as well as coinage figures and information from land and housing taxes. His key conclusions are that, were the national debt that of an individual, that man would be 'justly reputed in most flourishing circumstances whose *debts* do not amount to a *twelfth* part of his capital, or to *four fifths* of his annual *income*, and whose yearly profits in trade will, if appropriated to that purpose, actually discharge the whole within the space of *seven* years at *simple interest?*'[69] But of

---

[65] Ibid, p. vii.
[66] Ibid, p. viii.
[67] Ibid, p. 50.
[68] Ibid, pp. 51-2.

equal importance to him is his finding that, in 1600, 1660, 1688 and 1749, the ratios of 'cash stock, personal stock [which included commercial and industrial property] and land stock' remained roughly constant at 1, 20, and 12.33, thus demonstrating that land was not the major source of wealth.[70] He also critiques Davenant's jeremiads about the negative consequences of the Glorious Revolution and subsequent wars, using a battery of indicators of a massive increase not only in the value of trade, shipping and other personal assets, but also in the value of land since 1688.[71]

Just as Hooke's works of political arithmetic dealt heavily with history, at least since 1600, so his two historical publications drew heavily on political arithmetic and were intended to illustrate the centrality of commerce to historical progress. Had they been published beyond the early medieval period they would undoubtedly have been presented his Protestant and Whig interpretations of both British and Bristol history. Indeed for Hooke these two were indistinguishable, both demonstrating the progress of trade and liberty until the crisis of 1688, when God stepped in to save both through William's intervention.[72] Unfortunately, only a fraction of Hooke's historical material was ever published: several collections of historical information remain in manuscript.[73] These reveal the thoroughness with which Hooke collected and analysed historical information, not just from the city archives but also from various national collections, reflected in his correspondence with antiquarians such as Browne Willis, and from all the available printed sources.[74]

---

[69] Ibid, p. 31.

[70] Ibid, p. 33.

[71] Ibid, pp. 38-50.

[72] A. Hooke, *Dissertation on the Antiquity of Bristol* (London, 1748), dedication.

[73] Bristol Central Library, Bristol Collection (hereafter BCL), 4504-5 notes for history of Bristol by Hooke; BA 45934/121 biographical notes on bishops, deans and prebendaries of Bristol by Hooke (formerly BCL 5009).

[74] Hooke, *Dissertation*, thanks the Corporation for the 'readiness and unanimity with which you granted my request of having free recourse to the city archives' (p. iii) and acknowledges his Oxford correspondent, probably Charles Godwyn of Balliol (pp. 27, 33) and Browne Willis (pp. 52-3) whose work is also cited in BA 45934/121. A March 1747 letter of Hooke to the Rev. Samuel Rogers, asking him to intercede further with his friend Willis for assistance in transcribing Domesday book entries and other materials, refers to Willis's earlier provision of lists of MPs, through the help of Robert Hoblyn, M.P. for Bristol since 1742 (Ken Spelman, Rare Books of York,

The title page of his unfinished *Bristollia: or Memoirs of the City of Bristol, both Civil and Ecclesiastical* also promised a second part, after the historical, with 'a topographical view of Bristol, describing the city in general, with every parish, and extraparochial precinct in particular; containing their respective extents, boundaries, squares, streets, lanes, number of houses and inhabitants; parochial and other officers; annual taxes; publick edifices and select private buildings; alphabetically digested according to the parishes, Together with a brief account of its shipping, navigation, commerce, riches and government, civil, ecclesiastical and military.' So, Hooke planned to combine history with geography as well as political arithmetic.[75] However, when he failed to attract the requisite 500 subscriptions to enable him to proceed directly with the book, he decided to publish it in his newspaper and then, when that failed, to publish it serially, reprinting his introductory work on Bristol's antiquity first.[76]

It has not aided Hooke's reputation as a historian that his only complete publication on Bristol, his *Dissertation on the Antiquity of Bristol*,[77] is devoted to what we might now regard as an ahistorical (or certainly historically incorrect) endeavour to prove, contrary to Camden's *Britannia*, that Bristol was not a late Saxon foundation but as ancient as London or York, during which he even gives some credence to the myth of its foundation by the Trojan prince Brennus, echoing medieval and annalistic accounts largely

---

Catalogue 77, January 2014, item no 7 at https://issuu.com/spelman/docs/cat_77_mss). See also BCL, 11161 27 July 1747 letter to the other M.P, Sir Edward Southwell, regarding lists of Bristol M.P.s. Both Southwell and Hoblyn were moderate Tories.

[75] The printed prospectus for *Bristollia*, detailing the proposed chapters, can be found in Bodleian MS Willis 43, fo. 87.

[76] See *Bristol Oracle* 28 May 1748. To accommodate gentlemen who had subscribed he would reprint quarterly from his paper what relates to Bristol by itself and deliver books in numbers to those who were quarterly subscribers to his paper at 6d and to all others at 12d per number. See also his note at start of Godwyn's copy of *Bristollia* in Bodl. Gough Som Add 8o 12, stating that 'his circumstances s are too well known to need any other apology' and that he has 'greatly suffered by the undertaking'.

[77] London: printed for W. Owen, publisher at the Homer's Head, near Temple Bar (no date given, but 1748) (ESTC T197669). The *Dissertation* was then reprinted as the introduction to *Bristollia* later in 1748. See *Bristol Oracle* 10 December 1748, *Bristollia* no 1 'speedily published', starting with the *Dissertation*, confirmed in the following week's *Oracle and Country Advertiser*, at one shilling per number.

abandoned by early modern scholars. Yet though clearly based on civic patriotism, his argument for antiquity is made not only using historical scholarship regarding the various settlement names that had been associated with Bristol by chroniclers and antiquarians, but also on the basis of geography. His fundamental argument was that Bristol's location made it such a natural trading centre that it must have been important, recorded by topographers but ignored by monkish historians only interested in religion and monarchy: once it became a centre of church and royal power then it attracted their attention. Hooke denigrated as pedantry Camden's humanist learning and undue respect for his scholarly authority, presenting himself, as in his political arithmetic, as a man who argued scientifically from raw historical and geographical facts to reach conclusions which must be true even if previous learning did not support them.[78] Using the Bills of Mortality to estimate gaps between generations and postulating a 400-year period of natural growth for a town to obtain a 'rank among the capitals of its country', he explained that while 'the generality of readers' may not see the force of such reasoning, those 'acquainted with the doctrine of annuities and political arithmetic know very well that arguments founded on a series of observations on the general law of nature or providence, notwithstanding the appearance of change or contingency, conclude with greater probability than other philosophical reasonings and approach as near to mathematical certainty as any other arguments whatsoever'.[79]

However, once he began his detailed annalistic history of Bristol in 1066, Hooke offered a well-informed critical digest of the traditional sources of medieval history. Perhaps too well-informed, because the early issues of his *Bristollia* were essentially a national history of the reigns of William I and II, with almost no reference to Bristol, so it is perhaps hardly surprising that he gained few subscribers and abandoned the publication after 56 pages, having only reached 1097![80] It is already clear from this section, however,

---

[78] I have explored Hooke's historical work in more detail in 'Chatterton in Bristol', *Angelaki,* 1:2 (winter 1993/4), 55-81, at pp. 56-8, 61-3, 69-70.

[79] Hooke, *Dissertation*, pp. 39-41.

[80] He began printing the memoirs in *Bristol Oracle* 25 June 1748, where they form the whole back page, but unfortunately the next four issues are missing, and by *Oracle and Country Advertiser* 30 July 1748 there are no memoirs. *Bristol Oracle* 7 August 1748 states that the third number of *Bristollia* is not to be printed till 500 stated customers,

as well as his manuscript notes for later periods, that he would have been highly critical of papal and clerical claims to authority while lauding the growth of constitutional liberty and local rights. He discusses, for example, whether the crown was hereditary or elective, judging that 'the rule of succession in the Saxon age stood in the same principles of reason and policy and was supported by the same inviolable maxims of the law of nature and nations as at present' so that 'hereditary or testamentary right' was 'always connected with, at least, the tacit consent of the people and whenever that was wanting, as appears from the whole tenor of English history, our ancestors never failed to assert their innate right of election'.[81]

Conclusion

A distinct irony runs through the life and writings of Andrew Hooke. Literally a child of 1688, he spent his career defending the Whig cause of Protestant liberty and exalting the rapid growth in Britain's wealth and power since 1688, which he sought to document through political arithmetic. Stressing the role of commerce and of cities like his native Bristol, he sought to educate his fellow citizens (local and national) in the geographical and financial knowledge which underpinned this progress, and to take advantage of new financial devices, such as annuities, to fund improvements. Yet his personal finances followed exactly the opposite trajectory: heir of a substantial estate built on brewing and sugar manufacture, he chose the life of a 'scholar and gentleman' and lost his estate, entered debtor's prison, could not sustain his highbrow newspaper against the competition of a mere printer whose values he despised, and ended his life dependent on an annuity from the Whig merchant elite from whose ranks he, and his family, had fallen. His attempts to enlighten his fellow citizens failed to attract wide support (at least in terms of sales), probably appealing largely to those already converted to his Whig enlightened values, who could appreciate his attempts to explain and justify government policy as built on long-term geographical and economic principles. Unlike other newspaper proprietors, such

---

which was clearly never achieved, though he tried again in December (see above).
[81] Hooke, *Bristollia*, pp. 12-13. Cf. pp. 33-4 on the rise of 'papal intrigues' to extend their authority and 'undermine the sovereignty of the crown and subvert the liberties of the people'.

as Robert Raikes in Gloucester or Robert Goadby in Sherborne,[82] he lacked the entrepreneurial skills to build up a long-term customer base for a regional paper built on Whig values. Hooke's career reminds us that, as Black has so ably demonstrated, the 'Whig supremacy', in so far as it was ever achieved, was no inevitable outcome, but the much-contested product of strenuous effort, at both national and local levels, with many setbacks. Yet Hooke might have taken some comfort from the electoral success, the year after his death, of Robert Nugent as a Whig candidate for Bristol, who drew heavily on the services of Josiah Tucker, Bristol's more famous (and heavyweight) Whig intellectual, in developing much the same case for the Whig government of Newcastle, as Hooke had for his brother's administration.[83]

---

[82] David Stoker, 'Robert Raikes, 1690-1757', *ODNB* https://doi.org/10.1093/ref:odnb/70911; Jonathan Barry and George Tatham, 'Robert Goadby, the *Sherborne Mercury* and the urban renaissance in south-west England' in Catherine Armstrong and John Hinks (ed.) *The English Urban Renaissance Revisited* (Newcastle, 2018), pp. 57-95.
[83] Shelton, *Dean Tucker*, pp. 133-61.

Lord Grantham and the Foreign Secretaryship, 1782-83: personalities and peace making during the 'Crisis of the Constitution'

Nigel Aston

From the start of his academic career, eighteenth-century international relations have been a primary focus for Jeremy Black's research and writing. From his 1982 Durham doctorate *British foreign policy 1727-1731* to his most recent extended coverage of the same subject across the reigns of the first two Georges, foreign policy as it was variously and contingently constructed by diplomats, politicians, Parliament, the press, and public opinion, has repeatedly claimed his attention and disclosed a rare archival and analytical mastery.[1] As much as any scholar in his generation, he has kept diplomatic history alive by reimagining ways of writing it and thereby shown how superficial was its unfashionability. Black's interest in the slightly later George III era –the inspiration for this essay– was awakened by Tim Blanning at Cambridge well before the Durham move and he began archival work on it in 1978, originally planning that it should be the subject of his doctoral dissertation. That was not in fact the case (he ceded precedence to another historian who never completed) but Black still published three articles on British foreign policy after the end of the American War of Independence in 1984 and 1987.

His research culminated in the publication of one of his finest books, *British Foreign Policy in an Age of Revolutions 1783-1793*, published by Cambridge University Press in 1994, the work, as one reviewer rather prematurely put it, 'of an historian at the height of his powers'.[2] Black considered policy formulation from a variety of perspectives, including peripheral as well as central figures in Britain's diplomatic establishment, as efforts were made to create a new foreign policy in the aftermath of international humiliation. One of those who might reasonably have been foremost and instrumental in that task (but deliberately chose not to be) was

---

[1] Structural aspects of foreign policy over a long timeframe were treated, for instance, in *A System of Ambition? British Foreign Policy 1660-1793* (London, 1991) and more recently, in ed. J. Black, *The Tory World. Deep History and the Tory Theme in British Foreign Policy, 1679-2014* (Farnham, 2015).

[2] John K. Severn in *Albion*, 27 (1995), 316-17.

Thomas Robinson, 2nd Baron Grantham (1738-86), the subject of this chapter and the man who was Pitt the Younger's first choice as Foreign Secretary in December 1783. The essay is a further attempt to reinsert Grantham's importance in the complicated international and domestic politics of 1782-84, to recover his distinct contribution to peace-making as Foreign Secretary in the 2nd Earl of Shelburne's government (July 1782-March 1783), and to argue for an exceptional, overlooked clarity in his diplomatic outlook that contemporaries including Pitt recognised and drew on in the early years of his ministry.[3]

Grantham's premature death aged just 48 has worked against a proportionate recognition of his contribution to public life. If measured by dint of diplomatic and domestic administrative experience, he was as well-qualified as any of his contemporaries for the Foreign Secretaryship in 1782.[4] And his was a career path that turned out closely replicating one followed by his father, Sir Thomas Robinson (1695-1770), British ambassador to the Habsburg court in Vienna 1730-48 (where his eldest son was born), and later Secretary of State for the Southern Department and (ill-suited) leader of the House of Commons, 1754-5.[5] Indeed, their careers somewhat overlapped: the younger Thomas followed his father as MP for Christchurch in 1761 and entered government as a commissioner of trade and plantations in 1766, just as the 1st Baron left it.[6] It was thanks to the latter that his son had his first (false, as it turned out) start as a diplomat when named in 1761 as secretary

---

[3] Andrew Stockley contended that Grantham's importance had been underestimated in his *Britain and France at the Birth of America: The European Powers and the Peace Negotiations* (Exeter, 2001), 147-50.

[4] David, Viscount Stormont (1727-94), the outgoing Northern Secretary, would be an exception but he had followed Lord North out of office when the latter's ministry ended in March 1782.

[5] D. B. Horn, *The British Diplomatic Service 1689-1789* (Oxford, 1961), 107. The elder Robinson was also MP for Christchurch, 1748-61; a Privy Councillor, 1750; a lord commissioner of trade, 1748-9; Master of the Great Wardrobe, 1749-54, 1755-60; joint-Postmaster-General, 1765-6. Appointed KB, 1742; cr. 1st Baron Grantham, 1761, died 30 Sept. 1770.
http://www.historyofparliamentonline.org/volume/1754-1790/member/robinson-sir-thomas-1695-1770

[6] He missed only 11 out of 150 meetings between 1768 and 1770.
http://www.historyofparliamentonline.org/volume/1754-1790/member/robinson-hon-thomas-1738-86

to the British embassy for the intended peace congress at Augsburg.[7] When Lord North took office as First Lord of the Treasury in January 1770 Robinson was appointed vice-chamberlain of the royal household and named a Privy Councillor until succession to his father's barony led to a plum diplomatic appointment as ambassador at the court of Carlos III of Spain in Madrid in 1771.[8] Having discharged his duties with what was widely admitted to be consummate professionalism until Spain joined France in declaring war on Britain in June 1779, Grantham returned home to receive public office within eighteen months, resuming his post at the Board of Trade and Plantations, this time as First Commissioner on 9 December 1780,[9] an office he held until its abolition in 1782 (he quit on 11 July) under Edmund Burke's 'Economical Reform' legislation.

Lord Grantham's aptitude for public service at home and abroad would have come as no surprise to those who knew and nurtured him as a boy and young man. He was educated at Westminster School and Christ's College, Cambridge where he had the good fortune to have Beilby Porteus as his tutor.[10] Porteus, knowing that his charge was broadly intended to follow a career trajectory similar to his father's and finding in the son a receptive intelligence, encouraged his pupil to secure a thorough grounding in classical literature while reading in more modern literature that might be of value in shaping his perspective and attitude towards contemporary concerns.[11] After graduation, young Robinson spent eighteen

---

[7] For the circumstances of this appointment and the key patronage of Charles, 2nd earl of Egremont see T. Robinson to James Grant of Grant, 24 June 1761, Scottish National Archives, GD. 248/177/1/89, quoted in J. Black, *British Diplomats and Diplomacy 1688-1800* (Exeter, 2001), 25-6.

[8] As well as the title and the estate, the new Lord Grantham inherited the pension of £2,860 p.a. awarded Sir Thomas Robinson for diplomatic services. See below.

[9] He also acquired the lucrative sinecure of Chief Justice in Eyre North of the Trent the same month. *GM* 50 (1780), 51.

[10] Beilby Porteus (1731-1809), BA Christ's College, 1752; fellow, 1752. Later domestic chaplain to archbishop Secker of Canterbury (1769-2); chaplain to the king, 1769; bishop of Chester, 1776-87; translated to London, 1787. Supported the rising Evangelical party in both dioceses. There is no evidence that he made any attempt to imbue Grantham (a thoroughly conventional Anglican) with that approach to the faith. J. Gascoigne, *Cambridge in the age of the Enlightenment. Science, religion and politics from the Restoration to the French Revolution* (Cambridge, 1989), 264-5.

[11] 'dear Tommy', Sir Thomas Robinson hoped, would apply himself to civil law after classical learning: 12 June 1755, WYAS, 150/12205.

months on Tour in Italy (1759-61) and became personally acquainted with all the leading portraitists, Mengs and Batoni among them, and took lessons himself at the Academy in Turin.[12] And he had a life-long passion for architectural design within a palladian idiom loosely commensurate with the Robinson family's principal seat at Newby Park in the North Riding of Yorkshire between Boroughbridge and Thirsk.[13]

By the time he succeeded to his father's barony in 1770, Thomas Robinson's character was formed. He was genial and personable, possessed of an underlying seriousness but with a nice line in self-deprecation, the sort of individual whose participation would strengthen any administration. Robinson was close to his family members throughout life. Father-son relations were at all times strong and well-balanced,[14] and after the 1st Lord's demise, his eldest son's relations with his younger brother, the Hon. Frederick Robinson (always known as 'Fritz') (1746-92), were unfailingly congenial: Grantham took him to Madrid as Secretary to the Embassy in 1772 and, after their return to England, relied on 'Fritz' to act as his agent in local affairs in the Ripon vicinity so long as public duties kept him in London. Though eminently sociable, Grantham had no reputation for dissipation and remained unmarried until his return home from Madrid when, at the age of 42, in August 1780, he took as his wife Lady Mary Jemima Grey Yorke (1757-1830), youngest daughter and co-heir of Philip, 2nd Earl of Hardwicke, and Jemima, *suo jure* Marchioness Grey.[15] Their

---

[12] He impressed most of those who met him. Sir Horace Mann called him a 'glorious young fellow indeed and most amiable'. Quoted in J. Ingamells, *A Dictionary of British and Irish Travellers in Italy 1701-1800* (New Haven and London, 1997), 816-17. He was a member of the Dilettanti Club and FSA from 1763.

[13] See, for instance, his project for a hill temple for his brother-in-law, John Parker, of Saltram, Devonshire. J. Harris, 'The Importance of the Amateur in Innovation', in G. Worsley, (ed.) *The Role of the Amateur Architect. Papers Given at the Georgian Group Symposium 1993* (London, 1994), 40-3.

[14] See his letters to Fritz, 24 Oct 1765, WYAS (Leeds), Vyner MSS: 6015/14443, 24 Oct. 1765; Vyner MSS: 6015/14494, 23 Nov. 1765.

[15] WYAS (Leeds), NH [Newby Hall] 2753 for the settlement. The Yorke and Robinson families were well-known to each from their common Pelhamite allegiance. Indeed, the 2nd Earl had written to Robinson back in 1768: 'I consider the late D: of Newcastle, as the last of a very great & respectable set of men for whose memory & services all the Lovers of their Country & the Constitution must cherish an unalterable regard'. 17 Nov. 1768, WYAS (Leeds), Vyner MSS: 6033/12412

married life together was short, but it seems to have been an abundantly happy one.[16]

Like other Court Whigs, Lord Hardwicke had latterly abandoned his family's old Whig politics and Rockinghamite connection in favour of supporting Lord North's government,[17] a trajectory that the Robinson family had followed rather earlier. It would be an exaggeration to call the 2nd Lord Grantham a thoroughgoing Northite; eight years in Spain had kept him out of the mainstream of British politics and his involvement in government arose from a combination from an unarticulated sense of public duty, a proven capacity for business, and a need of the salary that office afforded him. But he continued to vote for the administration in the Lords – as did his brother in the Commons– until North's resignation on 20 March 1782.[18] Grantham was one of the very few individuals who did not lose his place in the new government when Lord Rockingham took over as First Lord of the Treasury. That decision is readily explained: the Robinson family had a long-standing political and neighbourly affinity with Rockingham and his connexion (both peers had their seat in Yorkshire) that had only recently been overlaid; both parties were aware that the Board of Trade and Plantations was slated for abolition; and Grantham's proven administrative competence was at a premium that spring.

The Rockingham government lasted barely three months before the marquess died on 1 July 1782 and a new administration was controversially formed around the previous Home Secretary and

---

[16] His new wife's sister was pleased with the choice. 'Though he cannot make great settlements, & is some years older than my sister she has chose him herself, as he bears an aimiable character, & seems good-humour'd & good natur'd'. Lady Ammabel Yorke, Diary, 68: 12 July 1780. West Yorks Vyner Add. MS. 2299. Diaries of Lady Amabel Yorke, vo. 5, p. 21, 10 Sept. 1776.] He was very much his new wife's own choice. Mary Yorke to Ly Amabel Grey, Beds and Luton Archives, L30/11/339/47. 23 July 1780.

[17] I. R. Christie, *The End of North's Ministry 1780-1782* (London, 1958), 74; G. M. Ditchfield, 'The House of Lords in the Age of the American Revolution', ed. C. Jones (ed.), *A Pillar of the Constitution: The House of Lords in British Politics, 1640-1784* (London, 1989), 199-236, at 224.

[18] His proxy vote had been lodged with ministers while he was in Madrid. House of Lords Record Office, Proxy books, 1770-82. The Hon. Frederick Robinson sat for Ripon from 1780 to 1787. The Robinson family had only indirect electoral influence in that pocket burgage borough. Christie, *End of North's Ministry*, 402.

George III's personal choice, Lord Shelburne. It led to a fracture in the Whig world over the next ten days as the majority of Rockingham's followers decided they could not serve under Shelburne, one whose principles and conduct made him, in their view, thoroughly untrustworthy. Charles James Fox resigned as Foreign Secretary on 4 July, other departures quickly followed and Shelburne was obliged to make up his ministry as best as he could.[19] Among the key Cabinet changes, Pitt the Younger became Chancellor of the Exchequer, the Secretary-at-War, Thomas Townshend succeeded Shelburne at the Home Office and led in the House of Commons, and Lord Grantham accepted the Foreign Secretaryship.[20] Whatever the latter's reservations about Shelburne's suitability for the Premiership, Grantham does not appear to have hesitated about taking high office.[21] He knew how government worked –or was expected to work– from the inside. He was personally acquainted with a high proportion of Britain's envoys currently accredited to foreign courts. And the immense policy challenge of peace making that lay ahead must have appealed to his honest assessment of his own capacities, even to his admittedly muted ambition.

More immediately, there was the need to conclude the war against the American colonists and the European powers –France, Spain, and Holland– in a manner that combined economy with dignity and on such a sufficiently successful basis that the shadow of defeat at Yorktown would be offset in the peace negotiations.[22] It would not be easy at a moment when, it has been argued, 'British standing

---

[19] For doubts about the new appointments see J. Cannon, *The Fox-North Coalition. Crisis of the Constitution, 1782-4* (Cambridge, 1969), 25-6.

[20] He was notified of his selection 11 July (*Daily Advertiser*, 12, 13 July), kissed hands 17 July, sworn of the Privy Council the same day (*London Gazette*, no 12314, 16-20 July); John Norris, *Shelburne and Reform* (London, 1963), 173-4.

[21] It may be that his name was suggested by the 4th Duke of Rutland, Pitt's Cambridge friend, and Lord Steward (and a Cabinet member) repacing Carlisle towards the end of the Shelburne government. Grantham was personally known to Rutland from at least 1779. A. Lock, *Catholicism, Identity and Politics in the Age of Enlightenment. The Life and Career of Sir Thomas Gascoigne, 1745-1810* (Woodbridge, 2016), 70, 79, 82, 83.

[22] Rodney's naval victory over the French at the Battle of the Saints in the West Indies in May 1782 was a means to that end. S. Conway, '"A Joy Unknown for Years Past": The American War, Britishness and the Clebration of Rodney's Victory at the Saints', *History* 86 (2001). The entire British naval position in the western Mediterranean still remained in the balance until Gibraltar was relieved for a third time in Oct. 1782.

across the continent was at rock bottom'.[23] In all this, Grantham was not constructing policy from scratch. He assumed office when its pattern had already been set during the brief Foreign Secretaryship of Charles James Fox in the Rockingham administration. He had wanted to proceed without delay to granting independence to the American colonists in order to isolate the Bourbon powers and had instructed his envoy in Paris, Thomas Grenville (responsible for negotiations with France and Spain), accordingly; Shelburne, as Home Secretary (under whose jurisdiction all colonies came), preferred to use any offer of independence as a bargaining chip in what would be a comprehensive overall peace settlement, and advised his envoy, Richard Oswald, to that effect. By early June 1782 Fox was so furious at what he saw as the deliberate obstructionism of Shelburne and Oswald in Cabinet and behind the scenes that it became a resigning issue for him quite separately from Rockingham's death, especially after the Cabinet on 30 June voted against the Foreign Secretary's proposal for the immediate grant of independence to America under the Great Seal.[24]

Fox's stormy departure at least offered the chance for the Shelburne ministry to proceed more harmoniously in its diplomatic manoeuevering and use public suspicion about excessive Whig partiality for the American cause to its advantage. There would, presumably, no longer be any danger of running together two divergent peace-making policies and Grantham, as Foreign Secretary, would be expected to complement and endorse those that the new Premier had attempted to run as Home Secretary. It is uncertain how far Grantham, on his appointment, felt able to do anything other than go forward on any other basis. Beyond the Yorke/Hardwicke connection and his own family, he lacked his own political following, had minimal electoral influence outside Ripon, and had made relatively little impact on proceedings in the Lords since his return to England in 1779. He was in post because of his proven professional competence, his personal decency, and, probably, because Shelburne considered him primarily a career diplomat whose lack of attachment to a party was a positive

---

[23] B. Simms, *Three Victories and a Defeat. The Rise and Fall of the First British Empire* (Harmondsworth, 2007), 658.

[24] L.G. Mitchell, *Charles James Fox* (Oxford, 1992), 48-55, for details from Fox's perspective.

advantage.[25] The very fact that he had been notified of his selection rather than negotiated it suggests Grantham's obedience to what he viewed primarily as a royal command[26] and his compliance could have given Shelburne further grounds for considering the new Foreign Secretary would play second fiddle in the construction of policy.

The working relationship of the two men would be crucial to the success of the administration formed in July 1782. Given that they were both essentially unknown quantities to each other in recent years,[27] it was something of a gamble for both men.[28] Shelburne would have known that Grantham was a steady, dependable figure, with a proven capacity for mastering detail. He was potentially vital to the felicitous outcome of ending the war with Spain for he spoke Spanish, knew that kingdom at first-hand, and was familiar with the Spanish court and politicians (and was known and liked by them). And that expertise and diplomatic finesse could be crucial in bringing Spain, the most belligerent of the Bourbon powers, to the negotiating table. Shelburne had none of those assets. The challenge for Grantham was to create promptly a transparent partnership with a First Minister whose reputation for that quality was chequered, to say the least, and was being publicly and privately bad-mouthed by Fox, Burke, and Sheridan throughout that summer. Of the other Cabinet members Grantham was slightly known to Lord Chancellor Thurlow (they had both served with North), and the Lord Privy Seal, the duke of Grafton (previously in office as First Lord of the Treasury, 1768-70); his fellow Secretary of State, Thomas Townshend (1733-1800), had moved in Opposition circles in the 1770s. All these figures and the rest —Pitt,

---

[25] The king was correct in his opinion when he wrote: 'I am certain to the corps diplomatique his nomination will be agreeable'. George III to Shelburne, 13 July 1782, Fortescue, *Correspondence*, vi. 83. Thus see, for example, the compliments of Sir Horace Mann from Florence, 6 Aug. 1782, TNA SP 105/299, f. 14.

[26] George III preferred a Secretary of State who had served abroad. D. B. Horn, *The British Diplomatic Service 1689-1789* (Oxford, 1961), p. 109.

[27] They had overlapped in office between 1766 and 1768 when Shelburne was Secretary of State for the Southern Department.

[28] Shelburne was not spoilt for choice given the factional division between himself on the one hand and North and Fox on the other. As one Northite noted: 'Some of the appointments made since Mr Fox's resignation are, perhaps, best accounted for from the difficulties Lord Shelbourne must have found in making his arrangements.' To William Knox, *HMC Various Collections*, vol. vi (Dublin, 1909), 14 July 1782, 187.

Ashburton, and Richmond- had an established political profile in 1782 and stood in some sort of recent previous relation to Shelburne. With the possible exception of the First Lord of the Admiralty, Augustus, Viscount Keppel, Grantham was the odd man out.[29] How far that disconnection would signify remained to be seen.

His immediate task was to get on with peace making and put the negotiations in Paris on a more stable basis than had been the case between April and June 1782. But Grantham also had to get to grips with a very complicated Foreign Office brief when leisure to do so was lacking and Shelburne had the advantage of first-hand familiarity with the diplomacy already undertaken plus the advice and resources afforded him by the so-called 'Bowood Circle.'[30] He retained primary and personal control of negotiations regarding the settlement with the thirteen Colonies.[31] Given these realities, Grantham had no choice but to follow in the Premier's wake rather than rush to carve out a negotiating stance of his own. Besides, there had been enough of that awkward diversity when Fox had been in office and Grenville his representative at Versailles. His request for a recall was gratified and Shelburne's replacement for him on 16 July was the precociously competent Alleyne Fitzherbert (1753-1839), known already to Grantham from his service as envoy at Brussels (1777-82). From his first years as ambassador at Madrid, Grantham was also personally acquainted with the chief Spanish negotiator in France and its ambassador there since 1773, the conde de Aranda (who received full powers to negotiate in August 1782).[32] It became gradually apparent in London that Aranda and his superior, the conde de Floridablanca, Carlos III's Secretary of State

---

[29] Both Keppel and Grantham had been in office alongside Shelburne in the Chatham ministry formed in 1766. For Grantham's tie to the Duke of Rutland.

[30] For Shelburne's role in the peace negotiations the fullest account remains V. T. Harlow, *The Founding of the Second British Empire, 1763-1793*, vol. 1: *Discovery and Revolution* (London, 1952), 223-447.

[31] The Home Secretary, Townshend, played a very minor role in the American negotiations. Jonathan R. Dull, *A Diplomatic History of the American Revolution* (New Haven, 1985), 144. See Charles R. Ritcheson, 'The Earl of Shelburne and Peace with America, 1782-1783: Vision and Reality', *International History Review*, 5 (1983), 322-45.

[32] For Aranda, his leadership of the so-called Aragonese party, and his enlightenment preferences see M. Artola, (ed.), *Enciclopedia de historia de Espana. Vol. 4, Diccionario biográfico* (Madrid, 1991).

since 1777, were both distrustful of each other personally and had
different policy objectives: Aranda most concerned on preserving
the integrity of the Spanish empire in America (if necessary,
conceding more autonomy), Floridablanca making the recovery of
Gibraltar his priority.[33] On 7 October 1782, Aranda presented
Charles III's peace terms to Fitzherbert with a comprehensive list of
territorial demands that included the return of Gibraltar.[34]
However, it coincided with the total failure of Bourbon forces to
take the Rock by assault and the French indicating their view
regarding the likelihood of ever recapturing it militarily by
withdrawing their troops from the besiegers. Even if the Spanish
had captured Gibraltar, Grantham wrote to Fitzherbert, Britain
would not relinquish Gibraltar for the territories Spain was
offering.[35] Orán was not viewed as an acceptable alternative.

Grantham's expertise regarding Spanish politics and policies made
an underrated input into the shaping of British policy during the
peace negotiations, but the crucial contacts were between
Shelburne personally and the French Foreign Minister, the comte
de Vergennes', de facto deputy as under-secretary [*premier commis*]
and personal representative, Joseph-Mathias-Gérard Rayneval, who
visited Shelburne at his Wiltshire estate of Bowood in September
1782 with a list of items Vergennes considered requisite for peace
preliminaries to be agreed.[36] He returned on a second mission on

---

[33] Orville T. Murphy, *Charles Gravier Comte de Vergennes. French Diplomacy in the Age of
the Revolution 1719-1787* (Albany, NY, 1982), 329-30.

[34] To facilitate negotiations, Aranda sent one of his scretaries, Don Ignacio Heredia to
London in Dec. 1782 to deal directly with Shelburne and Grantham. W. N.
Hargreaves-Mawdsley, *Eighteenth-Century Spain 1700-1788. A Political, Diplomatic &
Institutional History* (London, 1979), 138.

[35] Grantham to Fitzherbert, 21 Oct., 9 Nov. 1782', L. G. Wickham Legg, *British
Diplomatic Instructions, 1689-1789*, VII, *France, part IV, 1745-1798* (London, 1934)
[Camden third series, vol. 49], pp. 193-5; 195-99. Grantham ordered Fitzherbert to
refer to him immediately if Aranda ever mentioned Gibraltar along with a detailed
report about everything said on the matter. Letter of 23 Sept. 1782, ibid., VII, pp.
186-90. See generally S. Conn, *Gibraltar in British Diplomacy in the Eighteenth Century*
(New Haven, 1942).

[36] Grantham participated in a week of discussions with Rayneval after the initial
Bowood exchanges. Jonathan R. Dull, 'Vergennes, Rayneval [premier commis], and
the Diplomacy of Trust', in eds. R. Hoffman and P. J. Albert, *Peace and the
Peacemakers. The Treaty of 1783* (Charlottesville, VA, 1986), 101-31, at 120; H.
Doniol, ed., 'Conférences de M. de Rayneval avec les ministres anglais', *Revue
d'histoire diplomatique* 6 (1892), 62-89. Neither had Grantham been privy to the

20 November 1782 following Franco-Spanish negotiations driven by a keen French desire to end hostilities at the earliest opportunity and not allow the outstanding issue of Gibraltar's future to stand in the way any longer than needed.[37] Rayneval brought with him a Spanish ultimatum that proposed that Gibraltar would go to Spain; Minorca would be restored to Britain, and France would allow the islands of Guadeloupe and Dominica to became British. It was a tempting offer, and a protracted cabinet meeting on 3 December actually voted in favour of ceding Gibraltar.[38] Meanwhile, Vergennes, by this date the undoubted prime mover in Franco-Spanish foreign policy under the Bourbon Family Compact, had been working hard to persuade the Spanish to drop their insistence on retaining Gibraltar at all costs in the interests all parties shared of moving speedily to finalising peace.[39] Rayneval returned to England for a third time on 3 December just at a point when the British and American negotiators had reached an agreement that confirmed as much:[40] British parliamentary and public opinion would not accept the loss of Gibraltar and French acquisition of Santo Domingo on top of generous concessions to the Americans.[41] Following his master's bidding, Rayneval asked the Shelburne ministry to be frank about what peace terms they wanted with Spain and, much to the satisfaction of Vergennes (acutely aware that France did not have the resources to undertake year of war), they duly did so and offered what seemed to him generous compensation to Spain (including the two Floridas and Minorca) for keeping Gibraltar

---

preliminary meeting in early Aug. 1782 between the captured Admiral de Grasse and Shelburne. ibid., 101-2; Dull, *A Diplomatic History of the American Revolution*, 152.

[37] Richard B. Morris, *The Peacemakers. The Great Powers and American Independence* (New York, 1970), 397-9. Meetings took place principally at Shelburne House in Berkeley Square.

[38] Rayneval to Vergennes, 4 Dec. 1782, AAE-CP-Angleterre, vol. 539. Even George III had become reconciled to exchanging Gibraltar. George III to Grantham, 11 Dec. 1782; to Shelburne, 11 Dec. 1782', Fortescue, *Correspondence*, vol. vi, 182-3, 183-4. He reluctantly accepted the ministry's subsequent decision not to do so once it had become conscious of the force of public feeling. George III to Grantham, 19 Dec. 1782, Fortescue, *Correspondence*, vol. vi. p. 192.

[39] They finally did so on 16 Dec. 1782. J. Cannon, *The Fox-North Coalition. Crisis of the Constitution 1782-4* (Cambridge, 1969), 35.

[40] Grantham was not informed personally by Shelburne of Rayneval's impending return. See Richard Fitzpatrick to Lord Ossory, 2 Dec. 1782, *Memorials and Correspondence of Charles James Fox*, ed. Lord John Russell, (2 vols., London, 1853), II. 9.

[41] Dull, *A Diplomatic History of the American Revolution*, 157.

sovereign under George III rather Carlos III. Aranda was ready to endorse the package despite the misgivings of Floridablanca's government,[42] and, with France and the American colonists already having come to terms with Britain, peace had become a certainty.[43] An armistice and preliminary peace agreement with Britain was duly signed by the Americans, French, and Spaniards and on behalf of the Dutch on 20 January 1783. Grantham had held lengthy conferences with Rayneval and 'was responsible for much of the precise detail of the negotiation.'[44]

The challenge for the Shelburne administration was to secure parliamentary assent to the agreement. The original date for its reconvening was 27 November 1782 but that was put back to 5 December at a date when war was still being pursued. That Shelburne's angle on the provisional articles with America appeared in debate to be at odds with the views of Pitt and Townshend was inauspicious so that the Christmas recess could not come too soon.[45] It would in the the New Year so that a comprehensive, finalised package could be presented to MPs and peers for a simple 'yes' or 'no'.[46] Grantham stood aloof from the manoeuvering that preceded the meeting of both Houses. He had limited parliamentary influence and, for all the respect generally accorded him, remained something of an unknown quantity at Westminster. Yet, certainly as regards the Spanish dimension of the preliminaries, he had been as much an architect of their contents as Shelburne himself and his future as a Foreign Secretary might be reckoned to stand or fall with the Premier's own. Meanwhile, misgivings in Cabinet threatened to break out into the open about the channelling of business exclusively through Shelburne's hands with matters discussed (in as much as they were discussed) in an inner cabinet of Pitt, Ashburton, Grantham, and Townshend.[47] On specifics, it was

---

[42] Hargreaves-Mawdsley, *Eighteenth-Century Spain*, 138. Grantham's part in achieving this diplomatic outcome has been insufficiently credited.

[43] Grantham was corresponding personally with Aranda in Dec. 1782 to agree that the rights of British subjects in Honduras to cut and transport logwood would not be impeded, and the stipulation appeared in the the preliminary treaty of Jan. 1783. Fox reopened the question after resuming office as Foreign Secretary in 1783. Murphy, *Vergennes,* 366-7, 551.

[44] Stockley, 'Shelburne, the European Powers, and the Peace of 1783', 191.

[45] Cannon, *Fox-North Coalition,* 40-4 for details.

[46] Black, *A System of Ambition,* pp. 220-1.

[47] Grantham kept brief notes on twenty-six Cabinet meetings. Beds and Luton

less the content of the preliminaries than the manner in which they had been arrived at that was fuelling resentment about how Shelburne, Grantham and the king had kept the negotiation in their own hands with minimal consultation or involvement of other colleagues.[48] Shelburne was the principal figure in the firing line. Ministerial doubts about policy had been intensified by a resurfacing of all the unresolved questions concerning the first Minister's personality and his way of driving policy. He had proved to be insufficiently collegial, impossible to work with on a day-to-day basis, apparently incapable of either explaining the details of government policy or appreciating that taking colleagues into his confidence would actually strengthen the operational efficiency the ministry. It caused a haemorrhaging of the ministry: the duke of Grafton resigned as Lord Privy Seal mainly in protest that Shelburne was 'becoming Prime Minister' as distinct from holding the principal office in the Cabinet.'[49] Lord Carlisle also quit as Lord Steward of the Household and Keppel relinquished the Admiralty as a result of Shelburne's erratic, autocratic style.[50]

Lord Grantham had not accumulated sufficient political capital to act as either a lightning conductor for Shelburne or as forceful, reassuring presence within government in January-February 1783. Though he may have had his own disquiets about Shelburne's failure to consult with him personally he was reluctant to air them but focused instead on his primary responsibility for preparing the Peace preliminaries for legislative scrutiny.[51] Meanwhile efforts to win support from Fox had come to nothing and there was a general

---

Archives, L29/658-85; Norris, *Shelburne and Reform*, 242.

[48] Cannon, *Fox-North Coalition*, 36. The duke of Richmond, who had incurred the disfavour of his nephew, Charles Fox, for staying in office in July 1782, was particularly annoyed. Fortescue, *Correspondence*, vol. vi. nos. 3918, 4055. Along with Keppel, though he remained personally friendly with the Premier, he disliked the scale of Shelburne's concessions to the nascent United States and was averse to any idea of bartering Gibraltar. John Ehrman, *The Younger Pitt. The Years of Acclaim* (London, 1969), p. 96.

[49] Sir W. Anson (ed.), *Autobiography and Political Correspondence of John Henry Third Duke of Grafton KG,* (London, 1898), 361, 364.

[50] J. Cannon, 'Lord Shelburne's Ministry, 1782-3', in N. Aston and C. Campbell Orr, (eds.) *An Enlightenment Statesman in Whig Britain. Lord Shelburne in Context, 1737-1805* (Woodbridge, 2011), 161-76, at 166.

[51] They were laid before Parliament on 27 Jan. 1783. Norris, *Shelburne and Reform*, 267.

awareness that an anti-Shelburne alliance between his followers and those of Lord North was in the offing. It came about sooner than generally expected and proved fatal to the government's prospects of winning the vote on the Peace in either House. With British public opinion also inclined to consider that too many concessions had been made to the former Colonists, on 17 February 1783 ministers were beaten in the Commons by 224 votes to 205 and, again, on the 21st, by a motion directly censuring the treaty, by 207 to 190. Having, for once, informed colleagues in advance of his intentions,[52] Shelburne resigned in a pique on 24 February considering that it was less his tactical ineptitude that had blasted his key policy than insufficient support from George III.[53] In the Lords debate on the Peace Grantham took the reasonable line that it was 'as good a one as, considering our situation, we could possibly have had', a point made by Shelburne later in winding up.[54] It was a faint token of the team work in the Upper chamber that the two peers might have displayed together had Shelburne not precipitately given up the game.

Grantham, like other colleagues in the Shelburne administration, having been abandoned by their chief, were put on the spot as to whether to imitate his example and resign. It appears he was disinclined to do so. It was not for Grantham a matter of being loyal to Shelburne because he had never been a Shelburnite, and he suffered his own share of minor snubs and discourtesies from that direction.[55] He remained in post less out of any love of power and office for their own sake than because it was in Britain's best international interests not to give an impression of chronic instability.[56] And out of loyalty to George III who was desperate to

---

[52] Grantham, Pitt, Townshend, more junior ministers and the law officers of the Crown assembled at Shelburne House on 23 February to hear that the Premier planned to resign the next day. Lancs RO, DDKE/box 152/6, Shelburne to Lloyd Kenyon, 22 Feb 1783.

[53] Ehrman, *The Younger Pitt*, 99-101. For his part, George III blamed Shelburne for trusting too much that his measures would win support of themselves.

[54] *Parliamentary History*, vol. 23, co. 403. The treaties were approved in the Upper House by the narrow margin of 72 to 59 votes.

[55] Shelburne was critical of Grantham for hanging on to office. Morris, *The Peacemakers*, 426.

[56] Grantham was worried on that score hoping that 'our civil revolutions may not destroy all confidence from abroad in our councils'. BL Add. MS. 35528, f.22, to Sir Robert Murray Keith, 22 Feb. 1783.

hold what had been the Shelburne ministry together because the alternative of having Fox back in government was abhorrent to him. Grantham was one of those to whom the king was ready to unburden himself 'in the Closet' and Grantham produced a written memorandum of what the king had told him in confidence about his unsuccessful initiatives to keep Fox out.[57] It was not quite a case of business as usual for ministers after 24 February. Though Grantham was not privy to the proceedings, a sign of his insignificant standing as a political operator, some of his colleagues (led by Ashburton and the Attorney-General, Lloyd Kenyon) lobbied Pitt to head a government. His refusal on 26th February did not end increasingly desperate efforts to set up an administration without either Fox or North. Grantham could perhaps flatter himself that his was not one of the names put into the frame as a potential leader of one. By late March 1783, with Pitt having, on the 20th, refused again, it was plain to ministers that the game was up for all of them.[58] Grantham prepared himself to go and, after consultation about his official situation with Lloyd Kenyon in the Foreign Secretary's office at Cleveland Row on 21 March, duly resigned, having been granted a (second) pension worth £2,000 p.a.[59]

In discharging his office Grantham had displayed a level of professional competence that had been as apparent to Cabinet colleagues as it had to British diplomats;[60] judged by the standard of his predecessors as a Secretary of State, Grantham was on a level

---

[57] There is in this document a rueful comment that suggests Grantham's own grasp of Shelburne's angular character: 'The King said Lord Shelburne had constantly expressed that Pitt was cold, reserved & he even threw Gloom into Society. He betrayed great symptoms of Jealousy of Pitt. I can conceive this very easily.' Beds and Luton Archives, 29/596, memo. of correspondence with the king, 3 Mar. 1783.

[58] Ehrman, *The Younger Pitt*, 104; Brown, *The Chathamites*, 313-15. In the Commons Lord Surrey's motion deploring the absence of a government for six weeks (not strictly the case) was carried. *Parl. Hist.*, vol. 23, cols. 687-709.

[59] Lancs RO, DDKE/box 152/12, Grantham to Kenyon, 20 Mar. 1783. Their conversation was likely connected with his pensions. A comparable pension was granted to Lord Thurlow who left office as Lord Chancellor. Sir Thomas Robinson's pension (inherited) fell due every March. It survived Shelburne's drive for economies (as did that paid to Sir Joseph Yorke) and the intractable difficulties associated with reform of the Civil List. Norris *Shelburne and Reform*, 196-7, 252.

[60] He got on particularly well with Sir James Harris who recalled the time he had attended young Robinson in his post-chaise to Christs' College when Harris was 'a forward puppy, a spoilt over-grown school-boy,...' See Harris to Grantham, St Petersburg, 6, 17 Sept. 1782, in *Malmesbury, Diaries and Correspondence*, I. 541-2.

with the best of them and, as things stood in early 1783, his only obvious superior in experience was another former diplomat David, Viscount Stormont and he, at that juncture, was firmly in Lord North's camp. He expressed personal satisfaction that he had:

> ...knowingly done everything for the best, [and]...felt with satisfaction that I had largely contributed to the restoration of peace, and that I possessed the confidence of the Ministers of France and Spain.[61]

Any assessment of his tenure of the Foreign Office must confront the question of agency and it is quickly apparent that John Cannon's judgment that Grantham was 'little more than a clerk' to Lord Shelburne requires discounting.[62] One might better see him as a moderating influence on the Premier, a person whose talent for detail helped flesh out policy as it evolved.[63] Certainly, Shelburne took the lead in peace-making with America and France (though Grantham's involvement in the latter has been under-estimated) but it was actually with the neglected dimension of ending the war with Spain that Grantham had scope for displaying his expertise. It was, inevitably, a reactive policy as the negotiations wound their course with signs of Grantham briefly wobbling on the key issue of whether to sacrifice Gibraltar that would have made the final terms of the treaty still more unpopular. But he was not alone in this. Given that for the public Gibraltar was 'the Golden Image of English Idolatry',[64] retention was largely forced on him and Shelburne.

Apart from the primary policy of making peace, Grantham had the full range of Foreign Office business to master and direct *ab initio*, excuse enough to preclude him from involvement in the issues of economic and parliamentary reform that exercised Shelburne, Pitt, and other ministers in 1782-3. Down to his last days in post, he was busy plotting out British responses to international developments across the whole of Europe in conjunction with seasoned envoys

---

[61] Grantham to Harris, 22 Feb. 1783, ibid., II. 34-5.

[62] Vergennes, for one, acclaimed the patriotism of Shelburne and Grantham together. To Montmorin, (in Madrid) 1 Mar 1783, AAE-CP-Espagne, vol. 610. He had hoped that Grantham would retain influence even after Shelburne had quit.

[63] cf. Norris, *Shelburne and Reform*, 242.

[64] Conn, *Gibraltar*, p. 256.

such as Sir Robert Murray Keith in Vienna and Sir James Harris in St Petersburg,[65] and indicated distinct caution regarding membership of any northern powers alliance system while peace with France and Spain had yet to be ratified.[66] By contradistinction with Fox in office (Foreign Secretary April-June 1782; April-December 1783) Grantham preferred indirect pressure to weaken the Franco-Austrian alliance of 1756 and was hopeful that Russia's Balkan schemes against Turkey (France's traditional Mediterranean ally) would contribute to that outcome.[67] Away from peace with Spain, Grantham did not neglect Britain's Mediterranean interests. For instance, he required Sir Horace Mann in Florence to insist that the Duchy of Tuscany observe its neutrality (a condition of the duchy being made over to the Habsburgs) 'In all points' as it guaranteed the existence of Leghorn as a free port in which the Mediterranean fleet could be resupplied.[68] He took the lead with full Cabinet authority to pressurise the East India Company through its 'secret committee' to move towards scaling back or even ending the war in India and on the seas as a matter of urgency seeing that, as Shelburne put it, 'the sacrifices for peace and the chief risk of the war now lie with the India Company'.[69] And there were the usual duties within the remit of his office with the foreign ambassadorial corps that had an extra importance as Britain attempted to cultivate goodwill as peace approached, none more so than when, on 24 January 1783, Grantham introduced Rayneval to deliver his credentials to the king as minister from the French court.[70]

Though remaining primarily resident in London at Grantham House (6, Whitehall Yard),[71] he held himself aloof from party politics for much of the rest of 1783 and was averse to habitual House of Lords attendance.[72] Instead he took pleasure in the domesticity that he so much enjoyed in middle life with his third and last son born to Lady

---

[65] His letters and despatches as Foreign Secretary [Beds and Luton Archives, 29/559-685], stretch well into Mar. 1783.

[66] See, for instance, Grantham to Keith, TNA FO 7/6, 22 Feb. 1783.

[67] Discussed in Black, *A System of Ambition*, 224.

[68] Grantham to Mann, TNA FO 79/3, 17 Sept. 1782.

[69] Beds and Luton Archives, L30/14/306/6.

[70] *Caledonian Mercury*, 29 Jan. 1783.

[71] It was held on reversionary lease from his father. https://www.british-history.ac.uk/survey-london/vol13/pt2/pp160-161

[72] Beds and Luton Archives, L30/15/54/203, Grantham to Hon. Frederick Robinson, 6 Sept. 1783.

Grantham at the end of October.[73] But he had not been forgotten by his ertswhile colleagues and, as Pitt readied himself to form a government when he and the king judged it the moment to do so, Grantham was approached about resuming office as Foreign Secretary.[74] It was a mark of the esteem he had secured that Grantham was Pitt's first choice and, though he had already decided to vote against Fox's East India Company Bill, he turned down the offer. He had taken the Opposition's rejection of the Peace as disgraceful and had found sufficient evidence of 'the rank and universal corruption that prevails' to deter him from an early return to the political bear-pit.[75] Acceptance might also have required him to forego the additional pension he had recently been granted, one which would help him supply the needs of his wife and three young boys. Disquiet over the award had been aired in Parliament in July 1783 and it had not increased the peer's appetite for resuming a high public profile. He lacked the stomach –and the steady health– for what would be stormy times ahead alongside Pitt with limited scope for constructive diplomacy in a ministry that might well implode before it had properly begun.

That distinct possibility famously did not occur and, within a few weeks, Pitt successfully tempted Grantham to return to government, albeit in a minor key.[76] On 5 March 1784, he became a member of the Privy Council committee for the consideration of all matters relating to trade and foreign plantations headed by the former Thomas Townshend, newly ennobled (April 1783) as Lord Sydney, who had resumed under Pitt the Home Secretaryship he had held under Shelburne. It suited Grantham's temperament to be no longer in the front line of affairs in Whitehall and Westminster and, as a doting middle-aged father with three infant boys,[77] another ambassadorship was, for the time being at least, out of the

---

[73] Beds and Luton Archives, L30/11/339/80, Mary Yorke to Ly Amabel Grey, 1 Nov. 1783.

[74] Ian R. Christie, 'Lord Grantham and William Pitt, 12 December 1783: A Side-Light on the Fall of the Fox-North Coalition', *Historical Journal*, 34 (1991), 143-5. Earl Temple and Lord Sydney also urged him to accept. Black, *British Foreign Policy*, 22.

[75] To Harris, 22 Feb. 1783, Malmesbury, *Diaries*, II. 35.

[76] He also recommended Grantham's brother-in-law, John Parker, MP for Devonshire, for a Barony.

[77] For a vignette of the Granthams and their 'little men' in the country see Mary Yorke to Lady Amabel Grey, Beds and Luton Archives, L30/11/339/86, Aug. 1784.

question. He spent as much time as he could over the next two years happily domesticated on his estate in Yorkshire at Newby Park where Lady Grantham began to help poor families and he could assume, in lieu of his younger brother Frederick (or 'Fritz'), that involvement and influence in the civic life of the adjacent city of Ripon expected of the head of the Newby branch of the Robinson family.[78] But this marital contentment did not last long. Grantham's health was indifferent and he contracted an illness in the spring of 1786 that proved fatal. He died on 20 July 1786 at Grantham House, Putney Heath, and was buried the next day at Chiswick. He was only forty-eight years old. 'I never remember anybody more generally lamented', observed Lady Mary Coke, the high society chronicler.[79]

Grantham had limited scope to show his mettle in high Cabinet office but despite the distinctive challenges of working in Lord Shelburne's government, his performance as Foreign Secretary confirmed the aptitude on display earlier in his career, one that would, ministerially, be evident again in his sons.[80] This competence has been forgotten because of his early death. Contemporaries respected him and he had few enemies for he was always a diplomat before he was a politician, one who found political machinations got in the way of constructive government *pro bono publico*. He found the rough and tumble of politics in 1782-83 unpleasant and was stung by criticism of the pensions he felt he and his father had merited for their public service. But, while he was in office, he was far more than any cipher and had he accepted Pitt's offer of the Foreign Office in December 1783, would have been more of a heavyweight in policy formulation and implementation than the Marquess of Carmarthen proved to be.

---

[78] Beds and Luton Archives, L30/15/554/297, Grantham to Hon. Frederick Robinson, 21 Dec. 1785.

[79] 'tho so long and dangerously ill he never thought he should die till two or three days before. Journal (typescript) of Lady Mary Coke, 23 July 1780, Lewis Walpole Library, Farmington, CA. She had reported on 17 June that there was no hope of his recovery. For his earlier grave illness in autumn 1778 while resident in Spain see Beds and Luton Archives, L30/15

[80] Frederick 'Prosperity' Robinson (1782-1859), Chancellor of the Exchequer, 1823-7; created Viscount Goderich, 1827, and earl of Ripon, 1833; Prime Minister, 1827-8; ministerial offices under Grey and Peel; Thomas Philip Robinson (de Grey after 1833) (1781-1859), 3rd Baron Grantham, 1786; suc. as Earl de Grey, 1833; ministerial offices under Peel.

Selling the Lottery in Britain, *c.*1694-1826

Bob Harris

Lotteries were extremely useful devices for raising public money for European governments in the eighteenth and early nineteenth centuries.[1] As one British writer trenchantly declared in 1802: 'Of the expediency & utility of Lotteries in a political view, for raising a supply of money to Government there can be no manner of doubt.'[2] The first official lottery in England was staged in 1694, a subsequent, far less successful, one in 1697, while British government lotteries were annual events in most years from their revival by Lord Godolphin in 1710 until 1802, when their frequency increased sharply before their abolition was decreed by Parliament in 1823, the last official lottery being held three years after that.[3] In London and its environs lottery adventuring took hold rapidly, until by the end of the eighteenth century it was pervasive. One satirical writer observed in 1799, in terms which by that date were commonplace: 'During the drawing of a state lottery … trade is at a stand, mechanics pursue with eagerness the play till they are mere mendicants. *All ranks and degrees*, however, study to cheat the office-keepers, by every cunning art which the fertile mind of man can suggest'.[4] By the end of the eighteenth century, the spectacular reach of the lottery extended far beyond the British

---

[1] See *inter alia,* Marie-Laure Legay, *Les Loteries Royales Dans L'Europe des Lumières* (1680-1815) (Lille, 2014); Bernard Bruno (ed.), *Lotteries in Europe: Five Centuries of History* (Brussels, 1994); Robert Kruckenberg, 'The Royal Lottery and the Old Regime: Financial Innovation and Modern Political Culture', *French Historical Studies,* 37 (2014), 25-51; Larry Neal, *The Rise of Financial Capitalism: International Capital Markets in the Age of Reason* (Cambridge, 1990), p. 14. Between 1694 and 1784 state lotteries were involved with £144 million in public borrowing, debt retirement and joint stock operations (*National Debt: Report by the Secretary and Comptroller General of the Proceedings of the Commissioners for the Reduction of the National Debt, from 1786 to 31ˢᵗ March 1890,* British Parliamentary Papers, House of Commons Papers, 1890-91, C. 6539, vol. xlviii, pp. 696-703, cited in J. Raven, 'The Abolition of the English State Lotteries', *Historical Journal,* xxxiv (1991), 374). See also J. Cohen, 'The Element of Lottery in English Government Bonds, 1694-1919', *Economica,* xx (1953), 241-6.
[2] The National Archives [hereafter TNA], Treasury Board Papers, T64/324, 'Considerations on Lotteries', 31 Dec. 1802.
[3] Full details can be found in C. L. Ewen, *Lotteries and Sweepstakes in the British Isles* (London, 1932).
[4] *The Adventures of Lucifer in London* (London, 1799), p. 104 (*my emphasis*).

capital, encompassing much of Britain and Ireland. Nor was the market for British lottery tickets confined to the British Isles, for it had possessed a significant overseas dimension from at least the 1700s.

Modern historians have showed rather limited interest in the lottery of this period. Insofar, however, as explanations have been suggested for its popularity these have been normally framed in terms of either highlighting the investment features of early lotteries -the significant returns which they at times offered to investors and thus the rational grounds for participation- or, seemingly contradictorily, the supposed contemporary mania for gambling.[5] A comprehensive accounting for the phenomenon would need to examine both demand and supply sides. The former is the trickier given very patchy extant data on who bought lottery tickets, in what quantities, and with what regularity.[6] Much lottery adventuring involved collaborations of different kinds, in the form of lottery clubs, often based in public houses, or partnerships derived from kinship, friendship, neighbourhood or occupational connections. In the mid eighteenth century a Sheffield lottery society was established with a maximum membership of thirty six, each member being required to put in an initial sum of 5/- and a further 6d at every subsequent fortnightly meeting to contribute to a common fund for purchasing tickets, shares, and chances.[7] In 1787 members of a Hampshire whist club, which met weekly in the

---

[5] A. L. Murphy, 'Lotteries in the 1690s: Investment or Gamble?', *Financial History Review*, xxii (2005), 227-46; P. G. M. Dickson, *The Financial Revolution in England: A Study of the Development of the Public Debt, 1688-1756* (London, 1967), p. 45; B. Carruthers, *City of Capital: Politics and Markets in the English Financial Revolution* (Princeton, N. J., 1996), p. 76. But, for another kind of explanation, which is that the lottery offered 'ordinary people fictional capital', by which is meant the capacity to imagine themselves within a plot often borrowed from contemporary fiction, see Jesse Molesworth, *Chance and the Eighteenth-Century Novel: Realism, Probability, Magic* (Cambridge, 2010).
[6] For a start in analysing some of this, see Bob Harris, 'Lottery Adventuring in Britain, c.1710-1760', *English Historical Review*, 133 (2018), 284-322; idem., 'Fantasy, Speculation, and the British State Lottery in the Eighteenth Century', in *Revisiting the Polite & Commercial People: Essays in Georgian Politics, Society and Culture in Honour of Professor Paul Langford,* eds. Elaine Chalus & Perry Gauci (Oxford, 2019), pp. 119-35.
[7] Sheffield City Archives, NC/3/3, Rules and Orders Agreed Upon to be Kept and Strictly Observed by an Amicable Society for Raising a Sum of Money in Order to be Adventured in Every State Lottery For the Equal Benefit and Advantage of Every Member of the Said Society, 28 Mar. 1755.

George Inn on Winchester's High Street, agreed to subscribe three guineas each towards the cost of two state lottery tickets or more if the total sum collected allowed this.[8] Someone who regularly bought tickets in partnership with various sets of acquaintances was the Hampshire gentleman Tristram Huddleston Jervoise.[9]

Commercial schemes operated at different moments, which entailed pooling money to buy tickets and sharing the proceeds from any prizes won, less a portion taken by the organisers. The true extent and social reach of these aspects of participation in the lottery remain most resistant to our scrutiny, although they were very significant. This paper concentrates instead, therefore, on the mechanics of supply, on how ticket sales were organised and promoted, and how it was that individuals in remote parts of Britain might by the early nineteenth century have comparatively little difficulty in purchasing tickets or shares thereof. It is a story of energetic entrepreneurialism on the part primarily of Lottery Office keepers, but also the exploitation of new possibilities for market development and capture created by changing conditions of publicity, circulation, and communication in a rapidly commercialising society. It is a tale too in which London, the 'over-grown' British capital, looms large, in this context as the site for the development of what the Evangelical MP, abolitionist and moral reformer William Wilberforce condemned as a 'public system of gambling', one which encircled diverse worlds far beyond it.[10]

The paper has three main sections. The first seeks to bring into clearer focus the figure of the Lottery Office keeper. By the mid eighteenth century, Lottery Office keepers were the main sources of sales of lottery tickets; their well-honed entrepreneurial skills drove the expansion of the lottery market. The second examines the role of publicity and various promotional strategies as aids to selling lottery tickets. Those who ran lotteries or sought to sell tickets were notably innovative exploiters of print and the possibilities for communication with an expanding, ever more

---

[8] Hampshire Record Office [hereafter HRO], 181M84W/1, George Inn, Whist Club Minutes, 1777-1798, entry for 25 Jan. 1787.
[9] HRO, 44M69/E11/130, Account and Notebook of Tristram Huddleston Jervoise, 1785-94.
[10] Sheffield City Archives, RP/1/14, William Wilberforce to Samuel Roberts, 10 Feb. 1817.

geographically widely dispersed readership which it offered. As one historian of printing declared as long ago as 1960, 'there is hardly any device of the modern advertising agency that has not been anticipated during the lottery fever of 1800-1826'.[11] The final section briefly examines the business of a Glasgow lottery agent from the 1820s, thereby serving to underline the sheer extent of the Georgian lottery marketplace in its final phases, both geographically and socially.

We begin with several basic features of the official lottery in Britain in this period and its operation. Prior to 1769 nearly all of these lotteries were not winner-take-all affairs. Rather, tickets drawn blanks —in other words, those failing to win a prize in the draw- brought a return, which was usually in the form of government stock of a value significantly less than the face value of the ticket. Blanks thus retained a market value and were tradeable. This investment aspect ended in 1768. Thereafter blanks returned nothing, and lotteries became a simple gamble on drawing a prize. Tickets were subscribed for at and issued by the Bank of England. This gave brokers and subscribers an interest in driving ticket prices upwards following the subscription.[12] Prices normally rose appreciably before and often during the draw, which prior to 1793 could last anything up to forty two days.[13] How far they did so was determined by the state of demand for tickets, the numbers of capital prizes which remained in the draw, but also at times by the wiles of sellers, which were and are mainly hidden from view.[14]

---

[11] P. M. Handover, *Printing in London from 1476 to Modern Times* (London, 1960, p. 187, quoted in Rob Barnham, 'Lottery Advertising 1800-1826', *Journal of the Printing Historical Society*, new ser., 13 (2009), 17.

[12] There were frequent allegations that 'jobbers and engrossers' engaged in contrivances to inflate ticket prices. See e.g. British Library [hereafter BL], Add MS 70155, fo. 48, anon to Edward Harley, 9 Dec. 1713; *Caledonian Mercury*, 22 Nov. 1726, 4 Apr. 1743; *Salisbury Journal*, 15 July 1751. Similar allegations were made against the lottery contractors in the early nineteenth century, for which, see BL, Add MS 59309, fo. 10, Thomas Smith to Lord Henry Petty, 28 July 1806.

[13] In 1802 the maximum number of days was fixed at eight for any single lottery. Attempts were made in later years to encourage one-day draws for each lottery. One way of doing the latter was to issue multiple tickets bearing the same number, although this was evidently unpopular with the public who preferred as wide a range of numbers as possible from which to select their ticket(s) or share(s) thereof.

[14] Although, for the latter, see TNA, Treasury Board Papers, T64/324, T. Wood, 'On Produces of Lotteries', n.d. but 1800s. Produces were a form of speculation, usually engaged in by contractors, on the gain or loss per ticket relative to the

The market in 'scrip' —tickets subscribed for which had been paid only in part— and tickets was usually a source of quickly realised profits, and there was much dealing before and during the draw. This was, in essence, a bet on a climbing ticket price, which in most years is what occurred; by far the trickier judgement was when to sell.[15] The terms of the lotteries were before 1785 determined by the Treasury and enacted through parliamentary legislation establishing the specific lottery. From 1785 the Treasury ran an auction among so-called lottery contractors for tickets. The successful individual or partnership would then determine the terms of the lotteries for that year, although within fairly tight constraints set down by the Treasury and parliament. They would also sell tickets to the Lottery Offices, seemingly on a sale or return basis. The lottery draw - successful operation of which was crucial to maintaining public trust in the lottery - was managed by the Lottery Office and overseen by Lottery Office Commissioners who were appointed by ministers. Until 1801, the draw was held in the Guildhall. Thereafter, it moved for a year to the premises of Scottish Corporation in the City, before settling in 1803 in Coopers' Hall in Basinghall Street, where it remained until 1826.

With respect to the secondary market for lottery tickets —the most important one for our purposes— key agents in its development were middlemen; and to this extent its rapid growth owed much to the new financial markets taking shape in London from the 1690s. London's private bankers —pre-eminently, Coutts, Hoare's, Child's, and Drummond's- acted as important lottery agents during the first half of the eighteenth century.[16] Their clientele were mainly drawn from the ranks of the landed and professional elites.[17] In Edinburgh by the mid eighteenth century officials in the Bank of Scotland and Royal Bank of Scotland dealt in lottery tickets.[18] Some

---

contract price, and which led to significant attempts to manipulate prices of tickets.
[15] In the early nineteenth century, the Treasury received a proposal, which it rejected, that tickets be sold under contract for a fixed price to prevent jobbing, and that prices be reduced. TNA, IR55/19, Lottery Board, Lottery Office Papers, 1803-44, H. E. Swift, 'A Proposal for a New Mode of Disposing of a State Lottery by a Contract of Agency'.
[16] Harris, 'Lottery Adventuring', 294-6.
[17] D. M. Joslin, 'London Private Bankers, 1720-85', *Economic History Review,* new ser., vii (1954-5), 167-86; I. S. Black, 'Private Banking in London's West End, 1750-1830', *London Journal,* xxviii (2003), 29-59.
[18] Harris, 'Lottery Adventuring', 295.

people bought tickets through the banks not just for themselves, but others, sometimes on a substantial scale. One such individual was Sir Robert Walpole's political lieutenant and the MP for Worcestershire, Thomas Winnington. Winnington supplied tickets in 1740 and 1741 to, amongst others, Henrietta Cavendish Holles, Countess of Oxford.[19] Another was the Lincolnshire gentleman and MP Thomas Saunderson, who in September 1731 sent Henry Hoare and his partners a list of eight individuals who had ordered lottery tickets through him, distinguishing those who had already paid from those yet to pay. The bank extended credit to Saunderson to facilitate these transactions.[20] In terms of value, the role of the banks as lottery agents peaked early in the eighteenth century, with the valuable and much-in-demand Queen Anne lottery loans.[21] Nevertheless, the banks continued to act in this capacity on a substantial scale well into the middle of the eighteenth century.[22] Leading financiers and dealers were another potential source of tickets, although they often sold these on to other middlemen. Sir Richard Hill, whose career encompassed time as deputy paymaster of the forces in Flanders in the 1690s, several diplomatic postings, and at the Treasury, who, according to his father, had a talent of making money very quickly, and was certainly an experienced and substantial investor in stocks, bought tickets in the 1710s from his usual financial brokers, Sir James Bateman and Moses Hart.[23]

[19] Nottinghamshire Record Office, DD/P/6/7/2/2, Account Book of the Rt. Hon. Henrietta Cavendish Holles, Countess of Oxford, 1739-55; Harris, 'Lottery Adventuring', 298, n. 68.

[20] Hoare's Bank Archives, Fleet St, London, HB/8/T/11, Thomas Saunderson, Glentworth, to Henry Hoare, 4 Sept. 1731; Thomas Winnington to Henry Hoare, 5 Sept. 1739. I am grateful to the current partners of Hoare's Bank for allowing me to consult their records.

[21] See A. Laurence, 'Women Investors, "That Nasty South Sea Affair", and the Rage to Speculate in Early Eighteenth-Century England', *Accounting, Business and Financial History,* xvi (2006), 249-50.

[22] Banks continued to buy tickets for clients into the early nineteenth century, although on what kind of scale is currently unclear. The Northumberland gentleman, John Heaton Delaval was one of these, regularly buying tickets through Hoare's Bank, as well as, less frequently, several Lottery Offices. Northumberland Record Office, Delaval Papers, 2 DE 35/17, lotteries, 1771-1805. Another was the Kent gentleman, Edward Hussey, who bought tickets in most years through Child's Bank. Kent Archives and Records Centre [hereafter KARC], U1776/E73, Edward Hussey Esq., Bankers Book, 1783-1817.

[23] Shropshire Record Office, The Attingham Collection, 112/1/1968 & 1969, letters of Moses Hart, 1719, 1710-1719; 112/1/1929, Sir James Bateman to Sir Richard

Lottery Office keepers were usually stockbrokers who came to specialise in sales of lottery tickets. We currently know rather little about most of these individuals. Some who were active from an early stage were licensed stockbrokers based in and around Exchange Alley.[24] Others were goldsmith bankers. One of the latter was Matthew West of Clare Market, London. West dealt in Dutch lottery tickets, pioneered schemes for joint or collective purchase of tickets from 1710, and by the early 1730s was advertising his services in the Edinburgh press.[25] In the early 1710s, City coffee houses competed to provide up-to-the-minute information about the state of the draw, including keeping register books, where people could register their tickets and receive notice of their fortunes in the draw.[26] Andrew and William Bell, who were based in Cornhill at the heart of the City of London and pioneers in the production of printed benefit books authoritative printed records of successful numbers -also dealt in tickets, including eighth shares from an early date.[27] It was several goldsmith bankers who led the way in the provision of lottery insurance in 1719.[28] By at least the 1740s Lottery Office keepers had consolidated provision of these different services —sales of tickets and shares thereof, registration of tickets, and ticket insurance. Several of the major lottery businesses of the later eighteenth century emerged around this time, and it was during the central decades of the century that the Lottery Offices became a much more visible and important presence in the lottery marketplace.

From 1779, under the terms of the Lottery Office Keepers Act (1779 c. 21), Lottery Offices required licenses to operate. By the

---

Hill, 9 Mar. 1710; 112/1/1934, same to same, 2 Apr. 1711; 112/1/1933, same to same, 3 May 1711.

[24] For example, John Taylor from his office next to Jonathan's Coffee House in Exchange Alley (*Daily Courant*, 31 July 1711).

[25] For West, see Dickson, *Financial Revolution,* p. 497. See also *British Mercury,* 3 Aug. 1711; *Daily Courant,* 20 July 1711; *Original Weekly Journal,* 8 July 1719; *Daily Journal,* 5 Sept. 1722; *London Journal,* 25 May 1723; *Daily Journal,* 9 Sept. 1724; *Caledonian Mercury,* 9 Aug. 1731.

[26] *Spectator,* 1 Aug., 27 Sept., 2 Oct. 1711; *Post Man,* 4 Oct. 1711; *Post Boy,* 4 Oct. 1711; *Daily Courant,* 1 Aug. 1711; *British Mercury,* 1, 3 Aug. 1711.

[27] *Observator,* 15 Sept. 1711; *Post Man,* 13 Aug. 1719.

[28] *Daily Courant,* 27 Aug. 1719.

early nineteenth century, they were to be found across most of the capital, with particular clusters in Cornhill and Charing Cross. Richardson and Goodluck, for example, had offices in both, while Swift and Co. had offices in the Poultry, Charing Cross and Aldgate High Street.[29] For every licensed office, however, there were many more unlicensed ones. One estimate put the number of the latter at around 700 in 1787, although on what basis is unclear.[30] The impression, nevertheless, is of a small core of larger concerns, around which there existed a much larger number of much less heavily capitalized, marginal businesses, all of them operating in a highly competitive, even increasingly saturated market, a circumstance which fostered endless multiplication of new ways of selling tickets, including dividing tickets into ever-smaller shares, until shares smaller than sixteenths were prohibited (from 1787), new lottery-derived products, and much connivance at ignoring or circumventing attempts to regulate the lottery market. For many profitability it seems was dependent on the latter.[31] In the 1810s, the overall number of lottery businesses contracted somewhat, as the lottery market became dominated by a handful of concerns competing among themselves for the contracts to run the lotteries. Thomas Bish, who casts a lengthy shadow over the history of the lotteries of the early nineteenth century, ran one of these.[32]

Two related features of lottery salesmanship demonstrate very clearly the commercial ingenuity of the Lottery Office keepers. Both concerned lottery-derived products: 'chances' and lottery insurance. Chances were schemes which mirrored the official draw,

---

[29] TNA, IR4/210, Lottery Licences, 1810-20.

[30] TNA, Treasury Board Papers, T 1/652/68-75, Criticisms of the Present Law Affecting Their Lotteries, 1787.

[31] This was acknowledged by several witnesses who gave evidence to the 1808 Commons Committee on the lottery laws (Parliamentary Papers, 1808 (182 & 323), Reports from the Committee on the Laws Relating to Lotteries). One apparently quite common practice was for some Lottery Offices to give inaccurate information on which numbers had already been drawn or whether they had been drawn a prize or blank (University of Nottingham, Manuscripts and Special Collections, Mol 158, F. Plumtre to [Sir Molyneux], 22 Feb. 1766).

[32] For Bish, see G. Hicks, *The First Adman: Thomas Bish and the Birth of Modern Advertising* (Brighton, 2012). Between 1810-20, the number of licences issued ranged between 25-28 (TNA, IR4/210). In 1779, 47 individuals or partnerships had taken out licences (*Public Advertiser*, 4 Aug. 1779, Notice, Lottery Office, 27 July 1779), 45 London-based, one in Newcastle (the printer, Thomas Slack), and one in Edinburgh.

but where prices were lower and, indeed, prizes less valuable than for the official tickets. These were first prohibited in 1721, but with strictly limited effect, and many of them appear to have been fraudulent. They flourished spectacularly in the 1770s and '80s, when, against a background of seemingly heightened lottery fever, ever more elaborate schemes of this sort proliferated, covering many a column inch of the advertising sections of London's multiplying newspapers. They were eventually clamped down on by successful prosecution in the Court of King's Bench at the beginning of the 1790s of the printer of *The World* newspaper, which made it clear that newspapers would be liable to fines for publishing illegal schemes. To deny this was to cut off the necessary oxygen of publicity. As Lord Kenyon, the Lord Chief Justice, argued in his judgement, betraying a typically patronising view of the rational judgement of the lower orders and their susceptibility to bogus, exaggerated claims: 'If Hand Bills & Advertisem[en]ts were not inserted & delivered, the inferior ranks of Men might rest in their Houses & not go to the places where they are so extremely and scandalously plundered as they are, to the disgrace of the Governm[en]t of the Country.'[33] We will return below to the role played by newspapers in the promotion of lotteries.

Lottery insurance came in several different forms. Most straightforwardly it involved insuring tickets against being drawn blanks. All lottery insurance was prohibited in 1782 in the dying days of the North administration, in a bid to eliminate more controversial forms, but the legality of insuring tickets in the manner referred to above was restored in 1787, on the grounds that it underpinned the profitability of the lottery. The most controversial type of lottery insurance, however, were in effect bets on the outcome of the lottery draw. This was not really a form of insurance at all.[34] To give an example: in January 1788, Robert Sharman received six shillings from Raphael Solomons in return from which if a particular ticket –in this case, number 3,842– drew

---

[33] TNA, IR72/34, Board of Stamps, Miscellaneous Books, Solicitor's Department, Lottery Cases: Law Opinions, 1787-1799, King v. Smith, 1791, Case for the Opinion of the Court. See also *Critical Review* (1792), 616-9, 'English State Lottery'.

[34] To the extent that it was, this was because someone who bought large numbers of tickets, the value of which might fall significantly if one of the large capital prize was drawn might 'insure' against this occurring, through such a bet, in order to mitigate against any such loss.

one of the capital prizes, Solomons would receive certain sums, starting with £350 if it was the biggest prize of £20,000.[35] At around the same time, James Pegler paid Paul Groves 4 sh. 11d. in return for which if ticket number 1520 were drawn a prize in the Irish state lottery on either the 13th or 30th day of the draw he would receive a certain sum of money.[36] Or, to give one further example: in 1791 John Bligh paid a lottery insurance agent 20 shillings in return for which he would gain 20 guineas if the last drawn ticket was a number between 17 and 18,000.[37] Bets could be laid for any sum, and gambling of this kind was not merely engaged in by the poor, although it was the participation of this group which aroused the particular concern and hostility of the authorities. It had burgeoned from the 1740s, after new legislation was passed seeking to render more effective a prohibition on the hiring of tickets for set periods, a practice which was known as 'riding a horse'. The latter flourished from the 1720s and was seen as dangerously extending the market for lottery tickets far down into society. Its ban simply led to Lottery Offices finding new ways of reaching this same clientele through the development of so-called 'lottery insurance'.

The suppression of 'chances' produced a similar outcome, insofar as it, together with the reduction in the duration of the lottery draws after 1802, simply led to the rise of private lotteries -so-called 'little goes'- which were it seems often organised by the same individuals who ran unlicensed Lottery Offices, and which were typically held in periods when there was no official lottery draw. The battle to suppress lottery insurance in the later Georgian period, which began with an exemplary prosecution of the well-established lottery business of Richardson and Goodluck in 1774 by the magistrates of the City of London for selling illegal insurances, and involved passage of significant legislation in 1782 and 1787, as well as financial support from central government, including payments to informers, was notably protracted and had limited effect.[38] As one writer gloomily informed the Treasury in 1816:

---

[35] London Metropolitan Archives [hereafter LMA], CLA/047/LJ/13/1788, City of London Sessions: Sessions Papers, 17 Dec. 1787-6 Dec. 1788, 30 Jan. 1788.

[36] LMA, CLA/047/13/1788, 4 Feb. 1788.

[37] TNA, IR72/34, Case of Thomas Baker, 1791.

[38] TNA, Treasury Papers, T1/511/344-52, case of a city marshal acting under orders of the Lord Mayor to initiative a prosecution of Richardson and Goodluck, 1774. The

'With respect to insurance I beg leave to state that it never will be done away with by stopping the Lottery Revenue —more insurance goes on when the lottery is not being drawn than when it is.' What this referred to was the Little Goes, prosecution of which was the responsibility of the Solicitor of the Stamp Office.[39]

Many people bought tickets and, indeed, chances from Lottery Offices in person. One seemingly fairly common practice was to divide purchases between different offices, presumably in the hope of increasing one's chances of purchasing a lucky ticket.[40] Others used an intermediary to conduct the transaction. In the 1720s, the Scottish Patriot politician and landowner Sir John Clerk of Penicuik asked the artist William Aikman, then looking to forge his reputation and make his fortune in the capital, to keep an eagle eye on the fortunes of his lottery tickets.[41] Augustine Earle, who worked for the Excise Office, bought tickets for himself, his kin and several of his neighbours in north west Norfolk.[42] That very large numbers of people visited London in the long eighteenth century, often on a fairly regular basis, not just from among the elites, only made such practices more common. In some cases, moreover, these relationships and this activity continued over a good many years, especially where they involved kin, such as the Kent gentleman, Sir Edward Filmer and his brother, the London lawyer, Beavisham or James Harris of Hampshire and his siblings.[43] A big advantage of

---

City of London had petitioned the Commons against the lotteries in the previous year. See Bob Harris, 'The 1782 Gaming Bill and Lottery Regulation Acts (1782 & 1787): Gambling and the Law in Later Georgian Britain', *Parliamentary History*, forthcoming, 2021. What only further extended the grip of the lottery insurers on metropolitan society was the use by licensed and unlicensed Lottery Offices of agents, who often based themselves in inns and taverns, or were themselves victuallers. They were paid a commission on 'policies' sold. LMA, MJ/O/C/012, Middlesex Sessions: Orders of Court, 28 Oct. 1789-5 Dec. 1795, 1 Nov. 1792.

[39] TNA, IR55/13, anonymous letter, dated 29 Mar. 1816.

[40] See e.g. LMA, CLC/479/MS00205/1-9, personal diaries of Stephen Monteage, 1733-64; Derbyshire Record Office, D239/M/F/15894-15918, 'The Naturalist's Diary', kept by William Philp Perrin, 1773-80, 1783, 1793-1808.

[41] National Records of Scotland [hereafter NRS], Papers of the Clerk Family of Penicuik, Midlothian, GD18/4622, William Aikman to Sir John Clerk, n.d., but 1720s.

[42] Norfolk Record Office [hereafter NRO], MC 2782/A/1 & 2, pocket diary of Augustine Earle, 1757-8, 1759-60.

[43] KARC, U120/C25/3, 6, 8, 10, 11, 19, letters from Beavisham Filmer to Sir Edward Filmer (3rd Bart.), 1733-4; U120/C26/37, 40, 43, 44, 45, 46, 47, 48, same

purchasing tickets through a trusted intermediary was that, given the sometimes extremely volatile ticket price, they could decide when was the optimum time to buy.[44]

What greatly extended the scope for purchasing tickets from the Lottery Offices were the postal services. Lottery businesses were heavily reliant on the increasingly numerous and frequent posts in eighteenth and early nineteenth-century Britain. The main features of the development of postal services –the rise of cross posts, daily posts, mail coaches- are relatively well known and do not need rehearsing in detail here.[45] What does require emphasising is, firstly, the growing efficiency and geographical coverage of the post, measured in terms of regularity, speed and the range of places it served. By 1775, 277 towns across Britain benefitted from a six-day post, a rise from eighty-five in 1741. There was by the same date a five-day post between Edinburgh and London, and a six-day post between Edinburgh and Aberdeen, Glasgow, Greenock and towns between these places on the major Scottish post roads.[46] Fifteen or so years later, 507 places were linked to the G.P.O.[47] Improvements were relentless, both in terms of regularity of mail deliveries and places served. Cross posts ran every day throughout Britain, following their inauguration in 1784 mail coach services were extended, while penny posts were established in several major cities at the end of the eighteenth century -in addition to London, where the penny post saw substantial improvements.[48] Along these

---

to same, 1736-7; Hampshire Record Office, 9M73/G306/8, Thomas Harris, Lincoln's Inn to James Harris, Salisbury, 1 Dec. 1737; 9M73/G347/77, Thomas Harris to Elisabeth Harris, 14 Jan. 1752.

[44] For an illustration of how this might work, see NRS, GD124/16/129, Papers Concerning the Purchase of State Lottery Tickets for John Francis Erskine of Mar, 1780-81, 3, William Flint, St James's, London, to Mr John Jamieson, Alloa, 7 Dec. 1780.

[45] There is no systematic modern study of the development of postal services in this period and their impact. But see, K. L. Ellis, *The Post Office in the Eighteenth Century: A Study in Administrative History* (1958).

[46] Bodleian Library [hereafter Bodl], MS DD Dashwood (Bucks), C. 2, B2/4/5, printed notice, G.P.O., 5 Apr. 1775; Royal Mail Archives [hereafter RMA], printed notice, G.P.O. 1 July 1741.

[47] RMA, Post 24/1, papers relating to plans for increasing the revenue and circulation of the newspaper post, 1791-97, memorandum, Francis Freeling, surveyor, G.P.O., 20 Mar. 1791.

[48] Penny posts were established in Dublin (1773); Manchester (1793); Edinburgh (1793); Glasgow (1800).

routes flowed ever-growing volumes of letters, newspapers, and indeed lottery tickets and shares thereof. On a single day in 1770, for example, 500 letters and 135 newspapers were sent from London to Bristol. To take another place at random, Cardiff, the equivalent numbers were respectively forty five and thirty two.[49] The advent of the six-day post in Scotland in 1764 saw a pronounced rise in the revenues of the Scots Offices, of around a quarter in just three years.[50] In March 1796, a little over 8,200 letters were dispatched from Edinburgh to London, while slightly more were sent the other way. Around 7,000 were sent from the Scottish capital to other places in England and Wales, while 3,300 came the other way.[51] Susan Whyman has rightly emphasised the contribution of postal services to the conquering of the tyrannies of distance and separation in eighteenth-century England; they also had a major role in the 'shrinking' of Britain.[52] Lotteries were major beneficiaries of these trends. Lottery Offices would on request send lottery schedules through the post, sell and remit tickets to clients, and also inform them expeditiously of the outcome of the draw for payment of a fee. In the 1740s, for example, several London Lottery Offices sent tickets to the earl of Cassilis, owner of Culzean Castle on the Ayrshire coast, via the Maybole postmaster.[53] Other means of conveying demands to Lottery Offices were by carriers or coach services, two further key elements in the transformation of communications and markets which underpinned the deepening and broadening economic dynamism of British society in this period. By the 1780s letters

---

[49] Bodl, MS DD Dashwood (Bucks), C. 2, B2/4/4b, An Account of the Number of Letters, Newspapers, and Packets sent to the Several Post Towns in the Bristol Road, 28 July 1770.

[50] Bodl, MS DD Dashwood (Bucks), C. 2, B2/3/13a, Gross Produce of the Scots Offices.

[51] RMA, E298/1796, Edinburgh Post Office Establishment, 1797: North of Scotland, mail coach system, An Account of the Amount and Number of Letters Going From and Coming to Edinburgh & London, as also of Letter Coming, and Going to Places that are Dispatched with the English Mail, for One Month from the 1st March to 31st March 1796 Both Inclusive.

[52] Susan E. Whyman, 'Paper Visits: The Post-Restoration Letter as Seen Through the Verney Family Archive', in Rebecca Earle (ed.), *Letters and Letter Writers 1600-1945* (Aldershot, 1999), pp. 15-36.

[53] NRS, Papers of the Kennedy Family, Earls of Cassillis, GD25/9/24/4, Financial Papers, 1741-7.

could be sent free of charge to some Lottery Offices by means of the new mail coaches.

The business for postal services generated by the lottery was significant. In 1819 it was estimated by the Lottery Office that the annual postage on tickets and shares thereof amounted to £131,000, which may have represented between around 5-700,000 communications.[54] To this we would need to add letters which were sent between Lottery Offices, their agents, and other employees, as well as the printed notifications sent to registered lottery ticket owners informing them of the fate of their number in the draw, examples of which can be found scattered through the papers of many Georgian landed families.

From the final third of the eighteenth century, Lottery Offices developed networks of agents. In return for payment of a commission on tickets sold, agents were supplied with tickets (on a sale or return basis) and advertising bills (posting bills, window and hand bills). The first licensed Lottery Offices outside of London appear to have emerged in the mid eighteenth century.[55] From 1802, businesses did not require separate licenses for provincial agents, and thereafter they proliferated. In the early nineteenth century, all of the main London lottery businesses developed far-flung and extensive bodies of agents in towns across Britain. James Branscomb & Co., for example, had agents in the following places: Aberdeen; Bath; Bristol; Birmingham; Bury; Bolton; Coventry; Chatham; Chester; Chichester; Dorchester; Derby; Dundee; Exeter; Edinburgh; Gloucester; Glasgow; Gosport; Hull; Lancaster; Liverpool; Lynn; Marlborough; Newark; Newport, Isle of Wight; Norwich; Northampton; Newcastle; Nottingham; Plymouth; Portsea; Reading; Salisbury; Stamford; Shrewsbury; Sherborne; Weymouth; Wolverhampton; Winchester; Worcester; Warrington; Yarmouth; and York.[56] One estimate in 1816 put the

---

[54] Parliamentary Papers, 1819 (436), Return to Orders of the Honourable House of Commons, on the 7th Day of April 1819, For an Account of the Number of Lotteries Drawn Under Act of Parliament since March 1816, Together with the Amount of Revenue Derived Severally From the Same.

[55] *Whitehall Evening Post*, 28 Aug. 1758, advertisement for J. Hazard, Lottery Office keeper.

[56] Cumbria Record Office, Barrow-in-Furness, Soulby Collection, handbill for J. Branscomb and Co., n.d., but prob. post 1802.

overall number of provincial lottery agents at 3,000.[57] Very often they were booksellers. For example, Swift and Co.'s agent in Glasgow was the Trongate bookseller David Niven. Thomas Bish's was another bookseller, Thomas Ogilvie. In the early 1820s, Hazard & Co.'s Edinburgh agent was James Anderson, who ran a bookselling business from in front of the Royal Exchange on the city's High Street.[58] That booksellers and others in the print trade, such as stationers and printers, frequently acted as lottery agents is probably best explained by their versatility, the fact that they were used to acting as agents for all sorts of goods, but also because they had experience of dealing with London wholesale publishers and booksellers.[59] It was an aspect of the lottery business which was standardised and facilitated through the use of printed forms and instructions. At the local level, lottery agents relied, like their London masters, on postal services and carriers to transmit instructions from clients about purchasing tickets or shares thereof. The consequence was that there were few areas of Britain where people could not make contact fairly readily with a lottery agent or office. Agents also, as we will see further below, played an important role in the publicising of lotteries, the topic to which we now turn.

The vital relationship between lotteries and publicity in this period has been well noted by other historians.[60] It was true of the private and public lotteries which sprang up in large numbers in London in two waves in the 1690s. Lottery schedules, for example, were

---

[57] TNA, IR55/13, Return to the Honourable House of Commons Pursuant to an Order for 'An Account of the Number of Lotteries Drawn under Act of Parliament since 1811 Inclusive, Together with the Amount of Revenue Derived Severally from the Same, Shewing also the Terms Upon which the Said Lotteries were Disposed of to the Contractors' (1816).

[58] BL, 8229 k. 8 (1), handbills for D. Niven, Trongate, Glasgow, 1809; BL, LR 26 b. 1, handbill headed 'Success at Edinburgh'; BL, 8229 k. 8 (19), handbill for T. Ogilvie, bookseller, Glasgow. See also Trevor Fawcett, 'Some Aspects of the Norfolk Book Trade, 1800-24', *Transactions of the Cambridge Bibliographical Society*, 4 (1968), 383-95.

[59] James Raven, *The Business of Books: Booksellers and the English Book Trade 1450-1850* (New Haven and London, 2007), p. 240.

[60] Murphy, *Origins*, p. 95; Natasha Glaisyer, *The Culture of Commerce in England, 1660-1720* (Woodbridge, 2006), esp. pp. 155, 168-9, 179; *idem.*, 'Calculation and Conjuring: John Molesworth and the Lottery in Late Eighteenth-Century Britain', *Journal for Eighteenth-Century Studies*, 42 (2019), 135-55.

printed for their organisers on single sheets, which were then widely distributed.[61] Printed benefit books, already referred to, recorded the results of the lottery draw. Yet, the relationship was only more glaringly apparent in the case of the public lotteries of the early nineteenth century, when the market was becoming saturated and there is evidence of lottery fatigue with the increased numbers of lotteries. Indeed, the lottery contractors and Lottery Office keepers were notable adepts in the world of 'puffing' and promotion, and in the sphere of handbill design and printing in the 1800s, through the use of wood engraved illustrations, new large display types, colour printing, as well as the employment of literary devices such as acrostics, verses, songs, and even pictograms.[62] In 1820, one individual put together a collection of such material for his children and grandchildren as a record of the supposed 'national disgrace' represented by lotteries and the 'systematic series of tricks, puffs & deceptions' which had been resorted to by the Lottery Office keepers.[63] Before c. 1800, lottery handbills were fairly straightforward in terms of layout and content. Typically, they gave information about the distribution and size of especially the capital prizes, but also previous winners who had bought tickets at their 'lucky' Lottery Offices.[64] Such handbills continued to be produced in large numbers into the early nineteenth century, although they were, as referred to above, increasingly supplemented by more original, striking designs. One licensed office in Edinburgh, for example, advertised in 1804 that it had sold the 'largest prize that ever came to Scotland', a sum of £25,000 divided into shares. On the back of the same advertising handbill, it listed winners of parts of capital prizes, including, for example, a Dundee shoemaker who had won a sixteenth share of £10,000 and a similar win for a club of 18 people in Peterhead.[65] On a handbill for Pidding & Co., which gave details of a lottery scheme, the major part of the bill was taken up with a list of 'fortunate individuals'

---

[61] At the end of the eighteenth century, they were available free from mail and stage coachmen.

[62] See esp. John Strachan, *Advertising and Satirical Culture in the Romantic Period* (Cambridge, 2011).

[63] BL, 8228 bb. 78.

[64] See e.g. Bodl, John Johnson Collection, lotteries, vol. 6 (3), handbill for W. Hodges & Co., 1774; lotteries, vol. 9 (29), handbill for J. Branscomb and M. Swinney, Birmingham, 1801.

[65] NRS, GD99/229/13 (3). For another example of a similar handbill issued by the same business, see BL, 8229 k 8 (4). Both were printed in Edinburgh.

who had bought tickets winning capital prizes from their office, who included a Wapping publican, a Cirencester tradesman, and widow with three children from Guildford.[66]

One historian has estimated that in 1809, dependent on format and sizes and use of colour, anything between three to five and a half million handbills may have been produced to advertise a single lottery.[67] This estimate is based on figures for contracts between the lottery contractors and London printers. Other lottery handbills were printed by provincial printers, although on what scale is unknown. In 1816 the Treasury estimated that 'upwards' of 10 million lottery bills 'of all sizes' had been printed in the previous year.[68] A report on the contractors' accounts for the 1809 lottery shows payments for errand carts, town and country village boards, as well as travellers and trampers.[69] This is indicative of how sophisticated, extensive and intensive was the lottery advertising operation by the early nineteenth century, as towns were inundated and covered with bills posted on conspicuous buildings, boards and poles. Travellers were employed to follow circuits ensuring that provincial agents lived up to their responsibilities in this context, and to supplement these where they were deemed deficient. Inspectors checked on the activities of the travellers. Errand carts, meanwhile, carried handbills to places in and around London, and also served as mobile sites of advertising.[70]

Alongside the myriad handbills advertising particular lotteries, Lottery Office keepers used handbills and other printed ephemera to stir interest and custom during the draw itself. A fairly common device was a slip or single sheet advertising that a capital prize had been won by a ticket bought at their premises.[71] It was one such

---

[66] BL, 8226 cc. 27 (71).

[67] Banham, 'Lottery Advertising', p. 24.

[68] TNA, IR55/10, draft return to the House of Commons, 1817.

[69] TNA, T 64/324, *Report of the Four Auditors Appointed to Inspect the Accounts Delivered by Richardson, Swift & Co for Expences in the Third Lottery for 1809, Drawn 19th October 1810, in Which they were the Contractors* (London, 1811).

[70] Banham, 'Lottery Advertising'. The accounts of John Craske, a Norwich lottery agent of the 1810s and 1820s, include regular entries for posting bills, day boards (presumably advertising boards), circulars, and entries which read 'Bill Town' and 'Bill Fair' (presumably meaning for pasting up and circulating handbills in Norwich and at fair time. NRO, BR80/1&2, lottery register books of John Craske.

[71] Examples of these issued by Thomas Bish and J & J Sievewright are to be found in

notice that caused Johnson's biographer James Boswell in 1791 to break open the paper in which he had carefully enfolded his ticket to see if it was his ticket that was the lucky number. A quick peek revealing that it was not, Bozzy duly re-sealed his ticket to await the completion of the draw.[72]

However, if handbills and bill pasting by the early nineteenth century made the lottery a brazenly, and to some disturbingly, visible presence, viewing the period as whole, equally —even more perhaps- significant was the publicity made possible by an expanding, maturing newspaper press. Early official lottery schemes were announced in the official newspaper, the *London Gazette*, as well as on separate printed sheets, from where they rapidly found their way into other newspapers. London banker John Campbell could thus simply assume in 1711 that a client, Lord Yester, would have read about the first lottery of that year in the *Post Man*.[73] Newspapers of all types from the early eighteenth century typically reported the fluctuating prices of tickets and blanks before and following the draw, the state of the draw, including prize numbers drawn, and winners of the capital prizes. Indeed, it is because of press reporting that we know the identities of large numbers of lottery winners. The press furnishes, in short, ample evidence of the remarkable fascination which the lottery held for many contemporaries.

From the later eighteenth century it was the potential of newspapers as vehicles for advertising of the services of the Lottery Offices and lottery schemes which became more important. This was a function of the nationwide circulation of the metropolitan press, facilitated by the use from 1764 of the franking privileges of MPs, which meant that the papers could be sent free of charge through the post, but, and as importantly, the growth and ever-widening reach of the provincial newspaper, for which the number of titles is only a crude proxy.[74] From thirty five in 1760, this latter

---

the Lancashire Archives, DDHU/53/82/10, printed lottery material, 1796-c.1817.

[72] *Letters of James Boswell: 8 January 1778-19 May 1795*, ed. Chauncey Brewster Tinker, 2 vols. (Oxford, 1924), ii, 420-22: James Boswell to Edmond Malone, 10 Feb. 1791.

[73] Coutts & Co. Archives, Letter Book 6, 20r, Campbell to Lord Yester, 24 Feb. 1711.

[74] In 1787 the Post Office set up a separate office, comprising 16 people, to deal with newspapers. At the time of its establishment, 45,514 newspapers were being sent

figure climbed to sixty by 1790, doubling again by 1820. To these figures, we should add the smaller, but still growing, number of Scottish newspapers. It was symptomatic too of the growing volume of advertisements carried by the newspapers, facilitated by their growing size, and evident in all types of newspaper - London, provincial, and Scottish.[75] The rise of specialist advertising agencies after c.1800, of which the most important in respect of the lotteries was that of 'Jem' White, whose office was in Fleet Street, made placing advertisements and 'puffs' - notices disguised as news paragraphs - throughout the provincial and Scottish press much easier for the main Lottery Offices and lottery contractors.[76]

The amounts of money spent by the lottery contractors and office keepers on newspaper advertising – or, indeed, the importance of the contribution this made to the growing independence and financial strength of newspapers in later Georgian Britain - are very hard to estimate. Victoria Gardner notes that there were sixty-two lottery advertisements in the *Newcastle Courant* in 1791, which comprises 1.8% of the total. On the other hand, these were typically longer than most advertisements and paid notices and thus cost more.[77] Between 17 August and 23 November 1778 James Branscomb placed fifteen advertisements in the *Hampshire Chronicle*, paying between 5 and 12 shillings for each of them. On 16 October 1780, to take one issue of the same paper, five different lottery businesses paid for insertion of advertisements, while one of them also paid for insertion of a paragraph or so-called 'puff' in the news columns. In 1780, the total number of paid lottery advertisements was 110, which includes several 'lottery paragraphs' and

---

weekly through the post; three years later this figure had climbed to 67,419. In 1791, 3,944,093 newspapers were sent through the General Post Office. This does not include the numbers of provincial papers being sent through regional and local posts. RMA, Post 24/1, papers relating to plans for increasing the revenue and circulation of the newspaper post, 1791-7.

[75] Ivon Asquith, 'James Perry and the Morning Chronicle, 1791-1821', unpublished Ph.D. thesis, University of London, 1973, ch. 4, 'Perry's Advertising Policy'; Christine Y. Ferdinand, 'Selling it to the Provinces: news and commerce round eighteenth-century Salisbury', in John Brewer et al. (eds.), *Consumption and the World of Goods* (London, 1993), pp. 393-411; Hannah Barker, *Newspapers, Politics and Public Opinion in Late Eighteenth Century England* (Oxford, 1998).

[76] Victoria E. M. Gardner, *The Business of News in England, 1760-1820* (Basingstoke, 2016), p. 64.

[77] Gardner, *Business of News*, p. 57.

advertisements for the Irish state as well as British official lotteries.[78] In its issue of 9 February 1802, *The Cumberland Pacquet* carried thirty six advertisements, of which five were lottery related, all of which, however, were priced at the higher end of charges for advertisements owing to their length.[79] The 1809 audit report on the accounts of the contractors for the third lottery of 1809 is opaque on the issue of costs of newspaper advertising, although it includes substantial sums for what were termed 'town' and 'country' advertisements, which could refer to advertisements in the metropolitan and non-metropolitan papers respectively, as well as for the unspecified expenses of Lottery Office keepers.[80]

Whatever the costs and benefits to the newspapers themselves, the pattern of lottery advertising became fairly standard by the early nineteenth century. The contractors would place regular notices describing the terms of the lotteries, while the main Lottery Offices would place their own advertisements and 'puffs' in issues published in the weeks leading up to the draw, including information about their local agents. Some of the lottery advertisements spread across more than a single column and involved use of larger type.[81] In the 1770s and '80s, as referred to earlier, the advertising columns of metropolitan newspapers had been filled with long notices of elaborate, often dubious schemes of 'chances' run alongside the official lottery by many Lottery Offices.

How far press reporting on and advertising of the lottery drove or encouraged lottery participation is, of course, impossible to judge at this distance. Nevertheless, the repeated message they sought to convey was, apart from the opportunities which lotteries offered for winning dizzying sums through the major capital prizes, that people did win, and from across Britain and across the full spectrum of society. In the early 1790s, Andrew Armstrong, an Edinburgh woollen merchant, recorded several major lottery wins in his

---

[78] TNA, Exchequer Records, E140/90, Wilkes versus Collins and others, 1778-1783, sales ledger, 18 May 1778-19 Mar. 1781.
[79] Cumbria Record Office, Carlisle, office copy of the *Cumberland Pacquet*.
[80] TNA, T 64/324, *Report of the Four Auditors*.
[81] See e.g. *Kelso Mail*, 10, 14, 17, 21, 24, 28 Apr.; 16, 19, 20, 26 June; 3, 7, 17, 31 July; 14, 21, 25 Aug.; 1, 8, 25 Sept.; 2, 6, 23 Oct.; 6, 20, 24 Nov.; 15, 29 Dec. 1817; *Cumberland Pacquet*, 21, 31 Jan.; 7, 14, 25, 28 Feb.; 7, 14, 21, 28 Mar.; 11, 18 Apr. 1809.

journal.[82] He had almost certainly learnt about these from reading newspapers. Quite what motivated him to note these down remains obscure, although it was testimony to the potent appeal of the lottery. Armstrong was no gamester; rather he was a man of strong religious convictions, approving of sober, virtuous conduct by himself and others.

Just how widely the lottery habit had spread throughout Britain by the early nineteenth century is revealed very clearly by the records of Glaswegian stationer Thomas Murray. In the early 1820s Murray acted as lottery agent for John and James Sievewright, who ran one of London's largest contemporary lottery businesses.[83] Murray had his own agents in, respectively, the rapidly expanding, volatile industrial town of Paisley; the important Clyde ports of Greenock and Port Glasgow; Ayr, the county town of Ayrshire; and one of the other Ayr burghs, the port and manufacturing centre of Irvine. While the information provided in Murray's surviving lottery books is fairly patchy, the extensive geographical coverage of his business is, nonetheless, readily evident. Clients of Murray hailed from across much of west-central Scotland, including well-established burghs such as, to name only a few, Stirling, Renfrew, Ayr, Dumbarton and Hamilton, but also industrial villages such as Balfron, Stewarton, Neilston and Kirkintilloch. They also came from places throughout highland Argyllshire (Dunoon, Campbeltown, Arran, Inverary, Fort William, Oban, Arrochar and Tobermory on the island of Mull). Most of what Murray sold were shares of tickets, predominantly sixteenths, the smallest share.[84]

It has been argued that most sixteenths were sold to people from among the labouring classes or lower orders, and also that the middle classes tended to abandon the lottery from the later

---

[82] Edinburgh Central Library, DA 1861.789, Journal of Andrew Armstrong, 1789-93, fos. 96 r. (1 Mar. 1790), 175 (Feb. 1791), 261 (19 Mar. 1792).

[83] NRS, Court of Session Productions, CS96/2105, John and James Sievewright, lottery contractors, London, Thomas Murray, stationer, Glasgow, lottery ticket register book, 1824-6.

[84] For example, in the first lottery of 1823, he sold 1,185 half shares, 520 quarter shares, 688 eighth shares, and 5752 sixteenth shares. NRS, CS96/2106, lottery sales book, 1823-6. This pattern was repeated nationally, for which see Parliamentary Papers, 1817 (203), An Account of the Number of Tickets Sold and Shared in the Lotteries During the Last Two Years: Distinguishing Whole Tickets, Half Tickets, Quarters, Eighths, and Sixteenths.

eighteenth century.[85] The majority of the entries in Murray's records fail, frustratingly, to give occupations or designations, and where they do these can be disarmingly imprecise, such as, to pick just two examples, 'a tall pleasant gentleman' and 'sold to a country man'. Yet, it is apparent that even at this late stage the lottery continued to attract the custom of people from diverse backgrounds, and that sixteenth shares were bought by an equally wide selection of people. Murray sold sixteenths to, for example, George Jardine, Professor of Logic and Rhetoric at the University of Glasgow; military officers; various gentlemen and gentlewomen; a Paisley banker; professionals, including ministers of the Kirk; several manufacturers (including James Saunders, the linen manufacturer from Lochee, near Dundee, presumably visiting Glasgow for business reasons); various tradesmen and women, such as a female spirit dealer from Paisley; and a handful of farmers. Those among the labouring classes who bought shares of tickets from him included a weaver from nearby to Hamilton; Campsie slater; Beith corkcutter; Aidrie shoemaker; Stewarton tailor; and a Renfrew labourer. The practice of buying shares, including sixteenths, had long been common among the propertied classes, and one of the main effects of this was almost certainly to widen and deepen significantly the market for lottery tickets among the expanding, diversifying middling sort of Georgian Britain.[86] What makes this all the more plausible is that prices of whole tickets rose significantly after c.1800.

The lottery was, thus, a prime example of vibrant commercial forces which, together with widening prosperity, were reshaping opportunities for recreational gambling of different kinds in Georgian Britain, and of how entrepreneurial acumen and drive propelled the expansion of such markets far across Britain and down into society. One key to this was the ability of lottery contractors and Lottery Office keepers to harness the growing power of publicity in Georgian Britain presented by print in its various, diversifying forms. The lottery was one of the main beneficiaries of the transformations in communications which occurred in this

---

[85] P. Langford, *A Polite and Commercial People: England 1727-1787* (Oxford, 1989), p. 572; Lorraine Daston, *Classical Probability in the Enlightenment* (Princeton, N. J., 1988), pp. 162-3.
[86] NRS, Innes of Stow Papers, GD113/5/417, list of divided tickets sold for the state lottery 1775.

period. In this, and the development of the lottery marketplace, London, the British capital, played a crucial role. This was a function of its gargantuan size —while its position at the top of the urban hierarchy was cumulatively being eroded by the growth of large manufacturing towns and cities in industrialising regions, it remained by some distance the most populous city in Europe in 1800 - and magnetic attraction for people in this period, and the connections which were constantly being forged and renewed between Londoners, London businesses, and people in other parts of the British Isles, and, indeed, further afield. London Lottery Office keepers sat at the heart of a web of connections which extended ever further across British society in the eighteenth and early nineteenth centuries. The system of agencies which came into being in the early nineteenth century in many ways merely built on this reality, that and the ways in which standardised printed forms facilitated and expedited business transactions. Even advertising through the metropolitan and non-metropolitan press was made altogether simpler by the rise of agencies specialising in this area of business. Whether, therefore, you were in Whitehaven in Westmoreland or Kelso in the Scottish borders in the early nineteenth century, you could well have been reading in the early nineteenth century the same sets of printed handbills and newspaper advertisements from lottery contractors and lottery businesses for the lotteries in any given year. The multiplying carrier services, unheralded heroes of early industrialisation, carried instructions for purchasing tickets to lottery agents in provincial Britain from individuals and communities remote from the burgeoning towns and cities of the period which have often been identified as crucibles of economic, social, and cultural change.

To point out that adventures in the lottery were made possible for a growing and increasingly wide cross-section of the British population does not of course offer anything like a full explanation of why the lottery proved so successful. This is not the place to pursue this question in depth. Playing the lottery might be rationalized in all sorts of ways, as contributing to the public good, for example, or simply a harmless pleasure. People regularly, for example, bought tickets for their children. Henry Fox, for example, 'constantly kept a ticket in the wheel' for his youngest son, Harry.[87] Lotteries were undoubtedly popular, hence the many

---

[87] BL, Add MS 51,422, fo. 254, Lady Caroline Fox to Henry Fox, 27 Dec. 1771. See

illegal private lotteries for such things as, for example, selling off stock or goods of different kinds or staged by mountebanks at fairs, which is not to say that their appeal was irresistible. It emphatically was; and there were those who continued to oppose lotteries on religious grounds as a form of unwelcome gambling, destructive to the morals and industry of the poor, or built on unreason.[88] As one London correspondent declared to the Derbyshire gentleman, James Longsdon in early 1802: 'Enclosed is a Lottery Ticket ... I think you wou'd stand a much better chance of getting rich by playing whist at Guinea points – than playing for a piece of paper at almost a hundred p.ct. above its real value.'[89]

Another possible explanation, however, relates closely to the discussion above of how it was that many people were able to gain access to the services of the Lottery Offices. Modern behavioural studies of gambling suggest that people of all classes who have not previously gambled will decide to do so when they are confronted by increased economic security.[90] Who gained and who lost in these terms across the long eighteenth century, and to what degree, is of course a matter for lively debate. Much depended on place, chronology, and from which sector of the economy one derived one's living, or various lifecycle factors and patterns of household formation. Yet, it is what modern studies also claim which is of more interest in the present context. They emphasise that perceptions of one's economic wellbeing are relative. Risk taking thus increases on this account when people perceive threats to their economic security, but also when they are aware of others doing better than themselves. Whether Britain in the long eighteenth century was marked by unusual social mobility is impossible to assess given current knowledge. Nevertheless, the notion that money carried all before it, and could confer social status, was endlessly recycled in various media – novels, periodicals, and

---

also fo. 252, Lord Holland to Henry Fox, 20 Dec. 1771. I owe this reference to my DPhil student Geraldine Porter, to whom I am very grateful.

[88] The Quakers, for example, sought to discourage participation in the lottery as they viewed it as 'a species of gaming' (*Advices of the Yearly Meeting, 1791* (1791)).

[89] Derbyshire Record Office, D3580 C.17, William Whateley to James Longsdon, Esq., 27 Feb. 1802. For similar sentiments, see Lancashire Record Office, DDX 2743/M5797, Richard Blood, Lancaster, to Thomas Barrow, merchant, 24 Jan. 1801.

[90] See Reuven Brenner with Gabrielle Brenner, *Gambling and Speculation: A Theory, A History and Future of Some Human Decisions* (Cambridge, 1990).

newspapers. As the earl of Buchan, writing on education, bemoaned in 1782:

> They [the young] are taught to consider money, acquired by any profession, however mean or grovelling, nay even by gaming, by rapine, fraud, and murder, as the only roads to distinction, in a country become altogether venal, and that venality even sanctified by the monstrous nature of the constitution of the nation itself.[91]

Buchan was a reformer with his own axes to grind. Yet this same idea, albeit usually couched in less pointed terms, was hardly unusual. As Lorraine Daston has noted: 'The lottery did not create this levelling potential of money, but it was its most dramatic symbol.'[92] Rather more modestly, as well as covering an even bigger sub-section of society, aspirations to 'independence' remained very deeply embedded in British society in this period. That economic failure and downward mobility were probably the equally, if not more, prevalent fate of people hardly detracts from the point. It was, indeed, the looming counterpoint to the burgeoning ideal of meritocracy, and gave the lie to the notion that only talent and resolution were required to make one's way in the world. The lottery was parasitic on these deep cultural currents and behavioural dispositions, in that it depended for its success on recurrent advertisement of lottery wins, that and the fact that lottery fortune could strike anywhere. Not the least of the achievements of the Lottery Office contractors and keepers was to keep these notions strongly impressed on people's minds. It was their skilful, ebullient exploitation of the new technologies of communication of Georgian Britain which made this possible.

---

[91] David Stewart Erskine, earl of Buchan, *Letter from the Earl of Buchan to his Borther, the Hon. Thomas Erskine, Counsellor at Law; on the Subject of Education* (Edinburgh, 1782), p. 8.
[92] Daston, *Classical Probability*, p. 150.

The Jacobite Interpretation of Defeat[1]

Daniel Szechi

In early September 1745 Alexander Forbes, Lord Forbes of Pitsligo, was confronted by a crisis of conscience. Prince Charles Edward Stuart had landed in the western Highlands, gathered a small army and was on the march east, sending messengers before him with letters calling on Scotland's Jacobites to join him. Pitsligo had been out in the rising of 1715 and well knew that the personal consequences of involvement in a second failed rising would be dire. Nonetheless, he decided to come out in arms. Reflecting years later on his decision to go to war, Pitsligo recalled, 'I examined my motives as well as I could (for who can pretend to absolute purity), so being conscious to myself of no desire of any man's estate, and far less of his blood, I thought I might venture my own life in a cause that appeared to me to have so much to say in its behalf.'[2] He accordingly summoned his vassals, friends and neighbours and mustered the Earl Marischal's squadron of horse, a dormant, but still secretly extant, unit of Jacobite cavalry formed in 1715.[3] Gathered together at their first rendezvous, Pitsligo briefly addressed the assembled horsemen: 'Oh Lord, Thou knowest our cause is just. Gentlemen, march'.[4]

The Lord their God was a just God; the Jacobite cause was a just cause. God was, therefore, bound to vindicate the exiled Stuarts.[5]

---

[1] My thanks are due to the Royal Stuart Society for permission to reuse elements of my article, 'The Long Shadow of 1715. The Great Jacobite Rebellion in Jacobite Politics and Memory — a Preliminary Analysis', *Royal Stuart Journal*, 7 (2016), 20-47, in this essay.

[2] Aberdeen University Library, Special Collections, MS 2740/18/1/14 (Ogilvie-Forbes of Boyndlie collection), p. 2.

[3] MS 2740/18/1/14, p. 8.

[4] Murray G. H. Pittock, "Forbes, Alexander, fourth Lord Forbes of Pitsligo (1678–1762), philosopher and Jacobite army officer." *Oxford Dictionary of National Biography*. 23 Sep. 2004; Accessed 13 Aug. 2019. https://www-oxforddnb-com.manchester.idm.oclc.org/view/10.1093/ref:odnb/9780198614128.001.0001/odnb-9780198614128-e-9813.

[5] For examples of the ubiquity of this belief, see: Bodleian Library, Oxford, Carte 181, f. 629v: John Caryll, Jacobite Baron Caryll, to James Drummond, Jacobite Duke of Perth, [St Germain] 21/31 Oct. 1695; Anthony Aufrere (ed.), *The Lockhart Papers* (2 vols, London, 1817), i. 494; W. B. Blaikie (ed.), *Origins of the Forty-Five and Other*

These core beliefs lay at the heart of the Jacobites' dilemma as they struggled to understand their defeats.

For how could a just God countenance the defeat of a just cause? Yet defeated the Jacobites were, not once but on multiple occasions. Between 1689 and 1759 there were four major Jacobite wars. From spring 1689 to autumn 1691 Jacobite loyalists in Scotland and Ireland contested the Williamite triumph in England. In 1715-16 a Jacobite rising convulsed the greater part of Scotland and northern England. In 1719 the landing of a token force of Spanish infantry in western Scotland precipitated a rising there. In 1745-6 Charles Edward Stuart, the grandson of the king driven into exile in 1688, raised the greater part of northern and highland Scotland and marched a Jacobite army as far south as the English Midlands.[6] And in each of these conflicts the Jacobites were utterly defeated. In addition, France made strenuous efforts to invade the British Isles and restore the exiled Stuarts in 1692, 1696, 1708, 1744, 1745 and 1759. Likewise, Spain supported both the '15 and the '45 and launched its own attempt to invade Britain in 1719. And every one of these invasion attempts went awry. There were, too, deadly serious conspiracies to restore the main line of the Stuart dynasty in 1689, 1713-14, 1720-22, 1743-4 and 1750-52. Changing circumstances aborted some; others were discovered and thwarted by the British authorities.[7] In sum, the Jacobites had a lot of failures and defeats to explain.

Explaining why things had gone awry was, moreover, essential to the survival of the Jacobite cause. The ideology of Jacobitism was closely focused on duty. Duty to God, duty to God's anointed servant the Stuart king and duty to one's country.[8] All three co-

---

Papers Relating to that Rising (reprint, Edinburgh, 1975), 'A True Account of Mr John Daniel's Progress with Prince Charles', pp. 218-19.

[6] Daniel Szechi, *The Jacobites. Britain and Europe, 1688-1788* (2nd edn, Manchester, 2019), pp. 61-73, 133-44, 184-8, 193-202.

[7] Szechi, *The Jacobites*, pp. 73-90, 99-105, 152-6; Daniel Szechi, *Britain's Lost Revolution? Jacobite Scotland and French Grand Strategy 1701-1708* (Manchester, 2015); Daniel Szechi, 'Scotland and the Union in the Summer of 1714', *Swift Studies*, 30 (2015), 139-59.

[8] Daniel Szechi, 'The Jacobite Theatre of Death', in, Eveline Cruickshanks and Jeremy Black, *The Jacobite Challenge* (Edinburgh, 1988), pp. 63-70; Paul Kléber Monod, *Jacobitism and the English People, 1688-1788* (Cambridge, 1989), pp. 17-23, 308-42. And see for example: *A Faithful Register of the Late Rebellion* (London, 1718), pp. 88,

mingled in Jacobite thinking. Thus when James Dawson addressed the crowd assembled to watch him die in 1746 he forthrightly declared:

> I firmly believe, and in my conscience am persuaded, that James the third is my only true, lawful, and indisputable sovereign; that the present possessor of his crown and kingdoms is an intruder and usurper; that my taking up arms against him is so far from being a crime that it is my indispensible and bounden duty; and that if I had ten thousand thousand lives, I ought sooner to devote them all to my king and country's service, than to see right overpowered by oppression, or rebellion prevailing over justice.[9]

And ended by praying that God would extend his mercy to his servant Dawson, 'who is not only persecuted, but going to die for truth and righteousness sake.'[10] The fact that dutiful, righteous Jacobites kept on failing to overthrow selfish, evil Whigs was thus an implicit paradox within the Jacobite vision of the universe. If they could not somehow resolve it they were liable to doubt God's blessing upon their cause, and without his blessing their opposition

---

289-90, 323; *True Copies of the Dying Declarations of Arthur, Lord Balmerino, Thomas Syddall, David Morgan, George Fletcher, John Berwick, Thomas Theodorus Deacon, Thomas Chadwick, James Dawson, Andrew Blyde, Donald Macdonald, Esq.; the Rev. Mr Thomas Coppoch, the Rev. Mr Robert Lyon, Edmund Clavering, John Hamilton, Esq.; James Bradshaw, Alexander Leith and Andrew Wood* (Edinburgh, 1750), pp. 12, 13, 20.

[9] *True Copies*, p. 34. See also: Historical Manuscripts Commission, *Calendar of the Stuart Papers Belonging to His Majesty the King Preserved at Windsor Castle* (henceforth HMC *Stuart*; 8 vols, London, 1902-20), ii. 8: Harry Straton to John Erskine, Earl of Mar (Jacobite Secretary of State), [Edinburgh?] 28 Feb. 1716; *Lockhart Papers*, i. 498; ii. 93; Henry Paton (ed.), *The Lyon in Mourning or a Collection of Speeches Letters Journals etc. Relative to the Affairs of Prince Charles Edward Stuart by the Rev. Robert Forbes, A.M. Bishop of Ross and Caithness 1746-1775* (3 vols, Edinburgh, 1895-6), ii. 48 (A true Narrative of Captain Andrew Wood's conversion to the true Church, in a letter to a friend).

[10] *True Copies*, p. 36. See also: Aberdeen University Library, Special Collections, Macbean p Jam III ma: 'Manifesto and Declaration by the Noblemen, Gentlemen and Others, who dutyfully appear at this time in asserting the undoubted right of their lawfull soveraign James the 8th, by the grace of God, King of Scotland, England, France and Ireland, Defender of the Faith, etc, and for relieving this his ancient kingdom of Scotland from the oppressions and grievances it lyes under.'; HMC *Stuart*, iv. 414: Mar to [Charles Caesar], 22 June/3 July 1717; *Lyon in Mourning*, i. 28-9 (The Speech of Mr Thomas Syddal).

to the status quo in the British Isles was nothing more than rebellion, which is as much as to say, an egregious sin.

In a larger sense, too, explaining, and, in a sense, justifying defeat is vital to the survival of any subversive movement that suffers setbacks (and very few do not). If its adherents begin to believe that the movement's failure is inevitable and will serve no higher purpose, they will lose heart and become, at best, inactive. At the same time as the Jacobites were doggedly soldiering on from defeat through disaster to catastrophe, several contemporaneous European rebel movements were withering and dying for precisely these reasons. The last gasp of the French Huguenot community, the Camisard revolt, was crushed in 1705-7. The fugitives and exiles stemming from it were never again able to persuade the Huguenots still in France to rise up against their vicious oppression by the French state.[11] After the defeat of Hetman Ivan Mazepa in 1709, the Cossack exiles who followed Philipp Orlyk into exile in Sweden and the Ottoman Empire proved unable to instigate another uprising to liberate the Ukraine from Russian rule.[12] Despite his Hungarian noble followers' surrender in 1711 the Hungarian peasants clung to the legend of Ferenc Rákóczi the liberator into the 1730s and beyond, but their noble masters were completely demoralised and Hungarian resistance to Habsburg autocracy faded away until the mid-nineteenth century.[13] Likewise after the city of Barcelona was besieged and forced to surrender in 1714 Catalan resistance to the centralising aspirations of the Spanish state collapsed for well over a century.[14] Only the Jacobites persevered. They did so in part due to their higher sense of purpose, in part to the support intermittently given them by the great powers of Europe,[15] and in part because they developed a system of

---

[11] Laurence Huey Boles, *The Huguenots, the Protestant Interest, and the War of the Spanish Succession, 1702-1714* (New York, 1997), pp. 101-18, 129-43, 250-6.

[12] Orest Subtelny, *The Mazepists: Ukrainian Separatism in the Early Eighteenth Century* (New York, 1981).

[13] Linda Frey and Marsha Frey (eds), *The Treaties of the War of the Spanish Succession* (London, 1995), pp. 428-30; Ágnes Várkonyi, 'Rákóczi's War of Independence and the Peasantry', in Janos M. Bak and Bela K. Király (eds), *From Hunyadi to Rákóczi, War and Society in Early Modern Hungary* (New York, 1982), pp. 369-86.

[14] Linda Frey and Marsha Frey, *Societies in Upheaval. Insurrections in France, Hungary and Spain in the Early Eighteenth Century* (London, 1987), pp. 83-103.

[15] Szechi, *The Jacobites*, pp. 176-218.

explanation which (for a while) enabled them psychologically to minimise the importance of their defeats.

It is interesting to note that in this last respect they prefigured the approach taken by more modern subversive/revolutionary movements. Failure and defeat were, for example, simply milestones on the road to 'inevitable' victory for the Communists in Indochina 1945-73, and merely a passing phase in the struggle as far as the FLN were concerned in Algeria 1954-60.[16] Militant Irish republicanism has gone even further, turning its disasters to good account by metamorphosing them into heroic moments of mystical, self-sacrificial communion with epic resistance in the Irish past. By keeping the flame burning regardless of the consequences for themselves, so the argument goes, they will sustain the hopeful dream, and eventually bring in the reality, of a fully liberated, utopian Ireland in the future.[17] Thus the Jacobites' ability to explain away failure and thus deny it any consequence, was of profound importance. As long as they could maintain with conviction their rejection of the commonly accepted interpretation of events like Sheriffmuir and Culloden they could sustain their notorious optimism.[18] Once they accepted the orthodox interpretation: that these moments indicated they could never win, Jacobitism was finished.

* * *

In all likelihood entirely unconsciously, the Jacobites developed three common strands to their explanations of their defeats. These may be summarised as secular, in the sense of an interpretation that revolved around human actions and luck; conspiratorial, in the sense of a vision of events that centred on human treachery and malice; and cosmic, in the sense of an explanation that invoked the divine. None of them excluded the others, and Jacobites struggling

---

[16] Patrick J. McGarvey (ed.), *Visions of Victory: Selected Vietnamese Communist Military Writings* (Stanford, 1969), pp. 199-251; Alistair Horne, *A Savage War of Peace. Algeria 1954-1962* (London, 1977), pp. 403-8.

[17] Ruth Dudley Edwards, *Patrick Pearse: the Triumph of Failure* (London, 1978); Tim Pat Coogan, *The I.R.A.* (London, 1980), pp. 17-19, 27-38, 547.

[18] Daniel Szechi, *Jacobitism and Tory Politics 1710-14* (Edinburgh, 1984), pp. 36-42; William Donaldson, *The Jacobite Song. Political Myth and National Identity* (Aberdeen, 1988), pp. 34-5; Jeremy Black, *British Foreign Policy in the Age of Walpole* (Edinburgh, 1985), p. 138.

to come to terms with the bitter experience of defeat often blended all three on an individual basis so as to generate an interpretation that gave them maximum personal solace.

Because the watersheds in Jacobite history were dominated by battles, campaigns and plots, the secular interpretation primarily dwelt on military and political happenstance. The march of regiments to and fro; a miscarried letter; the poor timing of a charge; the selfishness, stupidity or cowardice of a particular actor; sheer bad luck, and so on, were used to imply that the Jacobites could have, or had very nearly, won the day on any particular occasion. Their 'secular' reflections on what had gone wrong were thus fundamentally concerned with detail, yet they were, perversely, also broad-ranging and individual.

This makes a historical analysis of the secular Jacobite interpretation of defeat potentially so broad and complex that it would be hard to say anything worthwhile in anything less than a major monograph. In the interest of keeping the subject manageable for the purposes of this essay the analysis that follows will accordingly only look at the Jacobites' secular response to the failure of the '45.[19] I have already conducted a similar analysis of the Jacobites' reflections on the '15 elsewhere, and these two analyses, plus the exploration of the conspiratorial and cosmic strands to Jacobite thinking more broadly that follows below, will, I hope, at least partially lay the foundation for a wide-ranging investigation of engagement and disengagement with the Jacobite cause between 1688 and 1788. A minimum of hundreds of thousands, but more likely millions, of inhabitants of, and expatriates from, the British Isles at some point in their lives embraced and (often) abandoned Jacobitism over the course of the century; this essay is an initial foray into thinking about how this social / intellectual / political / emotional process worked.

* * *

The Jacobites' pattern of secular explanation was unique in every one of the wars they fought against the English/British state and the '45 was no exception.[20] One aspect of this particular war that was

---

[19] See my essay 'Long Shadow of 1715' *Royal Stuart Journal*, 2016.
[20] For the best modern analyses of the '45, see: Jeremy Black, *Culloden and the '45*

crucially important in shaping the Jacobites' perception of it were their tactical successes. The Jacobites won two out of three of their major encounters with the British army, and as is the way of these things, success begat little critical thought. Though there are occasional comments in the sources to the effect that more should have been done to follow up on particular victories,[21] the Jacobites' focus was overwhelmingly on events immediately before, during and after their defeat at Culloden. There is also a special problem associated with the surviving sources, which is that our knowledge of the Jacobite commander-in-chief's interpretation of what went wrong is quite limited. This is because, unlike his grandfather James II and VII, Charles Edward showed no interest in writing up his memoirs and never compiled even the sketchy notes on the rising that John Erskine, Earl of Mar and the leader/instigator of the '15, jotted down during and after the conflict.[22] The prince did though, pass a few comments on the military conduct of the '45 in its aftermath that offer some insight into his analysis of what went wrong between 15 and 20 April 1746. For him a key moment came when the Jacobite columns marching through the dark to surprise the British army encamped at Nairn turned back on the night before Culloden. Charles Edward subsequently recalled that he pleaded with his commanders to persevere even though dawn was breaking, and when they refused was, 'so sensibly shocked …that, remounting his horse, he told them, with tears in his eyes, that he did not so much regret his own loss as their inevitable ruine.' Later, when he was on the run in the Highlands, Charles Edward told Captain Malcolm Macleod that, 'Lord George Murray … did not behave well at all with respect to obeying of orders; and that particularly for two or three days before the battle of Culloden [Lieutenant-General] Lord George [Murray] did scarce any one

---

(New York, 1990); Christopher Duffy, *The '45* (London, 2003); Frank McLynn, *Charles Edward Stuart. A Tragedy in Many Acts* (London, 1988).

[21] The battle of Falkirk in particular: Henry Paton (ed.), *The Lyon in Mourning or a Collection of Speeches Letters Journals etc. Relative to the Affairs of Prince Charles Edward Stuart by the Rev. Robert Forbes, A.M. Bishop of Ross and Caithness 1746-1775* (3 vols, Edinburgh, 1895-6), *Lyon in Mourning*, ii. 90 (account of Captain John MacPherson of Strathmashie); Chevalier [James] de Johnstone, *Memoirs of the Rebellion in 1745 and 1746* (2nd edn, 1821), p. 136.

[22] J. S. Clarke (ed.), *The Life of James the Second, King of England, etc, Collected out of Memoirs Writ of his own Hand* (2 vols, London, 1816); Stuart Erskine (ed.), 'The Earl of Mar's Legacies to Scotland and to his son Lord Erskine 1722-1727', in, *Wariston's Diary and Other Papers* (Edinburgh, 1896).

thing he desired him to do.'[23]

Taking Charles Edward's focus on the night march to Nairn as our starting point then, it is interesting to find that the prince's officers were seriously divided on the issue of whether it was ever a good idea. Lord George Murray essentially thought it the least bad option. James Maxwell of Kirkconnell disliked it from the outset and viewed it as having opened the way for, 'the fatal misunderstanding and confusion that prevailed upon the retreat from Nairn, and prevented any right measures being taken in consequence of that disappointment.'[24] But Colonel Sir John Macdonnell, one of Charles Edward's original companions (the 'Seven Men of Moidart'), disagreed. He believed that when Lord George Murray ordered the Jacobite columns to turn back, 'he was near enough to have defeated the enemy before they were drawn up before their camp'.[25] Likewise John Sullivan, the Jacobite Adjutant-General, felt that all that would have been necessary to avert the disaster at Culloden would have been for Lord George Murray to lead the Highlanders into the attack at Nairn the night before.[26]

The heated debates about the night march, though, are as nothing by comparison with the disagreements about how to interpret the battle of Culloden which came on the next day. Charles Edward, 'blamed always my Lord George as being the only instrument in loseing the battle', and specifically asserted that he did not want to fight that day, but was browbeaten into doing so by Lord George. The prince was supported in this version of what happened by a number of his officers.[27] In flat contradiction, James Johnstone

---

[23] *Lyon in Mourning* (Captain O'Neil's Journal of the Prince's Retreat and Escape after April 16th, 1746), i. 102; (Leith, Friday's Evening, 6 o'clock, August 7th, 1747, in the house of James Macdonald, joiner, who and Stewart Carmichael of Bonnyhaugh, were present, Captain Malcolm Macleod, second cousin to Malcolm Macleod (Laird of Raaza), gave the following Account or Journal) i. 135.

[24] John [Murray], Duke of Atholl, *Chronicles of the Atholl and Tullibardine Families* (5 vols, Edinburgh, 1908), iii. 279.

[25] Alistair and Henrietta Tayler (eds), *1745 and After* (London, 1938), p. 157, n. 1. See also: Johnstone, *Memoirs of the Rebellion*, p. 182n; *Lyon in Mourning* (Copy of a Letter, said to be written by Lord George Murray or one of his friends, 1746), i. 255-60, 263.

[26] *1745 and After*, p. 165.

[27] W. B. Blaikie (ed.), *Origins of the Forty-Five and Other Papers Relating to that Rising* (reprint, Edinburgh, 1975), 'Neil Maceachain's Narrative of the Wanderings of

accused Charles Edward of insisting on fighting despite his army's dire circumstances: 'The Prince ... would listen to no advice, and resolved on giving battle, let the consequences be what they might.' Others, such as Muster-Master Henry Patullo and Lord George Murray shied away from directly naming the prince, but the implication is clear: Charles Edward insisted on fighting despite the fact that his army was exhausted and starving.[28]

But why was the army in such a state, and why was the prince so pig-headed? There was no consensus on the subject among the veterans of the '45, but certain individuals were regularly singled out for their military incompetence and the pernicious influence of their poor judgement. Donald Cameron of Lochiel felt Charles Edward's former tutor, Sir Thomas Sheridan, 'had no other conception of waging war than to fight at every opportunity', and that he was responsible for persuading the prince to take many bad decisions, not the least of which was to blame Lord George Murray for the decision of the senior officers to retreat north after the battle of Falkirk: 'Distrust so ill-founded was the principal cause of all H.R.H.'s ills.'[29] David Wemyss, Lord Elcho, blamed Charles Edward's 'favourites', including Sheridan, for his poor decision-making, but singled out John Murray of Broughton's deputy, John Hay of Restalrig, 'a man of neither parts nor capacity', for sending the prince in the wrong direction and having by his incompetence reduced the army to starvation.[30] For James Maxwell of Kirkconnell the villain of the piece was the jealous and ambitious Murray of Broughton (Charles Edward's secretary) who, 'indisposed the Prince against those that were most capable of serving him, and committed the most important charges to such as were by no means qualified for them', resulting in the army going hungry while there was plenty of food in store.[31]

Prince Charles in the Hebrides', p. 240. See also: *Origins of the Forty-Five*, 'A True Account of Mr John Daniel's Progress with Prince Charles', p. 212; *1745 and After*, pp. 160, 162, n. 1

[28] Johnstone, *Memoirs of the Rebellion*, pp. 186-7; *Short Account of the Affairs of Scotland*, pp. 422-3, 430-4; GD1/53/86/2: Muster-Master Patullo's answers to John Home's queries [1790s?]; *Chronicles of ... Atholl*, iii. 321, 323.

[29] John S. Gibson, *Lochiel of the '45. The Jacobite Chief and the Prince* (Edinburgh, 1994), 'Mémoire d'un Écossais', pp. 180, 181.

[30] *Short Account of the Affairs of Scotland*, pp. 415-16.

[31] *Maxwell of Kirkconnell*, pp. 141-2, 155.

There was, though, an elephant in the room: administrators and advisors such as Murray of Broughton, Sullivan and Sheridan were only empowered by Charles Edward's confidence in them and support for them, and all the Jacobite army's officers knew it. So how far was he seen as personally responsible for the defeat at Culloden and the failure of the rising? Elcho's bitter memoir of the rebellion forthrightly contends the prince made many serious errors and thus fatally flawed the Jacobites' chances of success. The first of these was Charles Edward's failure to bring any French troops with him. Because of it various clan chieftains refused to turn out as they had originally promised, whereas if he had brought French troops so many more men would have joined his army that, 'very probably the thing might have succeeded.'[32] Similarly, Charles Edward's 'most extraordinary' decision not to await reinforcement from the Jacobite army in the north before marching into England in November 1745 is blamed by Elcho for the failure of the English campaign, for, 'had the prince had them with him in England he might very possibly have beat the Duke of Cumberland's army and gone on to London.'[33] For Johnstone, Charles Edward's not bringing a cadre of good officers with him from France was crucial, but a strategic error of equal if not greater significance was his Anglocentricity: 'The mind of the Prince', he opined, 'was occupied only with England'. Because of this the Jacobite army's conduct of the war was far less ruthless than it needed to be and the prince lost the opportunity to make himself the hero of Scotland by dissolving the Union and making his war a new war of Scottish independence.[34] Maxwell of Kirkconnell agreed with both men in their criticism of Charles Edward for not bringing a body of French troops and veteran officers with him because, he was too young himself, and had too little experience to perform all the functions of a general; and though there are examples of princes that seem to have been born generals, they had the advice and assistance of old experienced officers, men that understood, in detail, all that

[32] *Short Account of the Affairs of Scotland*, pp. 299-300.

[33] *Short Account of the Affairs of Scotland*, pp. 322, 323. See also: *Maxwell of Kirkconnell*, pp. 74, 77, 88, 137, 141-2, 153, 155; *Lyon in Mourning* (Journal by Mr. John Cameron, Presbyterian Preacher and Chaplain at Fort-William), i. 84, 86; *Lyon in Mourning* (account of Captain John MacPherson of Strathmashie), ii. 90; *Lyon in Mourning* (Copy of a Letter, said to be written by Lord George Murray or one of his friends, 1746), i. 265-7; 'Mémoire d'un Écossais', pp. 178-9, 180-1.

[34] Johnstone, *Memoirs of the Rebellion*, pp. 5, 45-6, 48, 51, 52, 166.

belongs to an army. The Prince had in his army abundance of good subjects, had he known them, but that was impossible, unless he could have read in people's countenances at first sight what they were capable of. Besides an eternal hurry of business, that allowed him no opportunity of making a general acquaintance, I have already observed what pains were taken to prevent it by Murray [of Broughton] and his associates, who laboured nothing so hard as to keep the Prince in ignorance of what he wanted [i.e. needed] most to know.[35]

Charles Edward also came under attack for his perceived favouritism towards the Irish officers who joined him in Scotland: 'Another thing the [Scots] officers took much amiss was the preference the prince gave the Irish to the Scots, which he did upon all occasions; his reasons for that were they were of his own religion, and paid always more court to him in their discourse.' According to Elcho, the prince also took it 'highneously amiss' whenever the Scots raised the issue.[36] Johnstone agreed: 'The natives of Ireland are generally supposed, in England, to have a great confusion of ideas; and they are, in general, very bad counsellors. But the Prince blindly adopted their opinions.'[37] As was often the case, Elcho and Johnstone were the most directly critical on the issue, but Lochiel's hostility to Sheridan and Maxwell of Kirkconnell's attacks on, 'sycophants, more intent upon securing [Charles Edward's] favour than promoting his interest', are simply veiled versions of the same.[38]

Following on from such criticism of the prince's conduct of the war up to and including Culloden, there is a vein of sharp disapproval of his decision post-Culloden to abandon his followers and return to France rather than fight on, guerrilla-style, from the clans' Highland fastnesses. For Donald Cameron of Lochiel Charles Edward's flight from Scotland was simply, 'dishonourable to himself and so harmful to the whole Scottish nation'.[39] Few of the

---

[35] *Maxwell of Kirkconnell*, pp. 156-7.

[36] *Short Account of the Affairs of Scotland*, pp. 416-17. See also: p. 383.

[37] Johnstone, *Memoirs of the Rebellion*, pp. 191-2. See also: pp. 4, 198, 202.

[38] 'Mémoire d'un Écossais', p. 182; *Maxwell of Kirkconnell*, p. 74.

[39] Gibson, *Lochiel of the '45*, 'Mémoire d'un Écossais', p. 183. See also: *Short Account of the Affairs of Scotland*, pp. 436-7; Johnstone, *Memoirs of the Rebellion*, pp. 198, 201-2; *Lyon in Mourning* (Conversations with Mr James Gib), ii. 160-1.

Jacobite veterans of the '45, however, took their criticism of the prince as far as Johnstone when he directly accused him of cowardice.[40]

There were, too, more positive opinions of Charles Edward's conduct of the war. Sullivan saw the military facts of life rather differently, particularly with respect to Culloden:

> no body that has the least notion of the milletary could imagine, that six or seven thousand men, for it was the utmost that the prince had in the field, for so long a time suffering without mony, or vivers, and being discouraged and harrised as they were two days before, could resist in a ranged battle, against above twise the number of regular troops that wanted for nothing, and had a considerable body of horse. We had nothing then for it, nor never can expect to conquor, without regular troops, but by surprise, or attacking them before they are prepared, which is the same thing.[41]

And what went wrong, in his opinion, had more to do with the jealous obstinacy of officers like Lord George Murray than military errors by the prince or Sullivan himself. Looking back on Falkirk, for example, Sullivan felt, 'There was such a Pannic among the enemy, that they durst not look at a highlanders in the face. If they (the Highlanders) wou'd but let themselfs be gouverned, they wou'd have done wonders, or rather if Ld George did not oppose every thing yt was proposed almost, the Prince would be stil in Scotland or the King parhaps restored.'[42] Macdonnell concurred, regarding Lord George as 'ignorant of war', but for him (as, indeed, ultimately for Sullivan), the Scotsman's conduct was motivated by darker motives which will be explored below.[43]

The troops were poor, the weather was bad, our allies let us down, etc; these are the timeless excuses for military defeats that can be found in many an unsuccessful general's memoirs.[44] And they

---

[40] Johnstone, *Memoirs of the Rebellion*, pp. 26, 191, 211. See also: *Short Account of the Affairs of Scotland*, pp. 93-5.

[41] *1745 and After*, pp. 165-6.

[42] *1745 and After*, pp. 120-1. See also: pp. 158, 164, 165.

[43] *1745 and After*, pp. 77n.2, 78n.1, 79n.1, 88n.1, 119n.1.

[44] Stearn, R. (2013, May 30). Percival, Arthur Ernest (1887–1966), army officer.

could, of course, be perfectly true, and have directly contributed to the defeat in question. Hence I do not wish to suggest that the Jacobites were simply indulging in a self-deluding exercise. What is striking, however, is the hidden burden of the secular mode of explanation. The implication throughout is that winning is merely a matter of getting the technical details right. In their reflections on what went wrong most Jacobites assume that factors such as popular support, economic power and the fiscal-military state were incidental and did not significantly affect the military decision.[45] If they won on the battlefield everything else would fall into place. By contrast their Whig opponents almost always assumed that such factors were of the first importance. Indeed, a major reason for the incredulity with which the Whig regime viewed the outbreak of both the '15 and the '45 was that they found it hard to believe that anyone could be so foolish as to throw the meagre military resources they could scrape up in Scotland against the might of the British state.[46] By focusing on the technical reasons for their defeats the Jacobites were really shying away from any deeper examination of the scale of the problem they were facing (i.e. the overthrow of what was in contemporary terms a highly successful military great power). For by doing so they could remain focused on what they saw as their great advantage versus the Whig regime: that they were God's soldiers in a righteous cause. And every good Christian knew that God could lay low the mightiest empire whenever he pleased.

Oxford Dictionary of National Biography. Retrieved 27 Aug. 2019, from https://www-oxforddnb-com.manchester.idm.oclc.org/view/10.1093/ref:odnb/9780198614128.001.0001/odnb-9780198614128-e-61472; Eric Pace, 'General Westmoreland Dies; Led U.S. in Vietnam', *New York Times*, July 19, 2005. For two Jacobite examples of this genre of explanation, see: *Life of James the Second*, ii. 399, 401; 'Mar's Legacies to Scotland', pp. 170, 174.

[45] For Hanoverian loyalism and the fiscal-military state, see: Jeffrey Stephen, *Defending the Revolution. The Church of Scotland 1689-1716* (Farnham, 2013); John Brewer, *The Sinews of Power. War, Money and the English State, 1688-1783* (New York, 1989); Linda Colley, *Britons. Forging the Nation 1707-1837* (London, 1992), pp. 11-101. For Jacobite views ignoring these factors, see: National Records of Scotland (henceforth NRS), GD 18/2099 (Baron John Clerk of Penicuik's notes of a journey to Perth), pp. 31-5; 'Mémoire d'un Écossais', pp. 178-9; *Short Account of the Affairs of Scotland*, pp. 299-300; 'A True Account of Mr John Daniel's Progress with Prince Charles', pp. 212-13. But cf. *Maxwell of Kirkconnell*, p. 158.

[46] Daniel Szechi, *1715: the Great Jacobite Rebellion* (London, 2006), pp. 76, 101; Frank McLynn, *Charles Edward Stuart. A Tragedy in Many Acts* (London, 1988), p. 134.

Like Christ, God's chosen can, however, be betrayed by secret enemies. The second, conspiracy-theory, strand in the web of Jacobite explanation directly stemmed from the political paranoia that persistently dogged the movement. Edward Gregg first pointed out the pervasiveness of this phenomenon in 1988, and his contention that it was largely responsible for the factionalism and disorganisation that characterised the Jacobite movement is a convincing one.[47] In part, this was the natural corollary of it being an underground, subversive organisation. Those who engage in genuine conspiracies and clandestine activities for any length of time seem particularly prone to see plots everywhere, often directed against themselves, as was the case with the professional spies of the Cold War era.[48] The Jacobites too, found spies and traitors to be involved in all their defeats.

The key theatre of war for the Jacobites between 1689 and 1691 was Ireland, so it was from here that the most generally accepted accusations of treachery emanated. Despite the Irish Catholics' manifest, overwhelming commitment to his cause, James II and VII and his chief minister, John Drummond, Jacobite Duke of Melfort, distrusted them.[49] James regarded Ireland simply as a stepping stone on his way back to England ('the king went to Ireland only in order to go to England', noted Melfort in 1689), and he and his ministers certainly envisaged a continuation of the existing imperial relationship between England and Ireland once he was restored.[50] The Catholic Irish, however, saw things rather differently. Though

---

[47] Edward Gregg, 'The Politics of Paranoia', in, Cruickshanks and Black, *Jacobite Challenge*, pp. 42-56. See also: Daniel Szechi, *George Lockhart of Carnwath 1681-1731. A Study in Jacobitism* (East Lothian, 2000).

[48] See for example: Jefferson Morley, *The Ghost: The Secret Life of CIA Spymaster James Jesus Angleton* (New York, 2017); Peter Wright (with Paul Greengrass), *Spycatcher. The Candid Autobiography of a Senior Intelligence Officer* (Sydney, 1987).

[49] *Life of James the Second*, ii. 636-8; T. W. Moody, F. X. Martin, F. J. Byrne (eds), *A New History of Ireland III. Early Modern Ireland 1534-1691* (Oxford, 1976), pp. 493.

[50] James J. Macpherson (ed.), *Original Papers; Containing the Secret History of Great Britain from the Restoration to the Accession of the House of Hannover* (2 vols, London, 1775), i. 334-7: 'Reasons why his Majestie ought to go with all diligence into England', [St Germain] 10/20 Oct. 1689; John Cornelius O'Callaghan (ed.), *Macariae Excidium, or The Destruction of Cyprus; Being a Secret History of the War of the Revolution in Ireland by Colonel Charles O'Kelly, of Skryne. or Aughrane, now Castle Kelly, County Galway. Edited, From Four English Copies, and a Latin Ms. in the Royal Irish Academy, with Notes, Illustrations, and a Memoir of the Author and his Descendants* (Irish Archaeological Society, Dublin, 1850), pp. 42-3.

they were deeply divided by ethnic and factional politics, virtually all the Irish Jacobites envisaged a wholesale recasting of the relationship between the two kingdoms, and they were quite prepared to lobby the French court in order to put pressure on James to accede to their wishes.[51] Thus when the French began to have doubts about committing further resources to the war in Ireland, Jacobite ministers soon began to accuse the Irish of treachery. Melfort advised James in October 1689 that Bishop John O'Molony of Limerick was acting as an unofficial representative of the Catholic Irish in France and that he was communicating independently with Louis XIV's ministers, 'to whom he shews letters of correspondence from Ireland of a most abominable strain; ...wherein the great things done in that kingdom before your Majesty's coming there are fully set out; and how you had by the advice of ill councillors, ruined all the good order you found in it, and hindered [the] duke [of] Tyrconnel's designs.'[52] For such an assault on the Jacobite war effort, Melfort maintained, there was only one appropriate punishment:

> I must conjure your Majesty, though I know it needless in this matter, where your honour and reputation in this country [France] is concerned, not to have compassion on him, nor have regard either to his relations or any thing else; but have him punished so, as the world may see he was a calumniator of his king: a crime merits more deaths than that ill man has hairs.

Moreover, O'Molony's, 'accomplishes here are as many almost as there are of Irish,' and, Melfort implies, they were secretly conspiring with the Williamite regime in England.[53] Small wonder the war in Ireland was being lost when those who were laying down their lives to defend the Jacobite cause in the kingdom were either in cahoots with, or dupes of, the enemy.

For their part, the Irish Jacobites were just as suspicious of James II and VII as he was of them. Bishop O'Molony's attempts to negotiate a separate deal with France did not arise out of Catholic confidence in the king's goodwill. And James's refusal to order an

---

[51] *Early Modern Ireland*, pp. 489-91; *Original Papers*, i. 342; *Macariae Excidium*, pp. 34-5.
[52] *Original Papers*, i. 320: Melfort to James, St Germains, [Oct.?] 1689.
[53] *Original Papers*, i. 321: Melfort to James II, St Germains, [Oct.?] 1689; i. 338: Melfort to James II, St Germains, Oct. 1689.

attack on the Williamite army when it was in dire straits over the winter of 1689-90 convinced Colonel Charles O'Kelly of Skryne that there was a secret conspiracy to abandon the Irish Jacobites, and let them be defeated, in order to please the English, and that the foolish James was part of it:

> This Resolucion was beleived to proceed from a wrong Maxim of State, which his evill Councellors prompted him to embrace, that the onely Way to recover [England] was to loose [Ireland]; for they perswaded him that, [Ireland] being once reduced, the [English] would imediately recall him, as they formerly brought in his [brother Charles II]; but this was a Favour he could not hope for whilst he headed a [Irish] or a [French] Army; and soe, like the Dog in the Fable, he must lett goe the Substance to snatch at the Shadow.[54]

Likewise, the Catholic Irish poets did not have much time for James II and VII, particularly after his flight after the battle of the Boyne. Tropes like James 'the beshitten' and James 'the coward' that appear in popular Irish-language poetry in the aftermath of the war drew directly on the perception that the king, 'came to us in Ireland with one of his shoes English and the other one Irish'.[55]

The 1715 rising also produced quite a number of candidates for the role of Judas, with even pathetic military incompetents like Thomas Forster being suspected of treachery,[56] but the most generally agreed-upon scapegoat was Henry St John, Viscount Bolingbroke, Queen Anne's former Secretary of State. Bolingbroke had fled to France when the Whig regime began impeachment proceedings against him in spring 1715, there met James and was appointed Jacobite Secretary of State by him.[57] Bolingbroke was correspondingly held responsible by many Jacobites for the failure of the French to intervene on the Jacobite side and the miscarriage

---

[54] *Macariae Excidium*, p. 42.

[55] Vincent Morley, *The Popular Mind in Eighteenth-century Ireland* (Cork, 2017), pp. 40-1.

[56] *Faithful Register*, p. 336; Robert Patten, *The History of the Rebellion in the Year 1715. With Original Papers, and the Characters of the Principal Noblemen and Gentlemen Concern'd in it* (James Roberts, London, 1745), p. 97; Blair Atholl Castle, Atholl Papers, box 45, bundle 12/77: account of Jacobite southern army's march to Preston.

[57] H. T. Dickinson, *Bolingbroke* (London, 1970), pp. 134-43.

of numerous attempts by the Jacobites in France to supply the rising in Scotland. Why had he been so inefficient? Mar, his successor as Jacobite Secretary of State[58] was in little doubt that Bolingbroke was criminally culpable and that there were dark doings afoot: 'Some attribute it to negligence, and others to a much worse reason, which I was unwilling to believe, but it is hard to think that negligence alone could have been the only reason, and the king as well as others thinks he has been very ill served, as is indeed too evident.'[59] Other Jacobites in the European diaspora soon endorsed this view, and within a few years it had become commonplace in the British Isles.[60] Thomas Hearne recording in September 1716, for example, that one Hugh Thomas had told him, 'that my Lord Bullingbroke hath been a great villain, and ruined all the measures for restoring the king. Bullingbroke is out of favour with the king for that reason', and in 1719 that John Lewis the bookseller had told him, 'that my Lord Bullingbroke is a great villain, and that King James turned him out of his court for being a spy and betraying his secrets. Indeed, as Mr Lewis said, he went over, by Marlborough's contrivance, purely to be a spy.'[61] For Hearne himself the clinching evidence came in 1723, when Bolingbroke was pardoned by George I, 'By which it appears that what I formerly heard asserted by several, that this Lord is not a man of integrity, but a traitour, and that he was one of those that hindered the restauration of King James III, is true.'[62] Which, of course, satisfactorily explained why the rising of 1715 had been such a disaster.

After the '45 the most influential protagonist of the conspiratorial interpretation of the defeat was no lesser an actor than Charles Edward.[63] The object of his suspicion was Lord George Murray, the

---

[58] Edward Gregg, 'The Jacobite Career of John, Earl of Mar', in Eveline Cruickshanks (ed.), *Ideology and Conspiracy. Aspects of Jacobitism, 1689-1759* (Edinburgh, 1982), pp. 179-200.

[59] *Stuart Papers*, ii. 3.

[60] *Stuart Papers*, ii. 262: Harry Maule to Mar, Leyden, 7 July 1716; ii. 418-19: John Menzies to Mar, 30 Aug. 1716; ii. 476: Lewis Innes to Mar, [St Germain] 26 Sept. 1716.

[61] John Buchanan-Brown (ed.), *The Remains of Thomas Hearne. Reliquiae Hearnianae* (reprint of 1869 edition, Carbondale, 1966), pp. 180, 219: 1 Sept. 1716 and 24 July 1719.

[62] *Reliquiae Hearnianae*, p. 254: 4 June 1723.

[63] McLynn, *Charles Edward Stuart*, pp. 230, 236, 260-1, 452.

most able general on either side of the conflict. According to Elcho Charles Edward's mistrust of Lord George had its origins early in the rising when Murray of Broughton planted the seeds of suspicion in Charles Edward's mind by dwelling on the fact that Lord George had taken the oaths to the government after he was allowed to return from exile in the late 1720s.[64] In all probability most of the officers in the Jacobite army had at some time in their lives sworn oaths of loyalty to the Hanoverian dynasty (it was the everyday cost of doing gentry business in the post-1714 British Isles), but from then on the Jacobite prince increasingly began to interpret Lord George's opposition to some of his more chimerical plans as proof of his unreliability. After the traumatic council of war at Derby where the officers of the Jacobite army, led by Lord George, united in insisting that they return to Scotland, Charles Edward even arranged with some of his Irish officers that if it looked as if Lord George was about to betray the Jacobite army in some future battle they would shoot him on the spot.[65] By the time the final defeat did come Charles Edward was so suspicious of the Scots Jacobites in general (and Lord George in particular) that he refused to try and rally the Jacobite army, apparently believing that the Scots intended to sell him to the Whig government as they had done his grandfather to Parliament in 1646.[66] Asked what had gone wrong with the '45 by Neil Macdonald, in whose home he was sheltering during his flight through the Highlands, Charles Edward was already edging towards blaming Lord George,[67] and his conviction that treachery lay at the root of his only grew with time. In 1747 he urged his father to have Lord George arrested and imprisoned in Rome as a proven traitor to the Jacobite cause, and in 1759 he declared that Murray's 'vilany [was] proved out of all dispute.'[68]

---

[64] *Affairs of Scotland*, p. 251. Maxwell of Kirkconnell agreed with Elcho, but Lochiel blamed Sheridan for Charles Edward's antipathy to Lord George Murray: *Maxwell of Kirkconnell*, pp. 155, 156-7; 'Mémoire d'un Écossais', p. 180.

[65] Frank McLynn, *The Jacobite Army in England, 1745* (Edinburgh, 1983), pp. 123-32; *Affairs of Scotland*, pp. 406-7.

[66] *Affairs of Scotland*, pp. 436-7; 'Mémoire d'un Écossais', p. 182; Johnstone, *Memoirs of the Rebellion*, p. 198.

[67] *Lyon in Mourning*, i. 135 ('Leith, Friday's Evening, 6 o'clock, August 7th, 1747, in the house of James Macdonald, joiner, who and Stewart Carmichael of Bonnyhaugh, were present, Captain Malcolm Macleod, second cousin to Malcolm Macleod (Laird of Raaza), gave the following Account or Journal').

[68] McLynn, *Charles Edward Stuart*, p. 334; *Affairs of Scotland*, p. 453.

It should be emphasised that a conspiratorial explanation of particular Stuart failures was not *ipso facto* misplaced or bizarrely paranoid. It is, after all, beyond dispute that there were genuine conspiracies against the Stuart dynasty in this period that were, on occasion, dramatically successful, the most obvious being that which underpinned the Glorious Revolution.[69] There were also *bona fide* spies and traitors in the Jacobite camp, such as Aleistair MacDonell the younger of Glengarry, who did the cause of the exiled Stuarts a great deal of harm.[70] Nonetheless, conspiratorial explanations of Jacobite defeats certainly overrated the potential damage one individual could cause a whole war-effort, and, as was the case with the secular interpretation of their failures, subtly begged the question of the Jacobites' likely prospects of success. If the only thing that had prevented them winning in situation x or y was human treachery, then all the Jacobites needed to do to win was to assemble the right collection of loyal, true Jacobites. The conspiratorial strand of interpretation is thus in a way another version of the technical explanations of Jacobite failure produced by the secular strand of interpretation. It, too, does not challenge their fundamental belief in their ultimate invincibility. Which necessarily brings us to the question of how they squared their belief that they were God's chosen warriors with the inescapable fact that, by whatever technical means, he was allowing them to be defeated.

* * *

So why would a good, just and all-powerful God allow such faithful instruments of his will as the Jacobites to go down to repeated, bloody defeat? The period 1688-1788 was manifestly still an age of faith and there can be no doubt that the great majority of Jacobites, both Protestant and Catholic, absolutely accepted the then-conventional view of the deity as interventionist and thoroughly engaged with everyday human affairs, so this was a very pressing question for them.[71] And the Jacobites' interpretation of their

---

[69] John Adamson, *The Noble Revolt. The Overthrow of Charles I* (London, 2007); Jonathan Scott, *Algernon Sidney and the Restoration Crisis, 1677-1683* (Cambridge, 1991); Tim Harris, *Revolution. The Great Crisis of the British Monarchy, 1685-1720* (London, 2006).
[70] Doron Zimmerman, *The Jacobite Movement in Scotland and in Exile, 1746-1759* (Basingstoke, 2003), pp. 83-4, 95-7; Hugh Douglas, *Jacobite Spy Wars. Moles, Rogues and Treachery* (1999).
[71] Jeremy Black, *Eighteenth Century Europe 1700-1789* (New York, 1990), pp. 183-90;

failures responded to the problem by elevating their disasters to a cosmic status. Thus the Jacobites were being defeated only because it served God's higher purpose; he still loved them and would, in due course, vindicate them.

There were three distinct versions of the cosmic explanation of Jacobite failure. One of these was singular and only prevailed amongst a tiny minority of Jacobites during the 1690s; the second generally dominated Jacobite thinking on God's role in their defeats throughout the lifetime of the movement; the third was an almost underground tendency within the Jacobite movement that put the blame specifically on the Stuarts themselves. The reason this analysis has to include the first of these: a cosmic explanation accepted by only a handful of Jacobites, is straightforward — its main proponent was none other than James II and VII himself, and thus it may have been highly influential in setting the tone and direction of Jacobite policy.

James's personal interpretation of defeat stemmed directly from the orthodox view of the role of princes in God's plan: as God's viceroys upon earth, they were meant to be both exemplars and shepherds to their people. James, therefore, personally took the blame for the downfall of his dynasty and the torments of faction and civil war his people were undergoing. For he believed that God had chosen to punish and abase him for his lewdness and fornication when he was a young man.[72]

> I must now speak as to myself, as a great punishment [sic] God inflicts on such as have had the misfortune to be led away by the unlawful love of women, even in this world, to reclame them and serve for an example and warning to all the world. I praise his divine goodness for all the mortifications and punishments he has been pleased out of his infinit mearcy to inflict on me, which had he not been pleased to repeat offten I have but too much reason to apprehend I should not have been awaked out of the leathergy and insensibility I was in, and that

---

Jonathan Clark, *From Restoration to Reform. The British Isles 1660-1832* (London, 2014), pp. 80-112.
[72] *Life of James the Second*, pp. 619-20, 622-3, 625-32; *Original Papers*, i. 247-8: 'Fatherly Advice to N.N.' [James II to his illegitimate son, the Duke of Berwick], 1695.

even from the very time of the restoration, by the losse of a brother, and a sister within the very first year, after which hardly a year past without some sensible mortification as losse of children, mother, wife, sister, or some of the best of my friends, and last of all, the letting me be driven out of my three kingdoms by the means and contrivance of a son-in-law, as well as a nephew, and my two daughters. For which all I praise God, and look upon myself as much happyer than ever I was in all my life, having that quiet of mind and inward peace which cannot be understood, or enjoyd, but by such as have an intire resignation for the will of God, Christian humility, a hearty repentence for sins past, and such a love of God, as has made one resolve by the help of his grace never to offend his divine goodness.[73]

Implicit within this vision of himself and his sufferings was James's removal to a higher plane. God was using the exiled king to teach a moral lesson (be chaste before marriage and faithful after it) to all Christians and simultaneously giving the peoples of the British Isles a poignant example of true Christian (and particularly Catholic) piety through James's humble submission to his will.[74] The exiled king, moreover, reinforced this impression, and signaled his continued conviction that his own sins lay at the root of all his problems by adopting an increasingly rigorous regimen of prayer and mortification and ostentatiously living in chastity with his queen from 1699 onwards.[75] Though James could only wistfully imply what he was hoping for: 'men of all ranks and conditions in life have been great saints and may be so still, providing they endeavour to improve their talents, and to make a right use of the grace of God, which will never be wanting to those who sincerely ask it',[76] his followers, friends and heirs could say it forthrightly: the trials and tribulations God was visiting upon James were giving him the opportunity to become a saint.[77] The more misfortunes he patiently

---

[73] *Life of James the Second*, ii. 631.

[74] *Original Papers*, i. 250-2: 'His Majesty's thanksgiving to God, for the particular benefits bestowed upon him', 1695; *Life of James the Second*, ii. 582-5, 614.

[75] John Miller, *James II. A Study in Kingship* (Hove, 1978), pp. 234-5; Edward Corp, 'The Jacobite Court at Saint-Germain-en-Laye: Etiquette and the use of the Royal Apartments', in, Eveline Cruickshanks (ed.), *The Stuart Courts* (Stroud, 2000), pp. 244-5; *Life of James the Second*, ii. 587, 613, 615.

[76] *Original Papers*, i. 249: 'That all Christians are bound to aim at perfection', 1695; *Life of James the Second*, ii. 413, 529, 589.

endured, and the more intensely pious he became in response to them, the closer he came to sainthood. And what greater gift could a kind and merciful God give a devout Catholic? Small wonder then, that there is a sense in which James was almost content to go down to defeat after defeat from the early 1690s onwards.[78]

In this, however, he was exceptional. The overwhelming majority of Jacobites believed instead that God favoured their cause because they were acting in accord with his express commandments, and, therefore, that the only reason he was not letting them succeed was because he wished to punish the peoples of the British Isles.[79] In their minds there was little doubt that the restored Stuarts would bring in an age of peace and prosperity;[80] God was only witholding these blessings so that the English, Welsh, Scots and Irish would fully taste the bitterness of their sins and thus (presumably) not repeat their error once the Stuarts again returned in glory. From which it followed that it was the Jacobites' duty, as the faithful remnant, to keep working away at getting the Stuarts back.[81] Eventually God would graciously permit them to succeed, and in the interim he would gather their martyrs to his bosom.[82]

The substance of this interpretation derived from that fruitful source of post-Reformation superstition and piety, the doctrine of providences.[83] The late Howard Erskine-Hill was certainly correct to argue that the Jacobites never accepted the providential

---

[77] Aberdeen University Library Special Collections, Blairs Letters 2/79/8: Charles Whyteford to [William Lesley?], [Paris] 10/21 Aug. 1702; 2/71/11: Perth to [William Lesley], [St Germain] 13/24 Oct. 1702; *Original Papers*, i. 591-7 and note; Miller, *James II*, p. 240.

[78] Miller, *James II*, p. 235; *Life of James the Second*, ii. 613.

[79] See for example, GD1/50/3: *Paper left by Mr. Archibald Burnet of Carlops before his execution for being in Arms at Preston, with a letter from him to his friend the publisher, January 10th, 1716* (I am indebted to my former student Prof. Margaret Sankey for this reference); *True Copies*, pp. 26, 29, 46; *Stuart Papers* ii. 114-15: Ranald Macdonald of Clanranald, Sir Donald Macdonald and 'J. Macdougall' to JIII, 11/22 Apr. 1716.

[80] Monod, *Jacobitism and the English People*, pp. 62-8, 70-80; Murray Pittock, *Poetry and Jacobite Politics in Eighteenth-Century Britain and Ireland* (Cambridge, 1994), pp.133-206.

[81] Szechi, 'Theatre of Death', pp. 69-70.

[82] *Faithful Register*, pp. 326, 329, 336; *True Copies*, pp. 13, 21.

[83] Keith Thomas, *Religion and the Decline of Magic* (London, 1971), pp. 90-129; Clark, *English Society*, p. 124. Cf. John Kenyon, *Revolution Principles. The Politics of Party 1689-1720* (Cambridge, 1977), pp. 24-9.

explanation of the Revolution of 1688 advanced by William Sherlock, and, indeed, that Jacobite intellectuals like John Kettlewell crushingly refuted it.[84] But they were nonetheless drawn to their own version of the providential interpretation. Hence Jacobite Secretary of State John Caryll observed in 1695 that, 'divine providence has not left the world to be governed by the passions and factions of men; he suffers them and makes use of them to his own great ends, which always terminate for the true best of those who serve him faithfully.'[85] The Jacobites should correspondingly view monsters like William III as, 'but a tool, perhaps a scourge in his [God's] hands, to bring about the great ends of his divine providence.'[86] For ultimately, Caryll was sure, 'so much suffering from all hands in so just a cause, with so much Christian resignation and perfect acquiescence in the will of God as is to be seen in both their Majesties, will sooner or later, for the edification of the world, be rewarded also here below with temporall blessings.'[87] This vision of God's providential role in the struggle between the Jacobites and their enemies, and of the ultimate outcome, prevailed among committed Jacobites until the disintegration of the movement in the 1750s and 1760s. In 1717, for example, Dr James Keith observed to Lord Deskford that, 'Our lot is faln indeed in perillous times, in which nothing is to be seen or heard from every quarter but trouble, confusion, distress. But the Lord reigneth and will make all turn to good in the end.'[88] Likewise John Daniel felt it appropriate to preface his memoirs of the '45 with the observation that providence, ... has screened,

---

[84] Howard Erskine-Hill, 'Literature and the Jacobite Cause: Was There a Rhetoric of Jacobitism?', in, Cruickshanks, *Ideology and Conspiracy*, pp. 50, 51, 54.

[85] Bodleian Library, Oxford, MS Carte 181 (Carte Papers), ff. 625r-626r: Caryll to Perth, [St Germain] 2/12 Sept. 1695. See also: ff. 626v, 629v: Caryll to Perth, [St Germain] 9/19 Sept. and 20/31 Oct. 1695; BL, Add. MS 29981, f. 103r: The Plagues of Nod; W. E. Buckley (ed.), *Memoirs of Thomas, Earl of Ailesbury. Written by Himself* (2 vols, Roxburghe Club, London, 1890), i. 123.

[86] Carte 181, ff. 627r-628v: Caryll to Perth, [St Germain] 3/13 Oct. 1695. For the Jacobite vision of William, see: Monod, *Jacobitism and the English People*, pp. 55-7 and *Reliquiae Hearnianae*, p. 411.

[87] Carte 181, f. 629r-v: Caryll to Perth, [St Germain] 20/31 Oct. 1695.

[88] G. D. Henderson (ed.), *Mystics of the North-East* (Third Spalding Club, Aberdeen, 1934), p. 142: [London], 13 Apr. 1717. See also: BL, Add. MS 29981, ff. 121-4: In Imitation of the 5th ode of Horace, Liber the 4th; Blairs Letters 2/89/3: William Lesley to Lewis Innes, Rome, 31 Mar./10 Apr. 1703; BL, Add. MS 31259, f. 171r: David Nairne to Cardinal Filippo Antonio Gualterio, Bar-le-Duc, 10/21 July 1715.

conducted and brought me safe out of so many miseries and dangers, [that] gratitude obliges me to be ever thankful to that omniscient power, by whose particular bounty and goodness I now live, and survive a cause, which, though it be now a little sunk, will, I doubt not, one day or other rise again, and shine forth in its true colours, make its hero famous to after-ages and the actors esteemed and their memory venerable'.[89]

As far as the Jacobites were concerned, providence was always actively engaged on their behalf. Given that they knew they were the faithful remnant, beloved of God, it logically followed that God was only allowing them to lose in order to punish the peoples of the British Isles.[90] George Lockhart of Carnwath directly linked the two when he contemplated the Jacobites' dismal record of failure from 1689 to 1714:

> ...on a review of the causes of the many disappointments of all the designs in favour of that prince [James III and VIII] and his father [James II and VII], it would seem that providence, as a punishment to these nations, wrought against them. For they were more occasioned by the immediate interposition and visible hand of God, than the power and contrivance of their enemies.[91]

Moreover, Lockhart's conjunction was typical of the Jacobite resolution of the problem. When Ranald Macdonald of Clanranald and Sir Donald Macdonald wrote to James in the aftermath of the collapse of the 1715 rebellion, they were quite certain that, 'though Providence for the punishment of our sins seems to smile on usurpation and rebellion, we are hopeful and shall always implore God that He will restore our natural, lawful and good King to rule over us.'[92] And in like vein, again in 1717, Dr Keith observed:

---

[89] *Origins of the Forty-Five*, p. 167: A True Account of Mr John Daniel's Progress with Prince Charles. See also: HMC *Stuart*, v. 244: James III and VIII to Dr. Charles Leslie, Urbino, 18/29 Nov. 1717; Blairs Letters 2/200/2: Dr Patrick Abercromby to Thomas Innes, Avignon, 6/17 Sept. 1716; *Lyon in Mourning*, i. 278 (Narrative of a Conversation betwixt Captain John Hay and me, Robert Forbes).
[90] *Faithful Register*, pp. 323-4, 333, 385; *True Copies*, pp. 12-13, 14-17, 20, 21-2; GD 24/1/872/1/3 (Memoirs of the Morays): 218, 221.
[91] *Lockhart Papers*, i. 180-1.
[92] HMC, *Stuart Papers*, ii. 114-15: Clanranald, Macdonald and 'J. Macdougall' to the Old Pretender, 11/22 Apr. 1716. See also: MS Carte 180, f. 258v: [Charles

...'tis lamentable that mankind will not be quiet, but rush forward to their mutual destruction. Nothing of all this happens by chance. The divine providence will overrule all to the advancement of his great and good ends. Let us chearfully submit to it in everything. Christendom seems to be universally convulsed at this time, and hastening to some great crisis. Men's minds are disturbed and at war even amidst an outward peace, and this certainly cannot last long whilst there is no real peace within.[93]

It could even become a kind of threat. Thus in Robert Lyons's scaffold speech in 1746 he warned his audience:

Consider, I beseech you, the evils already felt, the impending ruin of your country; consider the crying injustice and indignity offered to the best of princes; above all consider the guilt and high demerit of violating God's laws, and resisting his ordinance. And let these powerful and prevailing motives excite you quickly to mend your ways, and bring you to a thorough change in your life and conduct, and to continue forever firm and unshaken in your duty and subjection to that power ordained of God, not only for wrath but also for conscience sake, so shall ye arrest the vengeance and just wrath of heaven which is gone out against us. So shall ye be the happy instruments yet to preserve your languishing country from intire destruction, and save your souls in the day of the Lord.[94]

The message was clear: the only path to personal as well as national salvation lay through the Jacobite cause. The body of adherents to

---

Middleton, Earl of Middleton] to Jean Baptiste Colbert de Croissy, Marquis de Torcy, 18/29 Aug 1710; HMC *Stuart*, i. 506: James's, 'Letter of Adieu to the Scotch' [4/15 Feb. 1716]; Aberdeen UL, MS 2740/18/1/14, p. 7.

[93] *Mystics of the North-East*, p. 140: to Deskford, [London], 5 Feb. 1717. See also: Westminster Diocesan Archive, Old Brotherhood MSS, III pt 3, ep. 239: Melfort to Sir John Hales, Rome, 14/24 Mar. 1691; HMC *Stuart*, i. 424: Mar to Alexander Macdonald of Glengarry, Invercall, 11/22 Sept. 1715; Aberdeen UL, 2740/4/18 [pp. 3-4].

[94] *True Copies*, pp. 59-60. See also: Blairs Letters 1/121/7: Abbot Placide Fleming to Lewis Innes, Ratisbon, 15/25 Jan. 1689; BL, Add. MS 29981, f. 28r: Cato's Ghost; *Lyon in Mourning*, i. 62 (Speech of the Revd. Mr. Thomas Coppach of Brazenose Colledge, Oxford, commonly (but foolishly) called Bishop of Carlisle).

the Stuart dynasty had, in their own eyes, become Christ's true church. And the sufferings of the true church's martyrs were, in practical terms, of little moment in the divine plan. God would look after them in heaven, and on earth his will would be done regardless, hence Jacobitism's defeats were inconsequential. The net effect was to neutralise the experience. To paraphrase I Corinthians, 'O defeat, where is thy sting? O failure, where is thy victory?'[95]

The final strand of the Jacobite interpretation of defeat that will be explored here is the cosmic critique of the Stuarts themselves that has survived in a handful of sources. We have already seen that a few Jacobites were willing to blame individual Stuart princes for the failure of the risings on grounds of cowardice, incompetence or misjudgment.[96] But these were again technical errors; the writers concerned were not suggesting that God was smiting the movement because of some terrible impiety committed by the dynasty. And indeed, such dramatic and grave accusations-cum-interpretations are very few and far between. The reason is obvious: even among consenting Jacobites voicing such an analysis must have seemed very close to betraying the cause, and this in turn must have led many of those who held such views to keep silent on the subject or even suppress arguments that trended in this direction. For if the exiled Stuarts were being punished for some kind of dynastic original sin then God's plan might well be to keep them out of power indefinitely, which meant the loyal efforts of the Jacobites to restore the dynasty, while pleasing to him, were futile.

Where they have survived, Jacobite sources articulating such an interpretation are correspondingly idiosyncratic and often muffled. The Jacobite poet Jane Barker, for example, shied away from naming the specific offence the Stuarts had committed in the eyes of God to earn such a punishment. She viewed the suffering of the Jacobite court in 1694-5 as stemming from its pride and blasphemy, but did not specify what particular incidents of pride and blasphemy she was referring to. Similarly, in, 'Fidelia Walking the Lady Abess Comes to Her', Barker implied Ireland was lost because of 'other, earlier crimes', but was again non-specific.[97] The unknown Catholic

---

[95] I Corinthians 15:55.

[96] Johnstone, *Memoirs of the Rebellion*, pp. 191, 211; *Macariae Excidium*, pp. 6, 43-4, 48, 52; *Memoirs of the Insurrection in Scotland in 1715*, pp. 90-1.

Jacobite whose critique of James II and VII is preserved in the Rawlinson manuscripts in the Bodleian was deeply hostile to the king making any religious concessions to Anglican Protestants:

> And verily actuall condescensions and concurrences in the civill magistrate (such as are promises and declarations of support and defence to persons, religions and laws, repugnant to the law of God) redounding to the encouragement of the evill, the discountenancing of the good, and giving an occasion of fall to the wavering and weak, provoke God's wrath, and involve the condescending party in the same crimes.

This would make the king as obnoxious to God as the well-intentioned, but timid, King Amasias of Judah, who offended the Lord by allowing the Judaeans to continue worshipping false gods.[98] What the writer did not say explicitly, but what her/his audience would have known very well, was that James II and VII had already committed this sin while reigning in England. The deed was done. In the same vein, according to Abbé James MacGeoghegan, by ordering the plantation of Ulster by Protestant Scots and English settlers James VI and I invited divine retribution. This took the form of successful rebellions by these settlers against his posterity.[99] Which is to say that Charles I and James II and VII were overthrown because of James VI and I's egregious sin. This particular king of Scots featured, too, in George Lockhart of Carnwath's analysis of what had gone wrong with Scotland since the sixteenth century. To his mind the divine 'judgements' that had afflicted the kingdom for over one hundred years originated in:

> ...the mean-spirited behaviour of King James VI in not revenging his mother's murder. Ought he, with a view of not irritating Queen Elizabeth, been guilty of such an unnatural submission [sic]? Was it not a servile acknowledgement of

---

[97] Toni Bowers, 'Jacobite Difference and the Poetry of Jane Barker', *ELH*, 64 (1997) 857-869; Leigh A. Eicke, 'Jane Barker's Jacobite writings', in George L. Justice and Nathan Tinker (eds), *Women's Writing and the Circulation of Ideas: Manuscript Publication in England, 1550-1800* (Cambridge, 2002), p. 139.

[98] Bodleian Library, Oxford, MSS Rawl. D. 91, pp. [28-9].

[99] Vincent Geoghegan, 'A Jacobite History: The Abbé MacGeoghegan's 'History of Ireland'', *Eighteenth-Century Ireland / Iris an dá chultúr*, Vol. 6 (1991), p. 49.

England's dominion, to suffer the sacred person of the Queen of Scotland to be tried, condemned, and executed, without so much as daring to say it was ill done? And was it not a connivance at the greatest violation and encroachment that was ever offered to the divine rights of crowned heads, thus silently to see her treated after such a manner, who was accountable to none but God? How much was he degenerated from the illustrious stock from whence he sprung! And which of his royal progenitors would not have resented it with fire and sword? For my part, I'm afraid the indignation of God was stirred up upon this account against his posterity, and that particularly in the case of his son, Charles I.[100]

It is hard to see how those who cleaved to such interpretations of defeat could carry on the struggle, given they believed the Jacobite cause could not prevail, but they did. The Jacobites' sense of bounden duty must ultimately have trumped despair.

* * *

The elevation of the Jacobites and their cause, and the concomitant marginalisation of their defeats, lay at the heart of their survival and perseverance. It is a commonplace that religion was ideology in the early modern era — hence the Jacobites' transition from an inchoate, diverse scattering of malcontents and ultra-loyalists to a dedicated pseudo-church was crucial to their survival and endurance as a major force in the politics, society and culture of the British Isles for the best part of the century after 1688.[101] Turning Jacobitism into a neo-religious movement had, however, a hidden cost. God's wish to punish the peoples of the British Isles by denying them the blessings of being ruled by the main line of the Stuart dynasty could be used to explain Jacobite failure for one generation; thereafter it became a dwindling asset. For there was a countervailing interpretation of providence working against the Jacobite version. It pointed to the victories and the forces of nature that smashed so many Jacobite attempts to overthrow the new order as proof that God was on the side of the Revolutionaries and their heirs.[102] The Jacobites could contest this for one to two generations; they could not successfully contest it indefinitely.

---

[100] *Lockhart Papers*, i. 259-60.
[101] Szechi, *The Jacobites*, pp. 24-36.

There was, too, a worm in the bud of the Jacobite pseudo-church. If God's will (i.e. a Stuart restoration) was eventually going to prevail regardless of human striving, then demonstrating one's faithful adherence to the Stuart cause through quietistic, internal resistance to the new order could arguably be as satisfactory to God as mustering your tenants and servants, loading your pistols and riding off to join a Jacobite rising.[103] This is not to deny the role of Non-jury in England, Episcopalianism in Scotland and Catholicism throughout the British Isles in nourishing and sustaining Jacobitism.[104] But each of them implicitly offered two modes of resistance to the new British state: one external and military, the other internal and spiritual. And after two generations of defeats the military mode lost its appeal. The Jacobite interpretation of defeat, and its associated assurance of ultimate victory, could no longer persuade a sufficient number of Stuart loyalists to oppose the British fiscal-military state in arms to make a viable rebellion. Ironically, though, without the visible hope of a Stuart prince arriving 'like a Cyrus or a Trojan hero', commanding his supporters to, 'leave your nets and follow me,'[105] the internal, spiritual mode of resistance soon lost its savour too, and the pro-Jacobite religious communities declined or accommodated themselves to the new order.[106] In a sense, they no longer had any choice. The Jacobites disputed the new state's official interpretation of the defeat of the Stuart dynasty in the firm belief that God would soon vindicate them. Not the least of the successes of the new order was finally convincing them they were wrong.

---

[102] Clark, *English Society*, pp. 121-141.

[103] Monod, *Jacobitism and the English People*, pp. 138-45; *Reliquiae Hearnianae*, p. 412: 20 Feb. 1734.

[104] Szechi, *The Jacobites*, pp. 17-26.

[105] *Origins of the Forty-Five*, p. 168: A True Account of Mr John Daniel's Progress with Prince Charles.

[106] Szechi, *The Jacobites*, pp. 225-8; Holmes and Szechi, *Age of Oligarchy*, p. 232-4. The 1734 report (*Reliquiae Hearnianae*, p. 437: 9 Nov. 1734) that 'the superiors of the Nonjurors countenance the Nonjurors going to the sermons at the publick churches, but not to the prayers', if true (Hearne is not clear if it was or not), would suggest this process was well underway even before the failure of the '45.

What Happened at Culloden and What Happened Next?

Murray Pittock

The aftermath of the battle of Culloden is acknowledged as a brutal episode in British history. This has long been recognized: in 1769 for example, Thomas Pennant accepted the brutality of the episode in terms of a *felix culpa*: 'But let a veil be flung over a few excesses consequential of a day productive of so much benefit to the united kingdoms'.[1] Pennant's view is telling both for its recognition of this brutality and its acceptance, an acceptance born of a recognition that the British victory at Culloden was foundational in the establishment and success of Great Britain as a flourishing imperial state. The aftermath of the battle did indeed, as Pennant suggests, play a full part in this, as will be touched on in this essay.

Britain did not have to wait until the 1760s for the brutality of the battle's aftermath to appear excessive, however. There was almost immediate recognition that the prisoners taken were disproportionately composed of French regulars and that few of the Scots in custody were wounded. Despite circulation in London and the colonies of the forged battle orders of Lord George Murray offering no quarter to the British Army, which Cumberland countenanced if he did not originate, awkward questions began to be asked. As early as 1 May 1746, inquiry was made 'at a masquerade if the Duke had ordered his men to give no quarter to the rebels', and by the end of the month it was reported 'that when the duke came back to the capital he was to be made a freeman of the Butchers' company'. From thenceforth-and certainly after the appearance of famous pamphlets like *The Butcher* in December 1746-the epithet stuck to Cumberland. In the eighteenth century, when increasing urbanization increased both the demand for meat and urban density round places of slaughter, the reputation of the butcher was lower than it had been: the trade was associated with dirt, violence and brutalized and brutalizing behaviour.[2]

---

[1] Thomas Pennant, *A Tour in Scotland 1769* (Chester, 1771), ed. Brian D. Osborne, (Edinburgh: Birlinn, 2000), 103.

[2] W.A. Speck, *The Butcher*, (Oxford: Basil Blackwell, 1981), 159-61; Murray Pittock, *Culloden*, (Oxford: Oxford University Press, 2016), 102-04; Emily Cockayne, *Hubbub*, (New Haven and London: Yale University Press, 2007).

The aftermath of Culloden-how brutal is a judgement that has been made on a spectrum from excessive police action to genocide-was however only the beginning of a large-scale British Army occupation which has attracted far less attention, and which lasted many years. There were over 400 British Army cantonments in Scotland into the 1750s, and the traditional view of the post Culloden era as merely unsettled and subject to police action understates the case. There is a great deal of evidence for this extended occupation, more and more of which is being digitized and entering the public domain: it is thus very strange that there is virtually no secondary material on the occupation. This is a lack I intend to remedy with a full-length study in due course.[3]

But first to the battle of Culloden itself. As I argued in *Culloden* in 2016, no battle in British history is more systematically and widely misremembered, and this process is even reflected in our understanding of the footprint of the battlefield itself. The actual site of the battle of Culloden is a larger space than recorded in the designation of 1968, the Historic Scotland Battlefield Inventory of 2012 or Highland Council's Culloden Muir Conservation Area of 2015. The battlefield is in fact much larger than the 70 hectares now occupied by the National Trust for Scotland, almost entirely south of the B9006. As a consequence, the centrality of the British cavalry action to the outcome of the battle has been historically underestimated, an action which crossed land which has now been zoned for development. Both Jacobite and British deployment covered a longer front than is usually understood, and were in the British case substantially extended to avoid the possibility of being outflanked. The movement of the B9006 itself in the 1980s has helped to consolidate a more restrictive interpretation, and an assumption has perhaps grown up that the road was moved to allow all the battlefield to be accommodated south of it. Far from it. Jacobite troops first assembled after the night march in the grounds of Culloden House and the Jacobite left stretched all the way to them. As a consequence of this and in fear of flanking, Cumberland extended the British right by moving cavalry forward on to the wing of his front line. As a consequence, the British line stretched

---

[3] See for example the Stennis Historical Society, 'British Army Occupation of Scotland, 1746-55' based on the digitized Cantonment Register of the British Army (National Museum of Scotland, Edinburgh Castle): bit.ly/StennisHS.

for a probable 1200m, almost evenly distributed north and south of the B9006. The omission of the British dragoon and cavalry in action in particular, and its centrality to the battle, is one means by which the original zone of combat is separated from its aftermath, for the extended battlefield was not just larger, but mobile. From the moment that Kingston's Light Horse charged down the road to Inverness, the battlefield at its true scale was the epicentre of an explosion of violence beyond its confines. To take only the first 48 hours from dawn on the 16 April, Jacobite casualties more than doubled, and they did so over an area which stretches from Strathnairn to Inverness and beyond.

Why was this violence seen to be necessary? In the centuries since the battle, the Jacobite Army has frequently been portrayed as primitive, badly armed and in general weakly led: brave but of poor quality and hence doomed. In fact, the Jacobite Army was much closer to a regular army than has usually been admitted, despite the availability of regimental orders in print since the nineteenth century. Moreover, the presence of French regulars in significant numbers in its ranks emphasized the international threat it posed. Prior to Culloden, it was undefeated in three battles (Prestonpans, Inverurie, Falkirk) and a major skirmish (Clifton) as well as many minor engagements: only sieges had frustrated it. The extent of the violence following Culloden is only fully explicable only if the scale of the threat felt by the British Crown and Government is fully recognized. The conventional understanding of the Jacobite Army fails to do this. [4]

The two armies who took the field at Culloden were thus more similar to one another than the frequently misremembered history of this battle allows; and they are normally also misnamed, allowing the geopolitical framework of the battle to be reduced to the dimensions of an anachronistic dynastic squabble, savouring more of Stephen and Matilda or York and Lancaster than the age of David Hume. The victorious forces are normally termed 'the Redcoats', 'the Government Army' or the 'Hanoverian Army' which would be a confusing term if British history was not so frequently insular, as the Hanoverian Army was unsurprisingly the defence force of the Electorate of Hanover, being defeated-for example- by French

---

[4] See my *The Myth of the Jacobite Clans*, 2nd ed. (Edinburgh: Edinburgh University Press, 2009).

forces at Hastenbeck on 26 July 1757 and finally at Langensalza (after an initial victory) on 27 June 1866, which led to the incorporation of Hanover into the Prussian polity and thence from 1870 the German Empire. The correct term is 'British Army', a simple and factually accurate description of the forces who defeated the Jacobites, and one persistently avoided for what one can only attribute to feelings of political sensitivity, squeamishness or a desire to cast the conflict as a dynastic war removed from the direct threat it posed to the British state.

One small example encapsulates the need to use honest historical terminology. At Fontenoy on 11 May 1745, a British and allied victory was turned into defeat by the intervention of the Irish Brigade: Dillon, Bulkeley, Clare, Rooth, Berwick and Lally's battalions all contained men who fought with the Jacobites at Culloden, less than a year later, as did Fitzjames's Horse, all four of whose squadrons were sent to Charles Edward within months of their appearance in the French line of battle at Fontenoy. In the ranks of the British Army at Fontenoy stood the Royal Scots (front line at Culloden), the Scots Fuziliers (front) and Handasyde's (front), together with Sempill's (2nd line), Howard's (2nd line), Bligh's, Cholmondeley's and Pulteney's (3rd line) to say nothing of other forces, such as Hawley's and Bland's dragoons and the Inniskillings. The British Army at Culloden was far more British than the force commanded by Wellington at Waterloo, which fielded 25,000 British troops in a force almost three times the size, with the Hanoverian army (i.e. from Hanover) fielding 11,000 more from a German contingent of 26,000 on that day. Given the criticality of the Prussian relief at Waterloo beginning with IV Corp's attack on Lobau in the late afternoon, Waterloo can be seen as a clear-cut German victory, and a better understanding of its role in German memory might have made the war of 1870-71 more predictable to onlookers as the confirmatory conflict in the development of the German Empire.

This British Army was the force involved in the brutal aftermath of Culloden and the ensuing occupation of Scotland. It is important to note that its ranks included many Scots-indeed the incorporation of Scots into the English armed forces preceded the Union and arguably created the first 'British' institution. Scots held '10% of the regimental colonelcies' in the English army on the eve of the 1707 Union, with Scottish units (the Royal Scots and North British

Fusiliers) forming twenty percent of Major-General Cadogan's command which departed Ostend on 17 March 1708 (Cadogan later replaced the suspect Argyll as British GOC in the Jacobite Rising of 1715). Within Scotland, British forces also received support from the Independent Highland Companies, which had been formed on the recommendation of Lord Lovat in his *Memorandum Concerning the State of the Highlands* in 1724. The formation of these six companies was General Wade's concern after he came to Scotland in 1725, which in turn led to the incorporation of the Black Watch/*Am Freicheadan Dubh* -descended from the Companies, into the British Army following a proposal from Duncan Forbes of Culloden in 1738. Wade's 1725 plan saw the extensive renewal of fortified bases in northern Scotland to shore up the 'desultory programme of barrack building' which had been going on since 1717, and had led to the establishment of outposts at Glenelg to protect against crossings from Skye, Inversnaid near Loch Lomond, Kilcumein to secure Loch Ness and Ruthven in Badenoch. Wade built Fort Augustus near to Kilcumein, Fort George to control Inverness and reinforced Dumbarton and Edinburgh castles. These defences were not as effective as expected in 1745, and Wade's roads had in fact aided Jacobite manoeuvrability. Scotland was far from being militarily integrated into the United Kingdoms despite these efforts.

The five Jacobite Risings from 1689-1746 made that abundantly clear, and for their part, the British Government remained unwilling to countenance a Scottish militia because of the perceived military threat, which had been rumoured-even if it had not materialized- from Cameronian as well as Jacobite sources at the time of the Union. In 1706, four cavalry regiments and an infantry battalion had been deployed in the Scots Pale of the northern counties in Ireland alone, leaving aside the perceived Scottish threat, which led to multiple deployments in northern England at Leeds, Lancaster, Hull and along the border, to move into Scotland if necessary to support the Union against armed opposition. It is a safe assumption that given the number of Army units involved in this prospective police action, it remained embedded in the cultural memory of the British Army and its political masters, who were thus unwilling to countenance a Scots militia. In addition, the British Army's Scottish units were not altogether reliable, as in the case of the 43rd (later the 42nd), the Black Watch, who were suspect due to the mutiny against overseas service in 1743, and were consequently not used actively in the Rising. Indeed as late as 1759, the 2nd Black Watch were only given arms on landing at Guadeloupe.[5]

With a complement of only 23,000 in the aftermath of the Treaty of Utrecht in 1713, the British Army had been expanded by twenty-nine regiments to combat the 1715 Rising, which saw 12,000 soldiers stationed in Scotland in 1716. The army was double its post-Utrecht size in 1745, but another thirteen regiments were added in the face of Charles Edward's Rising. By the time of Culloden, the British Army was composed of 69 infantry regiments, all in single battalions of ten companies except for the Coldstream and Scots Guards (sixteen companies), the 1st Royal Regiment (two battalions) and the 1st Footguards (twenty-four companies). There were fifty-nine cavalry regiments, all with six troops to a regiment except for the Blues (Royal Horse Guards), and the 2nd Horse, which had nine. The Life Guards and Horse Grenadier Guards had mixed dragoon and horse regiments. The Jacobite Army was smaller but not dissimilar in organization, though there were no full-strength cavalry regiments and multi-battalion infantry regiments were more common.[6]

In 1745-46, Charles Edward's army had peaked at 15,000 men, which by the standard of British forces of the day represented a considerable military challenge.[7] This was the case to a greater extent than has often been realized, as the Jacobite Army was armed fairly conventionally and drilled in much the same way. The overemphasis on the sword as the primary Jacobite weapon was one of the key components in what I have termed 'The Myth of the Jacobite Clans', the construction by both British historiography and

---

[5] John Childs, 'Marlborough's Wars and the Act of Union, 1702-14', in Edward M. Spiers, Jeremy A. Crang and Mathew J. Strickland (eds), *A Military History of Scotland*, (Edinburgh: Edinburgh University Press, 2014 [2012]), 326- 47 (338, 339, 342-43); see also idem, Christopher Duffy, 'The Jacobite Wars, 1708-46', 348-79 (359-60) and Stephen Bramwell, 'The Scottish Military Experience in North America, 1756-63', 383-406 (387); Keith M. Brown, 'From Scottish Lords to British Officers: State Building, Elite Integration and the Army in the Seventeenth Century', in Norman MacDougall (ed.), *Scotland at War AD79-1918*, (Edinburgh: John Donald, 1991), 133-69 (149).

[6] Stuart Reid, *Cumberland's Culloden Army 1745-46*, (Oxford: Osprey, 2012), 11; Pittock (2009).

[7] Duffy, 'The Jacobite Wars, 1708-46', 360, 361, 371.

Highland romanticism of a narrative of difference and primitivism. Misremembered histories -Ireland in 1798 is another example- work best when the heirs to both sides in a conflict have an interest in seeing it in the same way. It did not suit either Scottish civil society or the narrative of British state integration to remember the Jacobites as a major military threat integrated into European power politics; a futile lost cause coloured by heroism better directed in support of the British Crown suited both stories better. Jacobite officers carried swords (as did British Army officers into the twentieth century), and often led the men they had raised from the front rank, but twelve times more muskets than swords were retrieved from Culloden, while weapons surrenders throughout the spring and summer of that year told the same story. Glengarry's, Keppoch's, the Mackintosh Regiment and others surrendered 281 guns and eighty-two swords, while the 19 August list of confiscated *materiél* at Stirling included twenty-two artillery pieces (the largest an 18-pounder), 1,365 roundshot, 430 muskets and 45 swords. The final surrenders-as late as May 1748-in Stonehaven and Laurencekirk in the Mearns brought in twenty-six guns and thirteen swords. This data is in line with British intelligence reports, which noted that guns and several pairs of pistols were commonly held by the Jacobite forces.[8]

Many Jacobite centres (including Aberdeen, Brechin, Doune, Dundee, Edzell, Elgin, Inverness and Oldmeldrum) were 'locations for the manufacture of firearms', with the 'heart-butt' and 'Celtic' pistols in particular providing distinctive evidence of native design. French and Spanish muskets with their shared 17.5mm bore were brought in in large numbers, with 7,500 coming in in three landings alone during the Rising, together with technologically advanced battlefield artillery, such as the 'Swedish' (in fact French) brass 4 pounders claimed to fire a shot every 5.5 seconds. One of these guns alone, deployed by Captain du Saussey and his gun crew, significantly delayed the British advance on the Jacobite left at Culloden. The Jacobites had some eighty-five artillery pieces in total in the campaign, though the need for mobility and the shortage of horses limited the effective use of siege calibre weapons, which were very heavy to transport.[9]

---

[8] Pittock (2009), 165-66, 171.
[9] Pittock (2009), 170-72, 176-77

The Jacobite army's movements were planned by the Quartermaster General, while its regiments (two largely neglected Order Book survive, one in print) were conventionally organized, sometimes even to the extent of having grenadier companies. There was no significant difference between the ordering of forces from the West Highlands and Forfarshire: Ardsheal's Appin regiment had standard parole words and orders, with eight companies and pay ranging from 2s 6d daily for captains through 2s for first lieutenants and surgeons to 9d for sergeants and pipers. Staffing and provisioning was largely efficient until the last phases of the Rising. As Christopher Duffy notes, the Jacobite forces exhibited a 'very high' quality of staff work. Drill was carried out in the earlier phases of the Rising on a modified British model, which was supplemented and perhaps largely replaced by French drill after the Ecossais Royales troops landed in Scotland. The army marched in column and orders seem to have been entirely in English or Scots, not in Gaelic: the term 'Highland Army' was one expressive of its patriot values rather than its ethno-linguistic composition: in reality no more than half its troops came from northern upland Scotland. The so-called 'Highland charge' involved a discharge of musketry at 50-55m and then closing with pistol and sword by company; the 'paired companies' of French practice may have been used, while Jacobite volley fire followed French models rather than the British 'firings' system. Pay was closely aligned to that of the last independent Scottish army. Jacobite soldiers averaged 162-166cm in height in 1745.[10]

The British Army was far from being a clearly superior force. While some regulars served for life and many of the soldiers raised for the War of the Austrian Succession were on six-year contracts, those raised for the 'Forty-five were on shorter terms. Soldiers had to be 'Protestant, not lame or prone to fits, with full use of both arms and legs', neither an apprentice nor a militiaman and over 168cm tall, with no Irish wanted. In his 'Orders and Instructions to the Recruiting Parties' on 19 October 1746, Cumberland specified a height an inch (2.5cm) lower and an age between 17 and 30. There was a £4 bounty on enlistment and privates received 8d a day (6d-8d in the Jacobite Army, though latterly this was more true in theory than in practice). Uniforms and equipment 'were provided

---

[10] Pittock (2009), 93-98; National Library of Scotland MS 3787 (Order Book of Appin's Regiment), ff. 48-49.

by the regiments from the money allocated to them by parliament and distributed by the quartermaster general'. This was in general not bountiful: the peacetime issue was only 60-120 charges per man per year, and the Ordnance office could take three years to replace worn-out weapons. Given the low issue of charges in peacetime and the infrequent replacement of broken weapons, British forces frequently had a high proportion of unserviceable muskets. Conservative military practice led to the retention of wooden rammers, which were affected by wet weather and deformed in frequent use. Even later in the century, 'two-thirds' of the 55th had bad firelocks, and 'an incredible 351 of the 34th's 390 stand of arms were defective'. Wives not infrequently travelled with the men, and could be up to 12% of regimental strength. Cumberland subjected them to military discipline, which, as James Wolfe (a colonel during the Rising) observed was generally 'bad'. In 1746, Cumberland's forces were reinforced by the 'Vestry Men', who were locally recommended poor whose dependents received £3 bounty for their enlistment under the terms of 18 Geo II c.12. They were the rough equivalent in the British Army of the 'manrent' offered by burghs and landholders to the Jacobite Army. Commissions were purchased (sometimes for children as an investment) by 'petitioning regimental agents, colonels or commanders'. Some 40% of officers were nobles or gentry. [11]

British forces were drilled after the practice of General Humphrey Bland's *Treatise of Military Discipline* (1728, revised 1743). They were formidable in full array, marching ten file width for a platoon and twenty-four for a division, but this lessened their manouevrability. The Independent Companies marched with a width of three files, like the Jacobite Army.[12]

On the battlefield itself on 16 April 1746, the armies drew up over a wide front, with the Jacobite left extending to the grounds of Culloden House. Glengarry's, Keppoch's and Clanranald's regiments were the first line here, with Chisholm's double company and the few men of Cromartie's not absent in the luckless search for French gold beside them: 1000 men in all and very much

---

[11] Victoria Henshaw, *Scotland and the British Army, 1700-1750: Defending the Union*, (London: Bloomsbury, 2015 [2014]), 21, 22, 54-57, 61-62, 64; Pittock (2009), 167; (2016), 49-50; Reid (2012), 18.
[12] Henshaw (2015), 39.

under strength (Glengarry's by a whole battalion), with fresh recruits still to come up. Two 3-pounders screened Clanranald's on the inner left. MacLean's regiment and MacLachlan's stood left of centre, where Monaltrie's and Balmoral's and Mackintosh stood, screened by three or five 3-pounders, battlefield guns. Right of centre was a Lovat battalion and Ardsheal's, behind two more 3-pounders. Beyond on the far right were both battalions of Lochiel's and the 2nd and 3rd battalions of the Atholl Brigade, possibly screened by four more guns. The front was 1100 metres, drawn up four-deep with a metre file, with Culloden Park walls screening on the left. The guns on the left may have been as far out as this.[13]

On the left of the second line stood the Perthshire Horse, Bagot's Hussars and possibly some of Balmerino's Life Guards, with the Irish Picquets on the inside left, all commanded by Brigadier Stapleton. The 1st battalion, Duke of Perth's, Glenbuchat's and the Earl of Kilmarnock's Foot Guards stood centre left, with John Roy Stewart's Edinburgh Regiment at the centre-in column as a mobile reserve, according to French tactical doctrine- and both battalions of Ogilvie's Forfarshires centre right. Beyond them stood the 1st and 3rd battalions of Lord Lewis Gordons, the 1st and 2nd battalions of the Royal-Ecossais and Fitzjames's Horse, a detachment of whom also guarded Charles Edward's command post behind the second line. Perth's and Glenbuchat's were moved forward to support the Jacobite left, and John Roy's to the centre right to cover gaps caused by a full move into column, while a company of Ogilivy's and picquets from Fitzjames's and Elcho's Life Guards moved to avoid flanking on the Jacobite right, where Bland (in command of Hawley's dragoons) opened a 500 metres front to threaten envelopment, closer to the Nairn than the boundary of current National Trust land. There is some controversy over this exact deployment, but the preponderance of accounts of the battle are consistent with this disposition. The second line may have been as far as 800 metres behind the first. At the onset of the battle, large numbers of the Jacobite left and the whole second line and command post stood outside the current National Trust footprint.

Facing the Jacobite left stood the Royals of the British right under Lt.-Col. Ramsay, behind two guns and ahead of Cumberland's command post, sandwiched between the first and second lines,

---

[13] Murray Pittock, *Culloden*, (Oxford: Oxford University Press, 2016), 74-76

which stood 50 metres apart, 800 metres north-west of the 'Cumberland stone'. Campbell's 21st and Cholmondeley's 34th stood inside the Royals, again screened by two guns, with Price's and the Scots Fuziliers behind four guns in the centre. On the left were Monro's 37th and Barrell's 4th with two more guns. William Keppel, Earl of Albemarle, commanded the front line. Major General John Huske had the second, with Howard's 3rd (the Buffs) on the right, with Fleming's 36th inside with three coehorns in front, then Bligh's 20th, and in the centre Sempill's 25th with three more coehorns and Ligonier's 59th and Wolfe's 8th on the left. The third line of the British Army consisted of Pulteney's 13th, Batterau's 62nd and Blakeney's 27th Inniskilling, with Kingston's Light Horse on both flanks and an additional mobile reserve on the far left of four companies of Argyll militia, together with three of the 64th and one of the 43[rd,], the Black Watch. Cobham's 10th and Kerr's 11th dragoons stood with them. The Moray Firth was lined with Commodore Smith's command. Alongside the British cavalry and dragoons, the Royal Navy was an unquestionable source of military superiority: its presence had damagingly delayed the planned night attack on the 15th, as the days were lengthening and the Jacobite Army was visible from the Firth.

As Cumberland formed line of battle, he moved Kingston's Light Horse to the right of his front line, backed by a squadron of Cobham's and Pulteney's and later Batterau's from the third line. Around 1.25 pm, less than half an hour after the start of the battle, Cobham's dragoons and Kingston's Light Horse on the British right and Cobham and Ker's on the left both began an attempted envelopment. Held off by the Irish picquets firing from behind the north-eastern Culloden Park walls on the Jacobite left, Kingston's began their brutal pursuit of fugitives down the road to Inverness. Lovat's 2nd battalion under the Master of Lovat, having arrived late at the battle, had already fallen back on the town. Captain Du Saussey's gunners held up further attempts to flank what was left of the Jacobite left until their rapid fire 4-pounder was in its turn destroyed by four 3-pounders and three coehorns moved up from the British front line. The Prince was trying to rally Perth's Glenbuchat's and the Edinburgh men at Balvraid, 1km from Culchunaig, before being forced to retreat towards the Nairn by the continued advance of Cobham's and Ker's on the Jacobite right. Both of Ogilvy's and Lovat's 1st kept battle formation and escaped mostly intact, with Ogilvy's forming square repeatedly to fire on any dragoons hardy enough to probe at them.[14]

On their way into Inverness, Kingston's-reinforced by the picquet of Cobham's on the British right-killed everyone in their path, irrespective of age, gender or arms, including the Mackintoshes who stood at the White Bog near Culloden House. Wolfe noted that as few prisoners were taken as possible and Cumberland noted that Bland's men gave no quarter; Maxwell of Kirkconnel agrees with this account of 'horror and inhumanity'. About 1,000 Jacobites died on the field that day, and another 2,000 in the days that followed. Cumberland had already mused at Perth in February on routes to the 'Speedy Punishment of these Wretches' who were 'the greatest Part of the Common People' and were too many for the criminal justice system to deal with. At Aberdeen a few days later he recommended death for anyone found carrying an offensive weapon, noting that there is 'so much Disaffection to any Government established upon an English Foot'. He may now have looked to put such musings into action. Nor was he alone: John Campbell for example writing to the Earl of Glenorchy in March, described the Jacobites as 'Vermine'.[15]

On the field, the advancing British infantry destroyed the wounded where they lay: Johnstone notes that Cumberland sent out death squads to finish off the wounded, while historian Bill Speck notes that the 'acts committed by the British army ... were outrages even by the standards of contemporaries'. The surviving MacDonald and Mackintosh regiments reached town ahead of the cavalry and took refuge in 'the enclosures of Castle Hill towards Inverness'. On 17 April, the Orders of the Day 'sent a captain and fifty men round all the houses neighbouring the battlefield with a "licence to kill"'. Only 154 prisoners were taken from the Scottish regiments; three fifths of those taken were French regulars. The lack of surviving prisoners was noted in London within a fortnight of the battle. Chambers in his *History of the Rebellion* noted that seventy were killed by firing squad on the 17th, and that 32 men were burnt alive in a building in which they had taken refuge. A similar atrocity with a variant number of victims is described by Ker of Graden, and the

---

[14] Ibid, 77-95
[15] Ibid, 97-98; SP 54/32 ff. 109-10; National Library of Scotland Adv MS 23.3.28 f. 121.

names of some are recorded in a document in the Thriepland papers in Perth & Kinross Archives: Colonel O'Reilly, attached to Lord Ogilvy's, David Stewart of Kynachan, Major in the 1st battalion of the Atholl Brigade and two Rattrays are all recorded as officers burnt alive, with Mercer of Aldie butchered on the field. Nineteen officers were shot or clubbed to death together, while thirty-six deserters were hanged in the British camp. John Fraser, an officer in Lovat's 1st, claimed that he was taken wounded on a cart to a place of execution where muskets were fired at 2-3 metres range into captured Jacobites, with the survivors being clubbed to death with the butts. Seriously wounded and minus an eye, Fraser nonetheless survived to tell his tale.[16]

Almost at once, locals became aware of the extraordinary levels of brutality, which in the words of one English commentator, would justify a 'Parliamentary Enquiry'. The Synod of Moray advised all its ministers 'to be very careful and cautious' in attesting to the guilt of anyone detained or suspected of complicity in the Rising. Major-General Bland's own 1743 *Treatise on Military Discipline* advised 'a respectful attitude by occupying military forces towards the civilian population'. Bland himself ignored it, ordering Loudoun on 22 May to 'destroy all persons you can find who have been in the rebellion or their abettors'. Nor was this a hot-blooded exception: as late as Advent 1747, Bland was noting to Newcastle the continuing need to be 'ridd of all Chiefs of Clans', the 'Barbarous Language' of their adherents, and the need to colonize northern Scotland with Anglophone Protestants. On 17 April 1746, Lt.-Col. Cockayne arrested 'Colonel' Anne Mackintosh at her home in Moy, and the next day Brigadier Mordaunt was sent in pursuit of the 3rd battalion of Lovat's command, still in the field, with orders 'to destroy all the rebels'. Mordaunt burnt Lovat's castle at Beaufort and drove off his cattle, also taking food so that the inhabitants, who had endured two bad winters in succession, should have nothing to eat. Lords Sutherland and Reay pursued and took Cromartie's men, while Cobham's Regiment marched to secure Montrose and the disaffected east coast against further French landings; Robert Cuningham wrote to the Earl of Crawford at this time that the north-east of Scotland was merely putting on 'the Appearance of being pleased' with 'Ringing of Bells, Bonefires, & drinking of

---

[16] Perth and Kinross Archives MS T69/7/3/32; Pittock (2016), 99-100; Christopher Duffy, *The '45*, (London: Phoenix, 2007 [2003]), 523-24, 529.

Healths, so much were they Convinced of the Total Defeat of their Friends'. Lord George Sackville took 500 men from Fort Augustus to Glenelg, with Cornwallis taking 300 along Lochs Lochy and Arkaig to meet up with Sackville. Major-General John Campbell (with the help of Captain Fergusson) laid Sunart and Morven to waste: the surrender of arms did not relieve the inhabitants. Captain Caroline Scott covered the country round Fort William and Loch Eil, while Captain Fergusson's *Furnace*, a 14-gun bomb vessel, patrolled the Western Isles, taking prisoners in Canna and Barra, and burning Raasay and MacDonald of Barisdale's house, though coming under fire from a battalion of Clanranald's. Later Fergusson was joined by Captain Duff of the *Terror*, and together they burnt Alan MacDonald's house at Morar and many more at Arisaig, though MacDonald of Borrodale's men fired on them at Arisaig and exploded mines at the shore approaches. Fergusson eventually captured Lord Lovat in Morar on the night of 4/5 June. The Campbell militia were sent to burn Atholl. British forces were reported to be 'shooting the vagrant Highlanders that they meet…and driving off their cattle' indiscriminately. Two men who owed their lives to the Jacobites: Lt-Col. Charles Whitefoord and Major Alexander Lockhart, joined many others in acting with brutality after Culloden. Lockhart was later shot by a sniper.[17]

While Cumberland remained at Inverness, the troops under his command were thus highly mobile. Under Lord Ancrum's overall command, six troops of Lord Mark Ker's dragoons set off from Inverness on 30 April to occupy Fochabers, Cullen, Banff, Fraserburgh and Peterhead, with six of Viscount Cobham's leaving on 23 April for Aberdeen, Brechin, Forfar, Inverbervie and Stonehaven as well as Montrose. Major General St George had mixed or broken troops at Arbroath, Coupar Angus and Glamis; Major General Hamilton had six at Dundee; Colonel Nezons had men at Crieff, Stirling and Drummond Castle, seat of the Dukes of Perth, about five kilometres from Crieff. On 13 May, Brigadier Mordaunt led a command of the Royals, Pulteney's and Sempill's with five pieces of artillery to Perth; on 23 May, Lt.-Col. Jackson

---

[17] Pittock (2016), 100, 107-08; Robert Chambers, *History of the Rebellion of 1745-1746* (London: Chambers, 1929 [1827]), 328; Duffy (2007), 528-29, 531-33; Bland to Newcastle, 4 December 1747 in *The Albemarle Papers*, ed. Charles Sanford Terry, (Aberdeen: Aberdeen University Press, 1902), 480-91; SP 54/32 ff.110-11; Cuningham to Crawford, NLS Adv. MSS 23.3.28 f. 277.

led Fleming's from Inverness to Aberdeen to support Cobham's single dragoon troop, as Cumberland was relocating overall command to Fort Augustus, where General Bland had already taken Howard's a week earlier. On the 23rd at 5am, Lt.-Gen. the Earl of Albemarle with General Skelton led Barrel's and Sackville's from Inverness to Fort Augustus in column, followed by the artillery and quartermaster stores. Major General Huske's 2nd column, composed of Dejean's, Fusiliers, Wolfe's, Haughton's, Conway's and Skelton's flanked them on the left, with Brigadier Haughton as second in command. Handasyde's, Mordaunt's, Blakeney's and Battereau's regiments remained at Inverness. The next day, the march was completed in a single column, though clearly with some concern of coming under attack, as a captain, two subalterns and 100 men formed both an advance and rear guard to the army on the march. Haughton's marched on to Fort William.[18]

The navy's role was largely policing for French shipping and carrying out raids on coastal districts at this stage in the occupation. An exception was the eviction of the Jacobites from Orkney. Andrew Fletcher, Lord Milton, the Lord Justice-Clerk, recommended a marine lieutenant, Benjamin Moodie, for this task: Moodie's father had been murdered by Sir James Stewart of Burray, Orkney's leading Jacobite. HMS *Exeter* (sixty guns), *Gloucester* (fifty) and *Glasgow* (twenty-four) were all to be deployed, and Moodie was briefed to lead the landing party. In the end it was the *Glasgow* and fellow 24-gun *Scarborough* that 'arrived in Deer Sound' at 8am on 26 April. The initial efforts made by Moodie's men were not successful, and on 17 May, Moodie-now a Captain- was sent again with the 8-gun *Shark* (the *Salamander, Tryal and Happy Jennet* having also been deployed), with Commodore Smith's orders to 'lay waste, take or Destroy any lands, Cattle, houses, Boats or anything also belonging' to the leading Jacobites, with a brief also to destroy all Episcopalian places of worship where George II was not prayed for by name. Servants of Jacobites were to be pressed. Despite the arrest of Sir James Stewart on 25 May, Moodie was not entirely successful this time either, but his marines remained at Kirkwall throughout the summer of 1746. It is noteworthy that considerable naval effort was expended on Orkney for very limited return; and the same was true at Loch Broom on the west coast, where while HMS *Glasgow* captured *Le Bien Trouvé* on 3 August, and Captain

---

[18] Cantonment Registers of the British Army, NMS.

Felix O'Neil in the French service was captured on land the next day, the Dunkirk privateers, *Le Comte de Lavendal* and *Le Comte de Maurepas*, who had thirty-three prizes between them, ranged the same waters.[19] The French navy brought off Lord Elcho, Sir John Hay of Restalrig, the Duke of Perth and Sir Thomas Sheridan on 3 May, and Lochiel, Charles Edward himself, twenty-three noblemen and gentlemen and 170 Jacobite soldiers on 20 September. Charles had travelled westwards after Culloden, and was on the Outer Hebrides until the end of June, after which he returned via Skye to the mainland, with the aid of Flora MacDonald and Neil MacEachain of South Uist. He crossed the British Army cordon to reach Cluny Macpherson at his Ben Alder hideout on 5 September, setting out just over a week later on receiving reports of French ships off Arisaig.[20]

Depopulation was very much in Cumberland's mind. It was his view (expressed in a memorandum of 30 April at Inverness) 'that this Generation must be pretty well worn out, before this Country will be quiet', and this was a process he set about accelerating. He recommended a summer session to Parliament to initiate 'total Change of this Constitution' and noted that 'It is wished here by the well affected, That some whole Clans could be transported, not as Slaves, but to make Them Colonies in the West Indies', as 'their rebellious & thievish Nature is not to be kept under without an army always within Reach of Them'. The 'well affected' here may be a reference to Lord Forbes of Culloden, who indeed favoured transportation, while the West Indies were notorious for high mortality rates, and Jamaica landholding in particular was heavily in the hands of the Campbell family. On 27 May at Fort Augustus, Cumberland reiterated the point, trusting 'Some Expedients' may be found by Parliament for 'Transplanting several of their Clans to some Part of the Indies'. On 5 June, he recommended the Camerons and MacDonalds for this treatment by having all of them appear 'under Penalty of Outlawry' before the authorities. Cumberland was not original here: he was building on seventeenth-century policy, implemented both by Cromwell and Charles II's government to transport the disaffected to the West Indies, as well

---

[19] R.P. Fereday, *Orkney Feuds and the '45*, (Stromness: Kirkwall Grammar School, 1980), 84-86, 89, 95-96, 111-12; James Ayton, 'Sir James Stewart of Burray (3rd Baronet): the Orkney Jacobite', *Royal Stuart Journal* 9 (2018), 55-59 (55).
[20] Duffy (2007), 534-36.

as the rather more recent capturing of men on Skye for sale as 'indentured servants' in America, practised by Sir Alexander MacDonald of Sleat and Norman MacLeod of Berneray in 1739, and possibly also similar practices carried out by merchants in Aberdeen.[21]

In the end, Parliament, although it ended feudal privileges of regality and placed other limitations on Scottish landlords, did not legislate as Cumberland wished. But in the military, where he was more influential a limited version of clearing off the land was practised in Lochaber and Morven. Cumberland's plans were in the end to bear fruit in a different place, when British forces initiated *Le Grande Dérangement* of 1755, which led to the expulsion of over eighty percent of the 14,000 French settlers in Nova Scotia, New Brunswick and Prince Edward Island. The circumstances were not dissimilar- continued sympathy for France while being subjects of the British Crown- and even further from the public eye, Cumberland's policies could be put into more thorough effect. As the Duke himself said, he looked forward to the French being 'drove out' as he had once hoped to do in Lochaber. The attacks on settlements and the killing of cattle in the Bay of Fundy campaign which opened the expulsions were entirely redolent of the post Culloden campaign, while the anti-Catholicism by which the actions against the Acadians were ideologically underpinned, was very close to the approach taken to Jacobitism. This was arguably compounded by the appointment of John Campbell, Lord Loudoun as commander in chief in North America in 1756. By 1757, half of the British Army manpower in the North American campaign were Scots (thirty percent) or Irish, with Cumberland being actively encouraged to send more Scots, and Loudoun suspected that deserters were Catholics: the horrendous casualty figures at Ticonderoga (Black Watch, fifty percent), Quebec (Frasers), Duquesne (Montgomery's, almost sixty percent) and the Caribbean campaign (sixty percent) testified to Wolfe's infamous 1751 comment, 'no great mischief if they fall'. Jacobitism and Catholicism were frequently conflated, despite the fact that there were far fewer Catholics than Episcopalians in the Jacobite Army. [22]

---

[21] SP 54/32 ff. 111-13; Alexander Murdoch, *Scotland and America, c1600-c1800*, (Basingstoke: Palgrave Macmillan, 2010), 40; David S. Macmillan, *Scotland and Australia 1788-1850*, (Oxford: Clarendon Press, 1967), 28.

[22] Pittock (2016), 108, 110-12; SP 54/32 f.111; Stephen Bramwell, *Redcoat: The*

In Scotland, the British Army operations were neither small-scale nor short in duration. In the absence of transportation of the population, Cumberland made good his view that the army should remain in reach, notoriously responding to Lord Forbes respecting 'the laws of the country! My lord, I'll make a brigade give laws'. That said, Cumberland cautioned his army against unfocused plundering, and areas like Lovat's fisheries were specifically noted as 'out of bounds' on pain of capital punishment. In compensation for such severities, he offered 16 guineas for the capture of Jacobite colours or a standard, 2s 6d for every Jacobite musket (usually French or Spanish pattern, so easily identified) or broadsword and a guinea to anyone captured by the Jacobites who had refused to join them. On 22-24 May, the Duke moved his main forces -eleven battalions and Kingston's Light Horse- to Fort Augustus, to begin the 'pacification' of the West Highlands. Sackville and Colonel Cornwallis destroyed Lochiel's house and huge garden at Achnacarry.[23] The British forces ranged widely from their new HQ: on 19 June men from Major-General Campbell's command even landed on St Kilda.[24] In autumn 1746 in Strontian, Patrick Campbell-on a mission from Albemarle- noted that there were still a 'great many...who have not as yet surrender'd', being 'in expectation of the Landing' of fresh Jacobite forces. After the arson carried out by British troops early in the year in a variety of locations from Laggan to Ardtornish, houses were beginning to be rebuilt in the Morvern area. MacDonald of Keppoch's and Cameron of Lochiel's lands were however still ruined from burning, and many of the inhabitants were reported as fled into Knoydart owing to fear of the British Army. Glengarry's lands were deserted except for some starving women. In Appin, Jacobite officers were reported as still paying their men. Campbell covered a wide swathe of Scotland between Glen Shiel and Edinburgh in October and November, to report on the mood of the people for the British commander-in-chief. Both Albemarle and the Lord Justice Clerk were also keen to locate rumoured hoards of Jacobite gold. It was typical for little intelligence and co-operation to be offered to British forces. Agents such as Patrick Campbell, John

---

British Soldier and War in the Americas, 1755-1763, (Cambridge: Cambridge University Press, 2002), 9, 60, 73, 267, 269; Bramwell (2014), 386, 390.

[23] Henshaw (2015), 67-68, 70-71, 103; Duffy (2007), 531.

[24] Cantonment Registers of the British Army, National Museum of Scotland.

Millar, John Wright and Alexander Robertson of Straloch found it hard going extracting information from the localities in which they were active in support of the British Government. In Glenmoriston, Major James Lockhart treated the Grants with savagery. So expected was government brutality that locals who wished to resort to banditry in Atholl or Mar on occasion dressed as Argyll Militiamen. In their turn, disbanded Argyll militia threatened to join the Jacobites. The situation was febrile.

On 18 July, Cumberland left for England, leaving Albemarle as Commander in Chief. Albemarle 'divided Scotland into four military division': north, north east (Strathspey to Dundee); south central (Great Glen to Perth) and Stirling and the south. He set cordons across the country.[25] Two regiments (Howard's and Cholmondeley's) moved to Newcastle, and three more (Wolfe's, Pulteney's and Sempill's) left for the Continent, while the Earl of Albemarle took over command from Cumberland in Scotland. Cobham's, Kerr's and St George's headed back to England in October. Over 12,000 troops remained in Scotland, however, including Nezons, the 2nd battalion the Royals, Barrel's (Edinburgh and Borders), Skelton's (Dundee and Angus), Price's (Glasgow), Handasyde's (north east), Mordaunt's (north-east), Sackville's (East Lothian), Haughton's (Stirling), Blakeney's (north east), Lee's (to Fort William and environs) and Battereau's (Inverness), together with twelve companies of Loudouns, nine companies from other units and 100 artillerymen at Perth. Three quarters of these garrison troops were regular Army. The British Army maintained deployments in Aberdeen, Arbroath, Ayr, Banff, Berwick, Cupar, Dalkeith, Dumfermline, Dumfries, Dundee, Edinburgh, Elgin, Forres, Glasgow, Haddington, Inverbervie, Inverness, Johnshaven, Kelso, Linlithgow, Montrose, Nairn, Newburgh, Perth, Stirling, Stonehaven, Stranraer.[26]

In September 1746, Cobham's were garrisoning Berwick, Duns and Kelso; Lord Ker's were at Haddington, Dalkeith and near Duns; St George was at Dumfries, Nezons at Ayr and Stranraer (moving to Musselburgh and Haddington on 17 October), and Hamilton at

---

[25] Duffy (2007), 532.

[26] Cantonment Registers of the British Army, NMS; National Records of Scotland GD 26/4/490; National Library of Scotland ACC 5039; NLS MS 3142 f. 154; NLS MS 17505 ff. 65ff, 78; NLS MS 17525 f.97; Pittock (2016), 108-9.

Cupar. Haughton's had nine companies at Fort William, and two more at Bernera and Mull, and 400 were deployed for the disarming of Cameron forces in October. Loudoun's had eighteen outposts from Inverness to Perthshire, including Aviemore, Dalwhinnie, Ruthven, Glenalmond and Amulree; Blakeney's and Battereau's were at Inverness, Mordaunt's at Findhorn, Forres and Nairn; Handesydes had most of their force (nine companies) at Elgin; Dejean's were headquartered at Banff, with half their force there and half at Cullen, Fochabers, Fraserburgh and Peterhead. Fleming's had five companies at their Aberdeen HQ and no fewer than five at Montrose, with roving units in Strathbogie and Angus, where Sackville also had over 100 men; Skelton had two battalions at Perth, with detachments at Crieff and Dunkeld; Conway and Price had almost two battalions at Stirling, with three companies at Alloa and 100 men at Doune Castle and Dunblane, a company at Buchlyvie and a small detachment at Balfron; half of Barrel's were at Linlithgow. Glasgow was deemed worth a battalion, with detachments from Kircudbright to Balfron; Lee's were in Edinburgh, while there were two companies of the Royals at Dumfermline, two companies of Sempill's at Ayr and three Highland companies from Ruthven to Inveraray. All in all, there were almost twenty battalions and five dragoon regiments at seventy-one locations throughout Scotland that autumn: the final escape of Charles Edward from Loch Nan Uamh on 20 September seems to have made little impact on the deployment of British forces.[27]

Cumberland and his commanders acted deliberately to move troops about every three months or so, 'to prevent Connections which may happen by their Staying too long in a place particularly Scotland', and also favoured concentrations of troops which could provide a sense of 'Awe'. In February 1747, the regiments underwent rotation accordingly, with concentrations in Edinburgh, Mussleburgh and Dalkeith (eleven companies), Stirling (ten companies), Perth (ten), Cupar (seven), Kirkcaldy (seven), Linlithgow (five) and Berwick (five), Aberdeen (four), Alloa (four), Dundee (four), Forres (four), Arbroath (three), Banff, (three), Burntisland (three), Dunfermline (three), Inverkeithing (three), Montrose (three), Nairn (three). Some three further regiments left Scotland at the beginning of March 1747.[28]

---

[27] Cantonment Registers of the British Army, NMS: Pittock (2016), 109.

Eleven battalions remained, together with the Highland regiments, two dragoon regiments and nine additional companies. Dundee, Edinburgh, Glasgow, Elgin, Forres, Inverness, Linlithgow, Perth and Stirling all had at least five companies posted to them. Troops continued to leave Scotland during 1747, but there was trouble from 'highland Thieves' in Dingwall on 15 July and 'the Disaffected' in Orkney on the 17th. In September, five Highland Companies were stationed in Moray and Nairn to defend the populace against 'Thieving Highlanders'. They were of course, however, an occupying force. Small units led by sergeants and corporals were stationed all over the north. Despite these challenges, though, by Christmas there were only some 1,000 British troops in the major outposts, with considerable units in reserve.[29]

There was a real threat for them to combat. Many Jacobite units were still in the field, even after the Ruthven rendezvous on 18 April, where between 1,000 and 3,000 men received a *sauve qui peut* order from Charles Edward which precipitated Lord George Murray's resignation of his command. On 18 April, Lord Milton heard from Aberdeen that Major-General John Gordon of Glenbuchat was rumoured to have a force in the field outside Aberdeenshire, while the Earl of Glenorchy reported 500 men lying in huts. On the 19th, Fitzjames's and the Royal-Écossais surrendered at Inverness. On 26 April, there were reported to be 120 in arms in Balquhidder in Perthshire, while the MacGregor regiment arrived home in full order. Before the end of April, four battalions of British troops had been deployed against Jacobite units. Reinforced by the gunpowder and £38,000 of Loch-nan-Uamh gold landed by the *Mars* and *Bellona*, Lochiel, Glengarry, John Roy Stuart, Glenbuchat and Clanranald decided to fight on (even though Lochiel was offered a secret amnesty by Cumberland), but only 600 men of their five battalions made rendezvous on 13-15 May; on the 17th, the Macpherson Regiment, not at Culloden and still in the field, surrendered. Nonetheless, Stewart of Ardsheal's Regiment of foot had yet to surrender in July, and Ardsheal was still dealing with back pay for his men. Eventually they and the MacDonalds of Glencoe surrendered to one of the few British officers who could be

---

[28] Cantonment Registers of the British Army, NMS.
[29] Cantonment Registers of the British Army, NMS.

relied on to keep his promises, Major-General Campbell of Mamore. Ogilvy's two battalions reached the Angus glens intact on 21 April. British forces and Campbell militiamen stood off the MacGregor Regiment as it returned to Balquhidder showing its colours and cockades: a single Jacobite battalion openly defied the occupying forces. 'Jacobite expresses were sent until August'. That summer, a British regiment was deployed across Banffshire, and in September 1746, Jacobite forces were reported in Strathdee and Angus, with Jacobite forces still being reported as being paid in November. In March 1747, two officers of Cromartie's 'carried out a raid on Dingwall' with the remnants of their command; in December 1747, Colonel Watson reported Jacobite rebels appearing publicly throughout the north-east, while months later, arms surrenders were still being secured in the Mearns. Assassinations of government officers or sympathizers (notoriously, Colin Campbell of Glenure on 14 May 1752) continued for years, while recruitment continued to the Irish Brigades in the service of France, Ronald MacDonald being banished for seven years at Edinburgh in 1754 for enlisting in the French service. Between 1749 and 1755, there were 'more battalions in Scotland than in the whole of the Americas'.[30]

Jacobites who surrendered did not have an easy time of it. The men who surrendered at Fort William on 2 June in expectation of the British Government's promised six-week immunity were drowned in salmon net by Captain Scott, while surrenders of poor quality weapons invited a vicious reaction. According to Chambers, General Hawley, Lt.-Col. Howard, Captain Scott and Major Lockhart were among the most vicious. 3,472 prisoners were taken: around twenty five to twenty seven percent of all those who had enlisted, but a far lower proportion of those from Scotland. None were tried in Scotland, and from 30 May 1746, a succession of vessels transported the prisoners from British HQ in Inverness to England. Many died in the poor and cramped conditions of the English jails in which they were held; those in the Tilbury transports had a mortality rate of seventy percent, with only 49 of

[30] NLS Adv MSS 23.3.28 ff. 203-05, 273; NLS MS 17514 ff. 26, 268, 271, 274-75; NLS MS 17527 ff. 76, 105; NLS ACC 5039; NRS GD 14/98; NRS GD 26/9.498; SP 54/35/53; Pittock (2009), 125-26; Pittock (2016), 49, 98, 107, 108, 111; Duffy (2007), 525, 529-30, 534; David Dobson, *Directory of Scots Banished to the American Plantations 1650-1775*, (Baltimore: Genealogical Publishing Company, 1984), 109.

the 157 surviving. 120 Jacobite officers and men were executed and almost 1000 men and women transported, many into slavery in the West Indies or the American colonies, although 149 were liberated when their transport, *The Veteran*, was captured by a French privateer off Antigua, being placed under the protection of Marquis de Caylus, Governor of Martinique, who refused to return them to the British authorities. Among those on board were George Keith, a 35-year old Aberdeen shoemaker who had served in Glengarry's, William Bell, a bookseller from Berwickshire, Anne Cameron, Flora Cameron, Barbara Campbell, Jane McIntosh and Mary McDonald. Women are not closely focused on in much Jacobite scholarship, but they were not infrequently transported, sometimes-as in the case of Isabel Chalmers of Glengarry's-with a regimental attachment noted. There are some indications that the destination of transports-for example Camerons and MacDonalds to Jamaica where there was extensive Campbell landholding-was not without purpose. The telling of these human stories is still at a very early stage, as we come to understand better the scale of the terror practiced in the wake of Culloden, and the complex backgrounds of those who served with the Jacobite forces.[31]

Eighty-one Grants of Glenmoriston who surrendered on assurances were 'transported into slavery' as were a company of Clanranald's under the command of Captain John Macleod. 750 joined the British Army and were 'pardoned on enlistment', although it turned out this was often a death sentence, as these were often sent to disease-ridden colonies in the West Indies in a transposition of Cumberland's hopes for mortality arising from transportation to mortality arising from military service. Between 500 and 1,000 Jacobites who evaded capture joined one of the three Scottish regiments in the French service, commanded respectively by Ogilvy, colonel of the Forfarshires, Major-General John Drummond and Lochiel. A further colonelcy was offered to the Master of Lovat, but he chose to join the British Army. Much later, he was to be-inaccurately but symbolically-depicted in Benjamin West's iconic painting of *The Death of Wolfe* before Quebec in 1759 as present at Wolfe's death, a symbolic bridge between the realm of the Native American and the civilized Englishman, who would

---

[31] Dobson (1984), 10, 19, 20, 28, 85, 109, 121; Douglas Hamilton, *Scotland, the Caribbean and the Atlantic World, 1750-1820*, (Manchester: Manchester University Press, 2005), 56.

rather have written Gray's *Elegy* than commanded at Quebec. This world, the world of British troops in the Seven Years' War, can seem a world away from the Jacobite era, but less than five years earlier Wolfe had written to Captain William Rickson at Fort Augustus, concerning his plan to take Macpherson at Ben Alder, kill him, and by so doing furnish himself with a pretext to kill all his followers and dependants. On the other hand, Captain Donald MacDonald of Fraser's, erstwhile captain in the Écossais Royale, had deceived the French sentry to secure passage for the British Army at Quebec, in whose ranks fellow Jacobite officers were still serving. It was a complex time.[32]

Trials were of course not entrusted to Scottish courts, wherever the alleged offences had taken place, and the deaths of the Jacobite leadership were deliberately rendered a public spectacle, but not theirs alone: five ordinary deserters were shot near Hyde Park, dressed in white by their coffins, 'their faces and breasts all tore to pieces by the balls'. Lord Balmerino wore both his uniform as a Lifeguard officer and a tartan cap for his execution on 18 August, while Lord Lovat's execution on 9 April 1747 was the last beheading in English history. The severed portions of those hung, drawn and quartered (how long they were hanged for was in the gift of the executioner) were displayed widely.[33]

Structural legislation aimed at destroying the social, cultural, religious and landholding rights and networks which sustained Jacobitism accompanied these demonstrations of raw power. While not engaging with mass transportation, Newcastle 'proposed six developments to Cumberland, including the destruction of superiorities and private jurisdictions, the suppression of clan names, the suppression of Episcopal chapels, and the annexation of forfeited estates to the Crown'.[34]

An Act of Attainder was passed in June 1746, then a Disarming Act then 'the use of Highland dress was forbidden' in 1748. 'Wardholding', which allowed for military service as a possible duty of a vassal to a superior, was abolished, as were heritable

---

[32] Pittock (2016), 109-10; Duffy (2007), 527, 529, 533, 536-7; *Original Letters of Major-General Wolfe*, (Glasgow, 1880), 583; Bramwell (2014), 388.
[33] Pittock (2016), 110; Duffy (2007), 538-39.
[34] Pittock (2016), 112.

jurisdictions, 'which could give holders of baronies and regalities rights of life or death over their tenants in criminal cases'. Baronies continued on a circumscribed basis; regalities were abolished, with compensation to Argyll and through him pro-British holders of heritable jurisdictions. The legislative offensive against tartan and the Episcopal Church (where any priest not ordained by an English or Irish bishop was now rendered illegitimate as a minister) disrupted the cultural networks of the Jacobites. Scottish Episcopalians were characterized as non-Protestants in public documents: General Bland noted that leaseholders in confiscated land should 'be Protestants, and ... suffer no Mass or Nonjuring Meetings within their bounds'.[35]

The annexing of Jacobite estates caused problems, 'not least the overstatement of debt burdens on the estates by those greedy for themselves or sympathetic to the politics of the Jacobite nobility'. The British Government looked to appoint factors who had no connexion with the owner or neighbour of the forfeited estate, but this was easier said than done, even though any 'unauthorised dealings' redolent of such connexions could lead to dismissal. In 1752, 'it was decided that fourteen of the forfeited Jacobite estates' (including Cluny's, Cromartie's, Lochiel's, Perth's and Robertson of Struan's) should be annexed 'inalienably to the Crown' in order to 'civilise' and 'diversify' the economy and 'promote Presbyterianism'. The Annexed Estates Commission did not succeed in these goals, but nonetheless broke up many estates in a disruptive way, not least through the provision of 'planned villages'. Tenants who were politically suspect were prioritized for pursuit for rent arrears; in some cases these arrears may have been the result of their paying a double rent to support the original owner of the estate in exile.[36]

The British Army occupation did not cease in 1746-47, nor did the opposition offered by Jacobite forces in the field. As late as 1748-9, five British companies were deployed against raiding in the north-east, while by the following summer there were still ten British regiments in Scotland, whose regular patrols (sixty of which remained as late as 1756) showed it be an occupying force.

---

[35] Pittock (2016), 112-13; *Albemarle Papers* (1902), 480-91.
[36] Pittock (2016), 113-14; Annette Smith, *Jacobite Estates of the '45*, (Edinburgh: John Donald, 1984), 7, 12, 13, 24, 58.

Increasingly devoted to infrastructure and garrisoning (1,350 of Guise's, Royal Welch Fusiliers, Pulteney's, Sackville's and Ancrum's were seconded to road building in 1749), the Army continued to be extensively billeted on the localities. Tents or huts were used when billeting was not possible: the tents were copious, about 4.3m long, 3m wide with a centre height of 2.4m and the half wall half of that. In addition, ancient barracks such as Corgarff or Braemar, forfeited after the 'Fifteen, were 'bought by the government in 1748 for the accommodation of soldiers', while some military settlements, such as Blackpark Barracks near Loch Rannoch, were used as a settlement for retired soldiers. This was to be a much longer residence than that of 1715 by an occupying and suppressing force; the British Army was in for the long haul. The same was true of the Royal Navy, with Captain Cook's early experiences closely linked to the occupation, not least as the Master of the sixth-rate *Solebay* of 20 guns, engaged in patrolling the seas round Scotland in 1757. The son of Scottish parents himself (he served haggis on *Endeavour*), Cook's christening of New Caledonia in the Pacific can be read both as an act of filial piety and a resurrection of the imprint of Scotland on the British Empire, which was to expand exponentially in the nineteenth century. The killing fields of northern Scotland were to begin a new national history that spanned the globe.[37]

---

[37] Pittock (2016), 109; Henshaw (2015), 81-83, 169; John McAteer and Nigel Rigby, *Captain Cook and the Pacific: Art, Exploration & Empire*, (London and New York: Yale University Press, 2017), 25; bit.ly/StennisDocs.

The English Response to the French Revolution: The Established Church's Prayers, Fasts, and Thanksgiving Days 1793–1802

Colin Haydon

In recent years, historians have stressed the importance of the Established Church in English society from the Restoration into the early nineteenth century (and, indeed, far later). They have rejected the Victorian caricature of a decaying institution and Marxists' or quasi-Marxists' dismissal of the Church as parasitic on, and culturally irrelevant to, the working population. *Inter alia*, they have emphasized the importance of the pulpit in fostering political awareness. Sermons, Tony Claydon maintains, 'played a vital role in creating and sustaining the public sphere after 1660'.[1] Clergymen 'were the sole representatives of a national institution in every locality and community', W. M. Jacob observes. They constituted 'the main channel of communication between government and people', and, addressing both the literate and illiterate, 'were potentially immensely influential'.[2]

From the sixteenth century, governments had appointed general fast days, with church services, at times of crisis, such as visitations of plague. During wars, they also ordered fast days, thanksgiving prayers for victories, said at ordinary services, and, following peace treaties, days of thanksgiving.[3] In the eighteenth century furthermore, they instructed parsons to preach on wartime fast days and thanksgiving days. David Napthine and William Speck have

---

[1] Tony Claydon, 'The Sermon, the "Public Sphere", and the Political Culture of Late Seventeenth-Century England', *The English Sermon Revised*, ed. Lori Anne Ferrell and Peter McCullough (Manchester and New York, 2000), p. 211.

[2] W. M. Jacob, *The Clerical Profession in the Long Eighteenth Century 1680-1840* (Oxford, 2007), pp. 10, 256, 304.

[3] H. R. Trevor-Roper, *Religion, the Reformation, and Social Change*, 2nd edn (London and Basingstoke, 1972), pp. 294, 295; C. J. Kitching, '"Prayers Fit for the Time": Fasting and Prayer in Response to National Crises in the Reign of Elizabeth I', *Monks, Hermits, and the Ascetic Tradition*, ed. W. J. Sheils, Studies in Church History XXII (Oxford, 1985), pp. 241-50; *National Prayers: Special Worship since the Reformation*, 2 vols, ed. Natalie Mears, Alasdair Raffe, Stephen Taylor, Philip Williamson, and Lucy Bates, Church of England Record Society XX, XXII (Woodbridge, 2013, 2017), *Past & Present* No. cc (2008), pp. 121-74.

examined sermons preached in time of war from 1660 to 1763.[4] James E. Bradley, Henry P. Ippel, and Paul Langford have analysed the sermons preached during the years of the American Revolution.[5] And Emma Vincent Macleod has investigated the clergy's preaching during the conflict with revolutionary France.[6] Between 1793 and 1802, a torrent of propaganda promoted loyalism and patriotism highly effectively in England;[7] and, along with 'Church and King' associations, Paine-burning demonstrations, newspapers, pamphlets, books, prints, and cartoons, sermons could vigorously encourage such sentiments.

The set occasions for loyalist preaching were many from 1793 to 1802. The French National Convention declared war on Britain on 1 February 1793; a month later, George III proclaimed a fast day, with three church services,[8] and, as in seventeenth- and earlier eighteenth-century wars, a fast was appointed annually while the conflict continued. Besides the fast days in 1797 and 1798, days of thanksgiving —usually ordered only after the resumption of peace— were proclaimed: in the former year, for the Navy's successes during the war, and, in the latter, for the victory of the Nile and the 'Deliverance of these Kingdoms from Foreign Invasion'.[9] In 1802, a

---

[4] D. Napthine and W. A. Speck, 'Clergymen and Conflict 1660-1763', *The Church and War*, ed. W. J. Sheils, *Studies in Church History*, XX (Oxford, 1983), pp. 231-51.
[5] James E. Bradley, 'The Anglican Pulpit, the Social Order, and the Resurgence of Toryism during the American Revolution', *Albion* xxi (1989), pp. 361-88; Henry P. Ippel, 'British Sermons and the American Revolution', *Journal of Religious History* xii (1982), pp. 191-205; Paul Langford, 'The English Clergy and the American Revolution', *The Transformation of Political Culture: England and Germany in the Late Eighteenth Century*, ed. Eckhart Hellmuth (Oxford, 1990), pp. 275-307.
[6] Emma Vincent Macleod, *A War of Ideas: British Attitudes to the Wars against Revolutionary France 1792-1802* (Aldershot, 1998), pp. 135-49, 156-7.
[7] Robert R. Dozier, *For King, Constitution, and Country: The English Loyalists and the French Revolution* (Lexington, Kentucky, 1983); Ian R. Christie, *Stress and Stability in Late Eighteenth-Century Britain* (Oxford, 1984); H. T. Dickinson, 'Popular Conservatism and Militant Loyalism 1789-1815', *Britain and the French Revolution 1789-1815*, ed. Dickinson (Basingstoke, 1989), pp. 103-25; Dickinson, 'Popular Loyalism in Britain in the 1790s', *Transformation of Political Culture*, ed. Hellmuth, pp. 503-33; Frank O'Gorman, 'The Paine Burnings of 1792-1793', *Past and Present* No. cxciii (2006), pp. 111-55.
[8] *The London Gazette*, 26 February - 2 March 1793.
[9] *A Form of Prayer and Thanksgiving ... to be Used ... on Thursday the Twenty-ninth Day of November 1798* (London, 1798), title page. For all the Forms, excluding that cited in n. 115, I have used those published by Eyre and Strahan, the royal printers in

thanksgiving day celebrated the Peace of Amiens. In order to affirm their importance, the fast and thanksgiving days were observed on weekdays, the practice since the 1560s. It was intended, as was traditional, that work would cease and the entire population keep them: in his proclamations (though presumably just rhetorically), the King warned of 'such Punishment as We may justly inflict on all such as contemn and neglect the Performance of so religious and necessary a Duty'.[10] In the churches, the government wanted parsons to champion its policies, justify the war, and denounce the Revolution in France. J. E. Cookson stresses the services' significance: there 'may well have been no other occasions', he contends, 'when the social influence of the Anglican establishment was so fully mobilized on behalf of the state'.[11] Prayers for good harvests were also included in some of these services. There were, too, several prayers of thanksgiving incorporated in ordinary Sunday services: for the naval victories at Cape St Vincent and Camperdown in 1797, and the Nile in 1798; and following the attack on the royal coach in 1795, Hadfield's attempt to assassinate George III in 1800, and the King's recovery from sickness in 1801.[12] Depending on the occurrence's deemed importance, these prayers were repeated on varying numbers of Sundays — the Church's standard practice in like cases.

Though there were a few exceptions,[13] most Anglican clergymen, when preaching at these services, supported the government's war policy.[14] In September 1793, *The Analytical Review* maintained that, 'upon the occasion of the late fast, the same political cry resounded through almost all the churches in England' in 'perfect harmony'.[15] Individuals assumed the same.[16] But plainly there were some

---

England.

[10] *London Gazette*, 26 February - 2 March 1793. The admonition's wording dated from the late seventeenth century, when the ecclesiastical courts might enforce the observance. It is unclear whether there was any enforcement in the eighteenth century.

[11] J. E. Cookson, *The Friends of Peace: Anti-War Liberalism in England 1793-1815* (Cambridge, 1982), p. 134.

[12] On George III's illness in 1801, see Jeremy Black, *George III* (New Haven and London, 2006), p. 383.

[13] Colin Haydon, *John Henry Williams (1747-1829) 'Political Clergyman': War, the French Revolution, and the Church of England* (Woodbridge, 2007), *passim*.

[14] Macleod, *War of Ideas*, pp. 135-49, 156-7.

[15] *The Analytical Review, or History of Literature, Domestic and Foreign* xvii (1793), p. 56.

variations in the treatment of political subjects none the less. Of course, it is now possible to examine only printed sermons –which may have been polished for publication– and a few manuscript texts. It is possible that clerics who published their sermons tended to proclaim exaggerated pro-government sentiments, thereby hoping to advance their careers. Others, doubting the wisdom of introducing 'politics into the pulpit', probably preached half-heartedly –though some parsons who had previously eschewed public political comment accepted the need for it in the alarming 1790s.[17] Even if the subjects which clergymen 'generally treat[ed] on ... [were] nearly the same in almost every congregation',[18] as one commentator believed, discrepancies in detail, political knowledge, and emphases were unavoidable.

However, though there was no sure guarantee of consistency for the sermons preached on the fast and thanksgiving days, there was for the Forms of Prayer for the occasions, prepared and issued by the archbishops and bishops. In 10,000 churches across England, the same denunciations of the French Revolution in those Forms of Prayer were to be read at the appointed times. Indeed, the Church authorities even hoped to standardize the delivery (as they did for ordinary services): parsons were instructed to read prescribed sentences from Scripture, and the subsequent exhortation, '*with a loud Voice*'.[19] Since the services were apparently well attended,[20] the fast and thanksgiving days provided golden opportunities for infusing the Church's and government's opinions of the French Revolution into the nation at large. Precisely what those opinions were, as proclaimed at the services, and the perceived implications of the Revolution's character for George III's subjects, constitute the subject of this essay.

* * *

---

[16] J. H. Williams, *Two Sermons Preached on the Public Fasts of April 1793, and February 1794* (London, 1794), pp. 8-10.

[17] E.g., William Mavor, *Christian Politics: A Sermon, Preached to a Country Congregation, on Friday, April 19, 1793*, 2nd edn (Oxford, 1793), pp. 13-14.

[18] *The Evangelical Magazine* iii (1795), p. 258.

[19] *A Form of Prayer, to be Used ... upon Friday the Nineteenth of April* [*1793*] (London, 1793), p. 3. The Book of Common Prayer ordinarily directed ministers to read in a 'loud' or 'audible' voice.

[20] Jacob, *Clerical Profession*, pp. 8, 193-4; Macleod, *War of Ideas*, p. 157. Cf. Williamson, 'State Prayers', p. 149.

According to the Forms of Prayer, which themselves followed the royal proclamations' time-honoured wording, the prayers and supplications to God on the fast days had four separable, though necessarily intermeshed, purposes. First, the days' prayers were for 'obtaining [God's] Pardon of our Sins', and second 'for averting ... [His] heavy Judgements which our manifold Provocations have most justly deserved'. Third, they were for 'imploring ... [God's] Blessing and Assistance on the Arms of His Majesty by Sea and Land', and, fourth, for His aid in 'restoring and perpetuating Peace, Safety, and Prosperity'.[21] The former two purposes were thus more austerely religious, and personal, than the two latter, with their political and national emphases; though, given God's anticipated agency, this division is somewhat artificial. The services stressed both the necessity of repentance in order to escape God's terrifying wrath and, simultaneously and comfortingly, His mercy, His protection of the righteous, and His smiting of their foes.

These purposes were underscored and balanced by the careful choice of readings from the Scriptures. Using the Forms for earlier fast days as models, the pattern for the usual Sunday services – morning prayer, followed by the ante-Communion,[22] and evening prayer- was easily adapted for the requirements of the fasts. Matins and evening prayer comprised scriptural verses, psalms, Old and New Testament lessons, collects and other prayers; the ante-Communion, besides the sermon, included epistle and gospel readings and prayers. The Forms were flexible and could easily be adjusted, with the replacement of some readings by passages that were more appropriate to prevailing circumstances and the insertion of fresh, sometimes specially-composed, prayers. The choice of psalms and New Testament readings for morning and evening prayer nevertheless remained the same from 1795 to 1800, with the exception of changes to the New Testament readings from 1798. The Old and New Testament readings for the ante-Communion were unchanged from 1794 to 1800. More changes were made to the readings for morning prayer and the ante-Communion in 1801, perhaps in anticipation of the making of peace.

---

[21] *Form of Prayer, Nineteenth of April 1793*, title page.
[22] I.e. the Communion service stopping after the Prayer for the Church.

At the start of morning prayer on the fast days, verses from the psalms proclaimed the need to trust in God's power and mercy: 'The Lord is King, be the Earth never so unquiet'; 'The waves of the sea are mighty, and rage horribly, but the Lord, who dwelleth on high, is mightier'; 'The Lord is my refuge, and my God is the strength of my Confidence'; 'Thou, O Lord God, art full of compassion and mercy, long suffering, plenteous in goodness and truth'; 'The Lord shall give strength unto his people, the Lord shall give his people the blessing of peace.'[23] Then, the psalms and the most–used readings from Scripture were, by turns, alarming and uplifting. Psalm LI stressed human sinfulness, while Psalms LXXXVI and CXXX celebrated God's mercy. Psalm XC –the Psalm which Isaac Watts partly paraphrased in 'Our God, our Help in Ages Past'– extolled God's power. Matthew III and Luke XIII respectively recounted John the Baptist's and Christ's calls to repentance, and II Peter II described God's justice ('[T]he Lord knoweth how to deliver the godly out of temptations, and to reserve the unjust unto the day of judgement to be punished').[24] Spiritual preparedness was all –disconcertingly so: 'be ye also ready: for in such an hour as ye think not the Son of man cometh'.[25] Yet God would assuredly spare the penitent as He had spared Nineveh, as the Book of Jonah recounted, when its King and people had worn sackcloth and fasted.[26] As for the war, God would decide the victory, and would not forsake a just nation. From 1795 to 1800, the first lesson at morning prayer was II Chronicles XX:1-15, describing the conflict of the Israelites with the Moabites and Ammonites and ending with Jahaziel's inspired words: 'Hearken ye, all Judah, and ye inhabitants of Jerusalem, and thou king Jehoshaphat, Thus saith the LORD unto you, Be not afraid nor dismayed by reason of this great multitude; for the battle *is* not yours, but God's.'[27]

---

[23] *Form of Prayer, Nineteenth of April 1793*, p. 4.

[24] II Peter II: 9.

[25] Matthew XXIV:44.

[26] Jonah III.

[27] At morning prayer in February 1794, the reading continued until verse 24, recounting God's destruction of the Israelites' enemies: *A Form of Prayer, to be Used … upon Friday the Twenty-eighth of February [1794]* (London, 1794), p. 5. But by 1795, this probably seemed inappropriate, given the French victory at Fleurus in June 1794 –the victory which secured France's military dominance on the Continent.

These passages from Scripture were, of course, applicable to any war (and, unsurprisingly, the framers of earlier fast day Forms had sometimes chosen them): they set the conflict of 1793 to 1802 in the general scheme of Jewish and Christian history. It was the prayers composed as *pieces d'occasion* for the fasts, thanksgiving days, and other services which specifically denounced the French Revolution, and which therefore now require examination. How did they depict events in France and continental Europe in the decade from 1793, and the Revolution's implications for the British state?

* * *

During most of the century preceding 1789, Britain's principal adversary was *ancien-régime* France. The French monarchy was easily depicted as tyrannous, and its foreign policy a threat to Britain and Europe generally. The French Catholic church appeared intolerant and obscurantist. Louis XIV had seemed the incarnation of 'Popery and tyranny', cruelly intent on European domination and heresy's extirpation; yet, even under the mild Louis XVI, France appeared a natural enemy of Britain and her empire, a view seemingly confirmed by French intervention in the War of American Independence. While British aristocrats and intellectuals might admire eighteenth-century French manners and culture, popular fears of cruel and bloody Popery were not easily dispelled. It is perhaps surprising how quickly, and with so little adaptation, the same denunciations of the *ancien régime* were employed from 1793 against the godless republic that had replaced it. Yet the centuries-old Popery/tyranny stereotype was itself protean. As the annual Fifth of November service reminded English congregations, if Papists favoured tyrannical kings, they might also plot, or indeed commit, regicide.

From the outset, the various services' and prayers' Forms presented revolutionary France as an appalling threat, politically and militarily, to Britain, the rest of Europe, and even the globe itself. Following the decree of 'secours et fraternité' (19 November 1792), offering aid to peoples wishing to regain their liberty, and Louis XVI's execution, the French Republic was 'an enemy to all Christian Kings, Princes, and States', the 1793 Form of Prayer proclaimed; she was 'labouring to overthrow the Religion, Laws, and Government of the World'.[28] The next year and in 1795, after her military successes and the crushing of the counter-revolution, her forces seemed to 'threaten ... desolation to every Country where they ... [could] erect their bloody Standard'.[29] Certainly by early 1795, France's neighbours were either 'exposed ... to the Violence, or groaning under ... [French] Oppression',[30] and the Republic's military dominance was confirmed by the peace treaties with Prussia, the Dutch, and Spain, of, respectively, April, May, and July of that year. By 1796, the French annexations of the Austrian Netherlands, Dutch Flanders, Nice, and Savoy appeared permanent, and her continuing dominance of the 'Batavian Republic' assured; and that year's fast day Form was pointedly adjusted, stating that the French '*have spread* desolation wherever they have erected their standard'.[31] We 'behold with compassion', it continued, 'the miseries they have inflicted upon the objects of their fury'.[32] But Britain was directly threatened too. With so much of the coastline facing England under French control, the enemy represented a monstrous danger to 'the Vessels of our Merchants'.[33] The challenge to the Royal Navy was also considerable. The Dutch navy worked with the French fleet from 1795, and, after concluding an alliance with France, Spain declared war on Britain in October 1796. The Spanish and Dutch fleets were defeated at Cape St Vincent and Camperdown respectively, and hence prevented from aiding the French in crucial manoeuvres in 1797, but the Dutch-French-Spanish alliance precluded British operations in the Mediterranean. As was noted at the 1797 thanksgiving service for the naval victories of the war, Britain faced 'numerous Hosts of confederate and mighty Foes'.[34]

Modern historians have maintained that violence and killing were integral to the Revolution, thus echoing its contemporary enemies'

---

[28] *Form of Prayer, Nineteenth of April 1793*, pp. 6, 9, 17, 20. The opening of the Scheldt in November 1792 showed the revolutionaries' disregard for earlier treaty obligations.

[29] *Form of Prayer, Twenty-eighth of February 1794*, pp. 6, 17; *A Form of Prayer, to be Used ... upon Wednesday the Twenty-fifth of February* [1795] (London, 1795), pp. 6, 15.

[30] *Form of Prayer, Twenty-fifth of February 1795*, pp. 6, 15.

[31] *A Form of Prayer, to be Used ... upon Wednesday the Ninth of March* [1796] (London, 1796), pp. 5, 13. My italics.

[32] Ibid., pp. 10, 15-16.

[33] Ibid., p. 7.

[34] *A Form of Prayer and Thanksgiving ... to be Used ... on Tuesday the Nineteenth Day of December 1797* (London, 1797), p. 8.

condemnations.[35] Edmund Burke prophesied in 1790 the Revolution's terrifying capacity for destruction; in 1791, he attacked the 'school of murder and barbarism' in Paris, and foretold that, if hostilities began in Europe, the 'mode of civilized war ... [would] not be practised'.[36] After the French monarchy's fall in 1792, he denounced the 'abominable, murderous and exterminatory' Revolution, the 'murderous Riot of the lowest people', and the 'Empire of Anarchy and Assassination'.[37] The Terror was appalling, especially in a country which had, until so recently, seemed so cultivated in the English élite's eyes. Such views were amply reflected in the various Forms of Prayer. The revolutionaries 'trusteth in Violence, and delighteth in blood', congregations were told.[38] In 1793, the French had 'plunged themselves into ... horrible iniquities, and cruelties', and, in 1794, 'into ... horrible Crimes and Impieties'.[39] The 'Ravages of their Cruelty amongst their Fellow-creatures' were terrible.[40] Such charges were reiterated year after year, along with prayers that God would strike the men of blood 'with Remorse and Compunction, before they fill[ed] up the measure of their Iniquities'.[41] When Parson Woodforde conducted the 1793 fast day service at Weston Longeville, there was 'a large Congregation', despite a 'rough N.E. Wind with Hail and Snow &c.'.[42] Unsurprisingly, the Form of Prayer's denunciation of revolutionary violence and bloodshed mirrored Woodforde's own loathing, following Louis XVI's execution, of 'the French Assassins', 'cruel, blood-thirsty' men.[43]

Besides the threat to other nations, and their domestic policies of repression, the revolutionary régimes were execrated in the Forms of Prayer for their attacks on Christianity. The revolutionaries, it

---

[35] Most notably François Furet in *Penser la Révolution Française* (Paris, 1978) and, more stridently, Simon Schama in *Citizens* (London, 1989).

[36] Edmund Burke, *A Letter from Mr. Burke, to a Member of the National Assembly* (Paris and London, 1791), p. 45.

[37] P. J. Marshall and John A. Woods, eds, *The Correspondence of Edmund Burke*, VII (Cambridge and Chicago, 1968), pp. 175, 176, 178.

[38] *Form of Prayer, Nineteenth of April 1793*, pp. 6, 17.

[39] Ibid., p. 13; *Form of Prayer, Twenty-eighth of February 1794*, p. 12.

[40] *Form of Prayer, Twenty-eighth of February 1794*, p. 12.

[41] Ibid.

[42] John Beresford, ed., *The Diary of a Country Parson: The Reverend James Woodforde*, IV (London, 1929, repr. Oxford, 1968), p. 22.

[43] Ibid., p. 4.

was stated in April 1793, had 'cast off their faith in Thee, the Living God':[44] a significant comment since, although the persecution of refractory clerics had by then begun (and mobs had butchered some priests in the September massacres of 1792), full dechristianization commenced later, in September 1793. In February 1794 (before the cult of the Supreme Being's inauguration), the revolutionaries were described as 'the impious and avowed Blasphemers of ... [God's] Holy Name and Word'; in 'the very Center [*sic*] of Christendom, [they] threaten[ed] destruction to Christianity'.[45] By 1795, they were 'Apostates from ... [God's] Truth and Despisers of ... [His] Holy Name'.[46] Sentences chosen from the Psalms targeted the Revolution's rejection of Christianity: '*Wherefore should the Heathen say, where is now their God?*'; '*Lo!* thine enemies make a murmuring, and they that hate thee have lift up their heads.'[47] Yoked to the French, other nations had also compromised their religion: in 1797, the Dutch and Spanish, with the French, were described as not only 'confederate and mighty Foes' but also 'enemies to ... [God's] Name'.[48] In all the services bar one,[49] no distinction was made between Protestantism and Roman Catholicism; there was no triumphalist rhetoric about the destruction of Popery in France, the fall of Antichrist, the French invasion of the Papal States in 1796, or the establishment of the 'Roman Republic' in 1798. Rather, the French Revolution was represented as the enemy of all *Christendom*, 'ourselves and other Christian Nations',[50] Protestant and Catholic alike, and the 'Prayer for the Reformed Churches', used in wars earlier in the eighteenth century, was discarded. From 1793, the 'Prayer for our Enemies' asked for 'the Repentance and Conversion' of the French revolutionaries, while simultaneously denouncing their crimes.[51]

---

[44] *Form of Prayer, Nineteenth of April 1793*, p. 13.

[45] *Form of Prayer, Twenty-eighth of February 1794*, pp. 6, 17.

[46] *Form of Prayer, Twenty-fifth of February 1795*, pp. 6, 15. The Convention decreed the separation of church and state on 21 February, but thereafter Catholic worship revived.

[47] *Form of Prayer, Nineteenth of April 1793*, pp, 3, 4.

[48] *Form of Prayer, Nineteenth of December 1797*, p. 8.

[49] Exceptionally, the 1802 Form of Prayer and Thanksgiving besought God 'to look down with pity on the Church ... particularly on the reformed parts of it': *A Form of Prayer and Thanksgiving ... to be Used ... on Tuesday the First Day of June [1802]* (London, 1802), p. 10.

[50] *Form of Prayer, Ninth of March 1796*, pp. 5, 13; cf. Tony Claydon, *Europe and the Making of England 1660-1760* (Cambridge, 2007), *passim*.

* * *

In his famous print 'The Contrast' (1792), Thomas Rowlandson juxtaposed 'British Liberty' ('Religion. Morality. Loyalty ... Happiness') and 'French Liberty' ('Atheism Perjury Rebellion ... Misery').[52] Comparably, the Forms of Prayer, while reviling revolutionary France, trumpeted the strengths of the British state and constitution, and the necessity of the war. They also denounced internal enemies to Britain's political *status quo*.

The monarchy was naturally extolled. As Linda Colley has delineated, George III enjoyed immense popularity in later life.[53] Publicly, he personified resistance to the enemy; in his private life, he was a devoted husband and affectionate father to his younger children; by nature, he was serious, moral, and god-fearing. The fast day and thanksgiving services, supposedly ordered by the King himself, appeared a testament to his own piety: George was, the 1802 Form proclaimed, 'the nursing Father of ... [God's] church'.[54] Prayers were accordingly composed for 'our most gracious Sovereign', God's 'faithful Servant', additional to those in the Book of Common Prayer used each Sunday; nothing, it was hoped, would 'obstruct his wise and salutary counsels'.[55] The King was the father of the nation, displaying 'anxious cares for the welfare of his People'.[56] From 1796, God was implored to assist George 'in all his Counsels for the preservation of these Kingdoms, and [to] crown them with ... [His divine] Blessing'.[57] The King was the Lord's anointed, his person sacred.[58] Unsurprisingly, there was a crescendo of such sentiments following the mobbing of the King's

---

[51] *Form of Prayer, Nineteenth of April 1793*, pp. 13, 21.

[52] British Museum, Catalogue of Political and Personal Satires, 8,149.

[53] Linda Colley, 'The Apotheosis of George III: Loyalty, Royalty, and the British Nation 1760-1820', *Past & Present* No. cii (1984), pp. 94-129.

[54] *Form of Prayer, First of June 1802*, p. 8.

[55] *Form of Prayer, Nineteenth of April 1793*, pp. 10, 20, 21.

[56] Ibid., pp. 10, 20-1.

[57] *Form of Prayer, Ninth of March 1796*, pp. 5, 13.

[58] *A Form of Prayer and Thanksgiving to Almighty God, For His Late Merciful Preservation of the King's Majesty from the Outrageous and Desperate Attempts against His Person* (London, 1795), pp. 3, 4; *A Form of Prayer and Thanksgiving to Almighty God, For His Great Mercy in the Providential Protection of the King from the Atrocious and Treasonable Attempt against His Sacred Person* (London, 1800), pp. 3, 4.

coach and Hadfield's attempt on George's life.[59] In 1796, God was asked to guard George, as He had previously done, against overt violence and covert plotting, while, in 1800, He was thanked for frustrating 'the atrocious Attempts ... against the sacred Person of Thy Servant, our Sovereign'.[60]

Besides praying for George III himself, congregations prayed that God would preserve the institutions of the state in this troubled period. Looking ahead to George's death, while contemptuously spurning republicanism, they asked that God would 'grant that ... [the King's] Sceptre ... [might] remain with his Children, and his Childrens [*sic*] Children, from Generation to Generation'.[61] Similarly, from 1797, 'the Prayer for the High Court of Parliament', from the Book of Common Prayer, was said.[62]

In 1793, as France was rent apart by federalism, counter-revolution, and civil war, the revolutionaries stubbornly insisted that the Republic was 'une et indivisible'. In England, the authorities, fearful of radicalism and riot, sought to bind the overwhelming majority of the nation to the Crown and the prevailing order. Unity was the order of the day. George III had 'unite[d] ... [his subjects] in prayer and supplication'.[63] From 1796, a collect at morning and evening fast day services asked God to 'unite our hearts, as the heart of one man, in loyal attachment to ... [the King's] Person, and in dutiful submission to his Authority, and to the Laws'.[64] The thanksgiving prayer for Camperdown and other prayers in 1797 and 1798 slightly shifted the emphasis to the necessary cohesion of society at large: 'Unite us in Zeal for Thy

---

[59] After the two events, special prayers were sent to all incumbents: they were to be used on the first Sunday after their receipt, and thereafter for fourteen days in 1795 and thirty days in 1800. 'Be Thou his Defence and Shield ... Cloath his Enemies with Shame', they implored. 'Long may the Crown flourish on the Head of thine Anointed ...': *Form of Prayer to Almighty God, For His Late Merciful Preservation*, title page, pp. 3, 4; *Form of Prayer to Almighty God, For His Great Mercy*, title page, pp. 3, 4.

[60] *Form of Prayer, Ninth of March 1796*, 5, 13; *Form of Prayer to Almighty God, For His Great Mercy*, p. 3.

[61] *Form of Prayer to Almighty God, For His Late Merciful Preservation*, p. 4; *Form of Prayer to Almighty God, For His Great Mercy*, p. 4.

[62] *A Form of Prayer, to be Used ... upon Wednesday the Eighth of March* [1797] (London, 1797), p. 8.

[63] *Form of Prayer, Nineteenth of April 1793*, p. 12.

[64] *Form of Prayer, Ninth of March 1796*, pp. 5, 13.

Truth, in Loyalty to the King, and in the Bonds of brotherly Love and Charity one towards another.'[65] Comparably, they contained prayers for both the military's officers and those that they commanded, whose different but complementary rôles were needed for victory: 'Continue, we beseech Thee, O Lord, to go forth with our Fleets and Armies. Inspire, as hitherto Thou hast done, the Leaders with Wisdom and Courage, and the Men with Intrepidity.'[66] In November 1798, the wording was minutely, but revealingly, adjusted: 'and the Men with Intrepidity' was replaced by 'and the Men with *Loyalty* and Intrepidity' —presumably a belated response to the naval mutinies of the previous year, which had so alarmingly imperilled the nation's defences and the war effort.[67]

For contemporaries, the army and navy seemed like microcosms of English society as a whole, with its ranks and gradations, and the concomitant importance of wealth and patronage.[68] Disloyalty in the armed services therefore apparently, and most ominously, suggested simmering, though largely invisible, domestic disaffection. From the start, the Forms of Prayer noted the dangers of 'secret conspiracy and open violence'.[69] From 1794 to 1800, the epistle at the ante-Communion was II Peter II, beginning 'BUT there were false Prophets also among the people, even as there shall be false teachers among you.'[70] Such teachers, the reading continued brutally, shall 'bring upon themselves swift destruction'.[71] Indeed, malcontents and the seditious risked damnation, for God would punish the wicked at the Last Judgement and 'chiefly them that walk after the flesh in the lust of uncleanness, and despise government': presumptuous 'are they, self-willed, they are not afraid to speak evil of dignities'.[72] After the attack on the King's

---

[65] *A Form of Prayer and Thanksgiving, For the Signal Victory Obtained through the Blessing of Almighty God by His Majesty's Ships of War, under the Command of Admiral Duncan* (London, 1797), p.4; *Form of Prayer, Nineteenth of December 1797*, p. 9; *Form of Prayer, Twenty-ninth of November 1798*, p. 8.

[66] *Form of Prayer For the Victory Obtained under Duncan*, p. 3; *Form of Prayer, Nineteenth of December 1797*, p. 8; *Form of Prayer, Twenty-ninth of November 1798*, pp. 7-8.

[67] *Form of Prayer, Twenty-ninth of November 1798*, p. 8. My italics.

[68] Cf. Timothy Jenks' analysis of the procession to St Paul's for the 1797 thanksgiving service in his *Naval Engagements: Patriotism, Cultural Politics, and the Royal Navy 1793-1815* (Oxford, 2006), p. 119.

[69] *Form of Prayer, Nineteenth of April 1793*, pp. 10, 20.

[70] *Form of Prayer, Twenty-eighth of February 1794*, p. 10.

[71] Ibid.

coach, it was hoped that 'desperate and bloody minded Men' who remained 'incorrigible in their Wickedness ... [would] perish by ... [God's] just Judgements, that others by the Example of their Punishment ... [might] take Warning'.[73] Acute and dangerous discontent was anticipated in 1796 and 1800, with high grain prices following wretched harvests, and, in consequence, the 'Prayer for Plenty', adapted from the Prayer Book's prayers 'In the Time of Dearth and Famine', asked God to end the shortages so that 'the Poor and Needy' might be aided.[74] The thanksgiving prayer for Camperdown deplored the possibility of civil insurrection, as did the service for the war's naval victories.[75] After the Irish rising of 1798, God was thanked for delivering the state from 'Intestine Commotions' and 'intestine Treason'.[76] Those who composed the Forms of Prayer, it seems clear, were genuinely troubled by the threat of clandestine sedition, civil unrest, and rebellion. Of course, denunciations of it could be dismissed as chimeras, calculated to cow the gullible into an unthinking acceptance of government policy.[77] Yet, the terrifying spectre of France's military power in tandem with domestic subversion was not easily banished.

The conflict battered the economy and produced great hardship. Crippling taxation was needed to sustain the war effort, and there was sustained harm to commerce, manufactures, and public credit. Despite the naval victories, and the inability of the French to invade Britain, the war was largely unsuccessful. The land campaigns in the Low Countries of 1793-95 and 1799 were failures, and, by 1796, 40,000 men had died in the West Indies (with 40,000 more incapacitated). When Britain and France concluded the Peace of Amiens in 1802, the former relinquished nearly all her overseas gains whereas the latter retained nearly all her continental conquests. It was therefore necessary to justify the lengthy, costly,

---

[72] Ibid., p. 11.

[73] *Form of Prayer to Almighty God, For His Late Merciful Preservation*, pp. 3, 4.

[74] *Form of Prayer, Ninth of March 1796*, pp. 8, 15; *A Form of Prayer, to be Used ... upon Wednesday the Twelfth of March 1800* (London, 1800), pp. 8, 15.

[75] *Form of Prayer For the Victory Obtained under Duncan*, p. 4; *Form of Prayer, Nineteenth of December 1797*, p. 9.

[76] *Form of Prayer, Twenty-ninth of November 1798*, title page, p. 7.

[77] One Warwickshire clergyman, who detested the fast day services, contemptuously dismissed the danger from 'Republicans, Levellers, Anarchists, Jacobins, Painists, or others of this obnoxious and seditious description (of whom one hears so much, and sees so little)': Williams, *Two Sermons*, pp. 2-3.

and increasingly questionable war in the church services. At the
outset, the 1793 Form of Prayer maintained that the enemy was
'unprovoked':[78] a problematical claim since, although it was France
that had declared war in February 1793, British diplomacy had been
sternly uncompromising in the preceding months.[79] From 1796,
the war was proclaimed 'just and necessary', and French
interference with the nation's 'lawful Commerce' decried.[80] After
Cape St Vincent, the gravity of the invasion threat was emphasized
(the Spaniards had projected an invasion): the nation's enemies, it
was said, had 'appointed our Land unto themselves for a Possession,
and, in their proud imaginations, seized upon it for a Prey'.[81] The
prayer of thanksgiving for Camperdown deplored the 'unjust
ambition' of the enemy, and that for the Battle of the Nile stated
that the struggle was for 'the Good of all Mankind'.[82] However, it
was for the Camperdown thanksgiving prayer that the most ringing
justification of the war was devised. The 'Battle is for more than
Gain or Glory', it stated. It was 'for Religion and for Public
Liberty, for the Independence of ... [our] Country, for the Rights
of Civil Society, for the Maintenance of every Ordinance, Divine
and Human, essential to the well-being of Man'.[83] This neat, if
extravagant, formula was employed again in the 1797 and 1798
thanksgiving services, but, rather surprisingly, was not incorporated
in the prayers for the annual fast days.[84] In the light of the Whigs'
campaign to topple Pitt's government and end the war in 1797,
such forceful propaganda was timely.[85] Overall, the services'
justification of the conflict was masterly. Year after year, the
prayers firmly reiterated that the war was both 'just and necessary'.
They highlighted the ideological, military, and economic threat
posed by the enemy; though, to balance this, the thanksgiving

---

[78] *Form of Prayer, Nineteenth of April 1793*, pp. 9, 20.

[79] T. C. W. Blanning, *The Origins of the French Revolutionary Wars* (Harlow, 1986), p.
157.

[80] *Form of Prayer, Ninth of March 1796*, pp. 7, 15.

[81] *A Form of Prayer and Thanksgiving to Almighty God; For the Victory Gained by His Majesty's
Fleet under the Command of Sir John Jervis* (London, 1797), p. 4.

[82] *Form of Prayer For the Victory Obtained under Duncan*, p. 4; *A Form of Prayer and
Thanksgiving, For the Signal Victory Obtained through the Blessing of Almighty God by His
Majesty's Ships of War, under the Command of Admiral Nelson* (London, 1798), p. 3.

[83] *Form of Prayer For the Victory Obtained under Duncan*, p. 3.

[84] *Form of Prayer, Nineteenth of December 1797*, p. 8; *Form of Prayer, Twenty-ninth of
November 1798*, p. 8.

[85] Cookson, *Friends of Peace*, p. 161.

services were calculated to raise morale and stiffen the political nation's resolve to continue the struggle. The naval successes seemingly presaged eventual victory. Necessarily, therefore, the services largely veiled military failures, the seeming invincibility of the French in their startling land campaigns, and Britain's inability to dent their dominance of the Continent. Only on the title page of the Form of Prayer for the Peace of Amiens' celebration was it admitted that the war had proved 'bloody, extended, and expensive' (following the royal proclamation and customary wording for Forms when wars ended).[86] It was then proclaimed that God's 'abundant loving kindness' had restored, 'to this and other Countries, the Blessing of Peace' and the Form maintained the need for reconciliation with former enemies.[87]

* * *

Like the political institutions, the Established Church was presented in the Forms of Prayer as an essential pillar of England's well-ordered society. It was the custodian of 'true religion', though almost nothing was said about its distinctive doctrines: instead, the national church, like the monarchy, was depicted as a focus for unity, a bulwark against the atheist French. Yet, while the fast day Forms showed the war partly as a religious struggle, from 1794 they also urged congregations to battle inner threats to the soul, and hence joined again the needs of the public and the individual: 'Suffer us not to return to our former sinfulness and disobedience, nor again to yield to those evil passions and desires which have brought down thy Judgements upon us: But save us, O God, from ourselves, as well as from our Enemies ...'.[88]

Since the services were predicated on the belief that God intervened in the world, it was natural to emphasize the importance of Providence at them. God was 'the supreme disposer of all events' and the 'Governor of all things', who alone ruled 'over the

---

[86] *Form of Prayer, First of June 1802*, title page; *London Gazette*, 27 April - 1 May 1802; *Form of Prayer, First of June 1802*, pp. 5, 6, 7, 10.

[87] Ibid., pp. 5, 6, 7, 10.

[88] *Form of Prayer, Twenty-eighth of February 1794*, pp. 9, 20. From 1796, the wording was strengthened: 'But save us, O God; save us, not only from worldly, but also from our spiritual enemies; and most especially save us from ourselves ...' (*Form of Prayer, Ninth of March 1796*, pp. 8, 15).

Designs and Counsels of Men' and determined 'their Issues by ... [His] Almighty Wisdom and Power'.[89] No creature could resist His power.[90] He preserved the godly and punished the reprobate.[91] Much stress was laid on God's protection of the British Isles: the nation was exhorted 'to recollect the many calamities from which ... [it had been] exempted by ... merciful Providence'.[92] Of course, that was scant comfort to those in the congregations who had sons, brothers, husbands, or friends serving abroad in the army or navy, or who had already lost loved ones in the war: where, for the fallen, had been God's shield? Death in battle, or even through illness, was not, therefore, presented as cruel misfortune, but rather as part of God's scheme: some, the Forms of Prayer maintained, were '*ordained* to suffer for ... [God's] sake'.[93] Prayers were accordingly said for them, and the hope expressed that, 'having glorified [God's] Name by their Sufferings upon Earth, they may obtain of Thee an Everlasting Crown of Glory'.[94] Comparable thinking resolved the other dreadful paradox of the conflict, the repeated victories of godless, regicidal France. As they were mentioned only obliquely during the services –when French oppression in conquered lands was decried– the lustre of the successes, notably at Fleurus and Marengo, was obscured. Yet, while it was acknowledged that God was 'the only giver of all victory', the presentation of war as His terrible punishment for sin simultaneously explained enemy triumphs,[95] and British losses. This had a profoundly conservative import politically: the sinful nation collectively, not just politicians' miscalculations or commanders' inadequacies or blunders, was responsible for failure. Overall, the providentialist interpretation of events in the prayers and services was intellectually convincing (if not, perhaps, always emotionally satisfying) because, with its oscillating applicability, it was self-confirming: defeat was God's chastisement for sin, victory betokened His forgiveness. Its protean character was captured in a letter of 1800 to George III from Richard Hurd, bishop of

---

[89] *Form of Prayer, Nineteenth of April 1793*, pp. 7, 9, 18, 20; *Form of Prayer, Twenty-eighth of February 1794*, pp. 6, 17.

[90] *Form of Prayer, Nineteenth of April 1793*, pp. 9, 20.

[91] *Form of Prayer, Twenty-eighth of February 1794*, pp. 10-11.

[92] *Form of Prayer, Nineteenth of April 1793*, p. 13.

[93] *Form of Prayer, Twenty-eighth of February 1794*, p. 13. My italics.

[94] Ibid.

[95] *Form of Prayer, Nineteenth of April 1793*, p. 9.

Worcester and the King's favourite prelate: 'Political subjects ... are directed by the Supreme Power at his good pleasure, & are always tending to some great & good end, let the means be ever so strange & unexpected.'[96]

Certain events during the war seemed to give good grounds for discerning God's intervention, thereby countering misgivings that the Forms' providentialism was mere elderly, conventional rhetoric. In December 1796, General Hoche endeavoured to land an army of 14,500 men at Bantry Bay in south-west Ireland. But the attempt was incompetently executed, and fog and a week of dreadful gales separated and scattered the ships and frustrated the landing, necessitating the expedition's abandonment. '[W]e were near enough to toss a biscuit ashore', lamented the dejected Wolfe Tone, who had sailed with the French; 'England has not had such an escape since the Spanish Armada.'[97] Unsurprisingly, a prayer was composed for the 1797 fast day '*For the Providential Dispersion of the Enemy's Fleet in their late Attempt upon the Kingdom of Ireland*'.[98] '[W]e presume to return thanks', it declared, 'for what appears to us a Providential Interference —when the Winds and Storms, fulfilling Thy Word, dissipated that mighty Armament, which threatened the Peace of our Sister Kingdom ...'[99] The victory at Cape St Vincent in February 1797 elicited a similar conclusion: again unsurprisingly. Fifteen ships of the line, under Sir John Jervis' command, defeated a much superior Spanish fleet — twenty-three ships of the line and five transports. God had blessed Jervis' 'Officers and Mariners ... with such success,' it was stated in the thanksgiving prayer, 'that, with far inferior strength and numbers, they ... fought and ... overpowered a mighty host, and disconcerted the Counsels of our Enemies'.[100] Later in the year, Camperdown was seen as a 'signal instance of ... [divine] Mercy, in that ... [God had] vouchsafed to bless the Arms of ... [the King] with Success, in the discomfiture of a numerous Host of a great and mighty Foe'.[101] In the battle, both

---

[96] A. Aspinall, ed., *The Later Correspondence of George III*, III (Cambridge, 1967), p. 310.

[97] T. W. Moody, R. B. McDowell, and C. J. Woods, eds, *The Writings of Theobald Wolfe Tone 1763-98*, II (Oxford, 2001), p. 420; Marianne Elliott, *Wolfe Tone* (New Haven and London, 1989), pp. 327-8.

[98] *Form of Prayer, Eighth of March 1797*, pp. 8, 15.

[99] Ibid.

[100] *Form of Prayer For the Victory Gained under Jervis*, p. 3.

[101] *Form of Prayer For the Victory Obtained under Duncan*, p.3.

sides had sixteen ships of the line, yet the British captured nine from the Dutch (and two frigates besides). Camperdown was indeed a 'signal' success: indeed, Professor Rodger observes that 'the British had never won a victory remotely equivalent against more or less equal forces'.[102] By ordering, after 'this glorious success', the naval thanksgiving day, George III, in Bishop Hurd's eyes, trumpeted royal approval of the providentialist interpretation of Britain's triumphs.[103]

Given the emphasis on Providence in the Forms of Prayer, it is scarcely surprising that they depicted the English as a nation peculiarly favoured by God –as they had from the sixteenth century. 'We have been signally blessed in the unmolested enjoyment of true Religion,' it was stated, 'and the Possession of abundant temporal Prosperity.'[104] In 1796, it was added that 'we have been blessed, beyond other nations'.[105] Naturally, the comparison was made between the British and the Old-Testament Israelites. On 19 December 1797, George III deposited enemy banners in St Paul's, and thanks were offered to God, Who didst wonderfully strengthen the hand of Thy Servant David to overthrow, and to despoil of the Arms, in which they trusted, great and numerous Hosts of the Syrians, of the Moabites, the Ammonites, and the Philistines, and didst permit the Spears, and the Bucklers, and the Shields, to be laid up in Thy Holy Temple at Jerusalem.[106]

Of course, the comparison with the Jews was also employed to reprove the nation for its sins: 'like the Israelites of old, we have too often turned our backs on Thee, and sought our Peace and Security in our own Inventions'.[107] And there followed an implicit warning that God would abandon a people who did not truly repent, as He had abandoned the Jews: 'Grant us Grace to put away all Ungodliness and sinful Lusts ... that Thy Judgements may be withdrawn from us, and we may become distinguished Objects of

---

[102] N. A. M. Rodger, *The Command of the Ocean* (London, 2004), p. 456.

[103] A. Aspinall, ed., *Correspondence of George III*, II (Cambridge, 1963, repr. 1968), p. 633.

[104] *Form of Prayer, Twenty-eighth of February 1794*, pp. 8, 19.

[105] *Form of Prayer, Ninth of March 1796*, pp. 6, 14.

[106] *Form of Prayer, Nineteenth of December 1797*, p. 6.

[107] *Form of Prayer, Ninth of March 1796*, pp. 6, 14.

Thy Mercy.'[108] God gave warnings of His anger. When grain prices soared in 1796 and 1800, the 'Prayer for Plenty', following the Book of Common Prayer, acknowledged that 'we suffer for our Iniquity' 'Scarcity and Dearth'.[109] And, from 1796, the wording '[w]e have been signally blessed in … the Possession of abundant temporal Prosperity' was altered to 'we have been blessed … in the *long* Possession of abundant temporal Prosperity' -a recognition that favourable economic conditions had, at least temporarily, ceased.[110] None the less, there were grounds for hope that God would show mercy or forgive a contrite nation, resolved to shun sin. In 1796, it was proclaimed that, despite the nation's sins, God's 'unspeakable Mercy' had ensured George III's safety when the royal coach was attacked.[111] In the thanksgiving prayer for Cape St Vincent, God was praised for His 'manifold mercies, so wonderfully multiplied upon us in various periods of our history'; and, in that for Camperdown, it was proclaimed that 'in numberless instances … [God's] Arm, stretched out in times of Danger, hath wrought Deliverance for this Land'.[112]

* * *

In the 1790s, three young lawyers, Thomas Amyot, William Pattisson, and Henry Crabb Robinson corresponded about politics. In November 1794, Amyot wrote to Pattisson about the Church's annual commemorations of Charles I's 'martyrdom', the Restoration, and the Gunpowder Plot. It 'is from their Recurrence that the lower Class of people derive the greater part of their Knowledge of the History of their own Country', he claimed. 'I believe an English Peasant', he continued, 'knows very little more of the Transactions of his ancestors that [sic] he is informed by

---

[108] *Form of Prayer, Twenty-eighth of February 1794*, pp. 8, 20.

[109] *Form of Prayer, Ninth of March 1796*, pp. 8, 15; *Form of Prayer, Twelfth of March 1800*, pp. 8, 15.

[110] *Form of Prayer, Twenty-fifth of February 1795*, pp. 8, 17; *Form of Prayer, Ninth of March 1796*, pp. 6, 14.

[111] *Form of Prayer, Ninth of March 1796*, pp. 5, 13. Cf. *Form of Prayer to Almighty God, For His Late Merciful Preservation*, p. 3: 'We acknowledge it to have been of thy unspeakable Mercy, O Lord, that … [the King] was not cut off for the Sins of the Nation, and that our Land was not filled with Violence and Blood.' See, too, *Form of Prayer to Almighty God, For His Great Mercy*, p. 3.

[112] *Form of Prayer For the Victory Gained under Jervis*, p. 4; *Form of Prayer For the Victory Obtained under Duncan*, p. 3.

Tradition on the return of the 30th of January 29th of May & 5th of November.'[113]

Given the barrage of loyalist propaganda, it is likely that 'an English Peasant' knew rather more of the French Revolution than just the special prayers' and fast and thanksgiving days services' depictions of it. Yet few depictions were perhaps so consistent; and arguably no others had the potential to reach so many people. Not only the 'English Peasant' and the Welsh, but the Church of Ireland's congregations too. Not only 'the lower Class of people', but also the middle classes and the aristocracy. Not only in England, Wales, and Ireland, but even in Canada and India; in February 1800, following the victorious Fourth Mysore War, a thanksgiving was held for 'the late signal and important Successes obtained by the Naval and Military Forces of HIS MAJESTY and of HIS ALLIES'.[114] George III enjoined the observance of fast days on Scotland,[115] and,

---

[113] Penelope J. Corfield and Chris Evans, eds, *Youth and Revolution in the 1790s: Letters of William Pattisson, Thomas Amyot, and Henry Crabb Robinson* (Stroud, 1996), p. 88.

[114] *A Form of Prayer and Thanksgiving ... to be Used on Thursday the Sixth Day of February, 1800* (Calcutta, 1800), title page. The thanksgiving was also 'for the ultimate and happy establishment of the tranquillity and security of the *British* possessions in *India*' (ibid.). The service's content paralleled the content of the services at home. Prayers were offered for George III's safety (ibid., pp. 14-15), his rôle as Supreme Governor of the Church (ibid., pp. 19-20), and for the royal family (ibid., p. 15). The 'enterprizes of all ... [the King's] enemies' and 'seditious tumults' in Britain were condemned (ibid., pp. 15, 17). The '*late ... War in Mysoor*' was deemed '*just and necessary*', and its '*prosperous issue*' and the securing of British possessions were held to manifest '*the signal interposition of ... [God's] good Providence*' (ibid., p. 18).

[115] *London Gazette*, 26 February - 2 March 1793. This essay's analysis partly endorses the central theme of Linda Colley's *Britons* (New Haven and London, 1992) –that the late eighteenth and early nineteenth centuries constituted a crucial period in the development of a British identity, shared by the English, Scotch, and Welsh alike. The war of 1793-1802 promoted this bonding, as previous wars against France had done. It awakened fears of a common enemy: French republicanism seemed as detestable as earlier French absolutism. English, Scotch, and Welsh Protestants' age-old hatred of Popery was quickly transmuted into a hatred of French atheism. Nevertheless, this endorsement requires some qualification.
Different strands of Protestantism could prove divisive. In these years, Unitarians and other Dissenters were vilified as an enemy within; the Methodists seceded from the Established Church; and Anglican alarm at proliferating Dissent increased. And when some Dissenters used the fast days to denounce the war, the stereotype of disloyalty seemed confirmed: Cookson, *Friends of Peace*, pp. 134-7. Scotland's religious self-identity was strong and proud, partly –- almost precisely -- because the Kirk's theology differed significantly from the Church of England's; George III's separate

though the Kirk used no set liturgy, most of its ministers denounced the Revolution from 1792.[116] English Protestant Dissenters, and Roman Catholics, largely observed the various fast days too.[117] For the period, this was indeed saturation propagandizing.

This investigation of the various services dovetails with modern reappraisals of religion's place in English society in the eighteenth and early nineteenth centuries. Principally, it endorses recent scholarly insistence on the Established Church's profound capabilities for ideological and political influence.[118] It also spotlights the very firm belief during these years in providential intervention, a belief which modern scholars are now carefully delineating.[119] Of course, a short essay cannot examine all the subject's facets comprehensively. The services from 1793 to 1802 invite further contextualization. They might be usefully compared with those composed during earlier wars and, particularly perhaps, with those devised in the conflict with the American rebels.[120] In part, the services illustrate the rapid decline of liberal thinking in the Church after 1789; and more could be said about that context too.[121] The providentialist interpretation of events which the prayers propagated deserves sustained comparison with other belief-systems that were likewise self-confirming.[122] Further questions might be asked: how far, for example, was there opposition to the prayers and services from radicals?[123] And,

---

proclamations for the observance of the fast and thanksgiving days underline not only each church's distinct legal status but also the churches' historic differences.

[116] Macleod, *War of Ideas*, p. 141. 'From what I can learn,' Henry Dundas informed Pitt in 1794, 'the clergy [in Scotland] with very few exceptions are all right in their dispositions' (ibid.). The Scotch Episcopalians used a Form of Prayer.

[117] Though the Dissenters might adapt them for their own purposes: Cookson, *Friends of Peace*, pp. 134-7.

[118] It incidentally contradicts Elie Halévy's elderly but famous contention that Methodists and Evangelicals constituted the chief bulwark in England against the French Revolution's doctrines.

[119] E.g., J. C. D. Clark, 'Providence, Predestination, and Progress: Or, Did the Enlightenment Fail?', *Albion* xxxv (2003), pp. 559-89.

[120] Cf. Henry P. Ippel, 'Blow the Trumpet, Sanctify the Fast', *Huntingdon Library Quarterly* xliv (1980), pp. 43-60.

[121] Nancy Uhlar Murray, 'The Influence of the French Revolution on the Church of England and its Rivals 1789-1802', University of Oxford DPhil thesis, 1975, pp. 95-103.

[122] Cf. Keith Thomas, *Religion and the Decline of Magic* (London, 1971), p. 641.

indeed, from others in a plural, if increasingly marshalled, society?[124] Given the strength of loyalist and patriotic sentiment, it is likely that the services' conservative theological buttressing was widely embraced, but further research may add nuances to this overall conclusion.

In November 1792, following the establishment of John Reeves' Crown and Anchor Association, one correspondent suggested to its secretary that loyalist tracts should be placed 'at the Church Door of every Church in the Kingdom'.[125] Yet, from 1793, that was scarcely necessary considering the depiction of the French Revolution, and its possible consequences for England, in the various Forms of Prayer examined in this essay. The Church was powerfully providing the desired admonitions for, ideally, the 'whole British Nation ... [in] one consentaneous Act of Devotion ... kneel[ing] before the Throne of the SUPREME BEING'.[126]

---

[123] Some radicals were simply disgusted by the fasts and thanksgivings: see Pasquin Shaveblock, *The Shaver's New Sermon for the Fast Day*, 3rd edn (London, 1795), p. 18. The pamphlet was 'RESPECTFULLY INSCRIBED TO THE REV. AND LABORIOUS CLERGY OF THE CHURCH OF ENGLAND' (ibid., title page).

[124] In time, the fast and thanksgiving days probably came to pall. (In January 1814, no-one attended a Thursday thanksgiving service at Milverton in Warwickshire: Warwickshire County Record Office, CR 1,707/120, Entry, 13 January 1814.)

[125] British Library, Add. MS 16,919, fol. 25r.

[126] *The True Briton*, 29 November 1798.

Monarchy and Nation in Modern Britain[1]

Bruce Coleman

National identity can involve multiple and complex associations. Charles Dickens, no admirer of patriotic assertiveness, listed some when he wrote in *Hard Times* (1853-54) that Josiah Bounderby, banker and manufacturer, was viewed in Coketown, the fictitious Lancashire industrial town, as a personification of national characteristics and qualities.

> They made him out to be the Royal arms, the Union Jack, Magna Carta, John Bull, Habeas Corpus, the Bill of Rights, An Englishman's house is his castle, Church and State, and God Save the Queen, all put together.[2]

Other items might have appeared (Britannia was conspicuous by her absence), but the monarchy featured prominently and inevitably. In modern Britain the Crown has served as a main symbol and formal representative of nationhood. Though its forms of government are effectively republican, Britain has retained a form of state that is monarchical. It is now largely a show monarchy –a matter of ceremonies and processions, formal visits and good works– but it retains enough constitutional significance to influence people's understanding of the state and to colour the national identity that supports it. This article examines the relationship between monarchy and nationhood since the early eighteenth century, both what the monarchy has contributed to national identity and how a changing nation and its circumstances have shaped and reshaped the monarchy itself.

The subject is not a simple one. One reason lies with the multiple, overlapping and sometimes clashing identities embodied in the unions that created first Great Britain and then the United Kingdom. Historians have come recently to explore more critically

---

[1] The present author wrote an earlier piece on the same theme: 'Monarchy and Nation in Britain since the Eighteenth Century', in Keith Cameron (ed.), *National Identity* (Exeter, 1999), pp.125-142. This new attempt is revised, rewritten and updated.

[2] Charles Dickens, *Hard Times* (1853-54), Book I, Ch. VII.

the problematic status of the territorial conglomerate gathered under the dynastic monarchy. Over the same period a colonial empire has come and now largely gone. Another reason is that the monarchy's status in both public esteem and constitutional theory has regularly shifted. It has often been uncertain, even ambiguous, and has tended to lag behind political realities. Those realities have forced themselves upon the monarchy as an institution and required successive reshapings. The Crown as an institution and some individual sovereigns have attracted strong loyalties as symbols of nationhood, but they have rarely been able to control or shape the development of their kingdoms decisively. The Crown has, not always to its comfort, become more the servant than the master of the nation or nations over which it has presided.

In 1603 the crowns of England and Scotland, each an ancient and self-governing nation, were joined in the person of James VI of Scotland, now also James I of England, the latter state having already incorporated the principality of Wales. Through the fortunes and misfortunes of the Stuart dynasty, the two countries remained associated until they were united under one Parliament and as one monarchy by the Act of Union in 1707. By the settlement Scotland retained its own systems of religion, law and education but otherwise settled for a monarch normally resident south of the border and for the legislative and political supremacy of a British Parliament based in Westminster. England brought other territories with it —not just Wales but, more problematically, Ireland, conquered in the name of the English crown and then consolidated under its authority and administration. Royal authority would, however, learn its own limitations. Parliamentary and sometimes popular resistance to Stuart essays in absolutism led to a civil war involving the three countries and culminated in the 'Glorious Revolution' of 1688-89 which established, in effect, a constitutional monarchy dependent on parliamentary consent. Behind this drama lay the issue of the security of the Protestantism established as part of the sixteenth century religious Reformation. England and Scotland had different religious characters and their established churches represented different forms of Protestantism, but in both countries dominant opinion rejected Roman Catholicism and the supranational authority of the Papacy. Rejected too were the Catholicism of the main line of the Stuarts and the royal absolutism associated with the Catholic monarchies of Europe. The triumph of Protestantism was confirmed by the crushing of Catholic and legitimist revolt in Ireland (William III's victory at the Boyne in 1690 would remain celebrated as the symbolic engagement) and by the 1701 Act of Settlement which determined the succession of the Protestant Electors of Hanover to the throne. Worries that this settlement would be less secure in Scotland than in England was one factor behind the Union of 1707. The Hanoverian succession on Queen Anne's death in 1714 would still have to be defended against Jacobite rebellions in 1715 and 1745. Scotland was more divided in confessional terms than England and the second Jacobite revolt had something of the character of a clash between the largely Catholic Highlands and the mainly Protestant Lowlands. The second rising's suppression provided the final underpinning of the Protestant monarchy of the new Britain.

This settlement had profound consequences for the future of both monarchy and nation. Though the political nation (or nations) had shown little enthusiasm for republican alternatives, it had established a particular and unusual form of monarchy, not the type prevalent over most of the European continent. A parliamentary-based monarchy now had to rule within the law and seek a significant degree of consent. Though the sovereign still appointed the executive, a parliament constituted by a system of representation had powers of veto over legislation and taxation, could limit government expenditure and could itself initiate and pass legislation. Queen Anne would prove to be the last sovereign to veto a bill passed by a parliament as well as the last to claim sacramental powers by touching for the King's Evil. In this mixed constitution, sovereignty lay with the Crown-in-Parliament, not with the Crown itself. The state which would shape and focus people's sense of nationhood was as much parliamentary as monarchical. The idea of 'the Englishman's liberties' had triumphed over monarchical absolutism and that idea became an element in national identity. In neither Britain nor the later United Kingdom could the Crown shape government and the state entirely in its own image. Patriotism would mean not simply loyalty to the Crown but to a broader form of state. The *de facto* recognition soon after 1714 of the position of first or prime minister was a matter not just of the political longevity of Robert Walpole and of the practical limitations of German-speaking kings but also of this broader system focussed on parliament and particularly the House of

Commons. The sense of British nationhood rested on Parliament and the rule of law as much as on any King.

The political nation that had settled its affairs thus was dominated by the landowning aristocracy and gentry, though the City of London was also tied into the regime by the institution of a traded national debt. Despite some differences in the legalities of landownership, England and Scotland were broadly similar in this respect. For these classes and for others who deferred to them or aspired to join their ranks, land helped to define the nation. That view coloured the political culture and gave the landed classes much of their self-confidence far into the nineteenth century. The Protestant landed elite could regard the nation as their creation more than the Crown's and the Hanoverians as a convenience dynasty. The attitudes displayed towards incumbents of the throne –ranging from distant coolness through amused contempt to sharp irritation– reflected such underlying assumptions. Behind these responses lay the realities of parliamentary politics. The surviving powers of the Crown were subject to parliamentary scrutiny and their long-term atrophy transferred much of their exercise to parliamentary leaders drawn largely from landed society. This landed oligarchy helped the integration of the several countries of what became the United Kingdom. The extent of intermarriage and inheritance, of shared education, culture and religion among the landed elites knitted them together as the ruling class of the kingdom, not just local notables.

The Hanoverians were an alien dynasty that initially had few roots, material or sentimental, in the kingdoms over which they reigned. This foreign character, emphasised by the continuing rule over Hanover (George I died and was buried there) and the practice of marriage with Protestant German spouses, was arguably part of their acceptability. The dynasty could not have built a Stuart-style absolutism (such as some, including the American colonists, suspected George III of trying to do) upon such limited Tory Church-and-King loyalism as survived and until mid-century that sentiment was anyway divided by the surviving appeal of the legitimist Stuarts. This distinctly German character provided an imperfect focus for the patriotisms of the United Kingdom and its component countries. The popularity of naval heroes even before Nelson scooped that pool and of the icons Britannia and, in cartoons, John Bull which all developed during the eighteenth century filled some of the vacuum left by the monarchy.[3] Attempts after George III's accession in 1760 to assert his true Britishness had only limited success initially and tended to spur Whiggish opposition to the implicit threat. Only with the loss of the American colonies (a humiliation for both Crown and nation) and then the determined resistance of his governments to the French Jacobins and then to Napoleon did George's image gain more public appeal. George's long reign (longevity has always tended to help the standing of monarchs) also saw a significant acceleration in the monarchy's involvement with philanthropic institutions, an aspect that would continue and grow under his successors. It aligned the monarchy more closely with a burgeoning social activism –health and educational concerns were the most favoured, with the new Evangelicalism and with various sorts of middle-class opinion. Some historians have seen these changes as the beginnings of 'bourgeois monarchy'. But gains in patriotic identification hardly obliterated the German connections. Hanover would be lost to the British Crown in 1837, but Victoria married the German princeling Albert and then their eldest child was married to the heir to the Prussian (later German) throne. (Had the succession not been by male primogeniture, the future Kaiser Wilhelm II would have inherited the British throne.) Until the Great War this patriotic ambiguity or limitation of the Crown was less damaging than it might have been, because for nearly two centuries after 1714 Britain had France as its main rival and recurrent enemy and tended to construct anti-French alliances with German states. The struggle against Napoleon which culminated at Waterloo in 1815 was a prime example. The acceptability and credibility of a semi-German monarchy were powerfully assisted by this Francophobia.

Another crucial element in the Hanoverian monarchy's relationship to nationhood was, of course, Protestantism. Without the overriding importance of the struggle against Roman Catholicism there would have been no Hanoverians crowned at Westminster, while numerous Roman Catholics continued after 1714 with better hereditary claims to the throne. Religion, though, brought its own complexities. In England the sovereign headed the established church and exercised considerable powers of patronage within it; in

---

[3] Some identified the weakness. Frederick, Prince of Wales, who would die before inheriting the throne, himself commissioned 'Rule Britannia' from Thomas Arne and James Thompson in the 1740s.

Scotland the relationship with the Presbyterian Kirk was more distant. In Germany, the Hanoverians had been Lutherans, a variant of Protestantism little represented within Britain, but such distinctions could be blurred in a generalised Protestant and anti-Catholic identity that served to give the Crown serious support among both the elites and the populace. (London's Gordon Riots in 1780 showed the dangers of royal government softening its resistance to Popery.) This religious status was, however, more secure in England than elsewhere. Scotland was more divided in religion, as the Jacobite risings had shown. In Ireland, where a Catholic majority survived under a Protestant ascendancy based on the landowning classes and centred on Dublin, the Crown's Protestant identity would be as much a weakness as an asset. Eventually, in the twentieth century, majority opinion in Ireland would reject the particular nationhood the Crown embodied and create for itself a state both republican and Catholic. That would, though, be a long process and until well into the nineteenth century Protestantism would remain a buttress of the monarchy, a cement of the relationship between Crown and Parliament and a central component of the national identity that developed around both. The sense of British nationhood, itself strengthening as the century wore on, interacted with a specifically Protestant interpretation of a providential dispensation.

Thus the Crown's position differed in each of the three countries. It was most secure in England, the most powerful and populous of the kingdoms; its greatest city, London, was the seat of Court, Parliament and government, and the monarchy had a mutually supportive relationship with the church establishment. Such Church-and-King loyalism that transferred itself from Stuarts to Hanoverians was strongest in England. Scotland was more problematic, both because of its regional and religious divisions and because of actual or potential resentment of domination by England. The Union of 1707 had been only one of several possible forms of association between the two countries. Though George III, who installed the first Scottish prime minister, and his successors worked to improve their Scottish credentials, Scotland would have more republican dissidence than England following the French Revolution. The greatest problem was, inevitably, Ireland where a Protestant monarchy embodied not just the victory of a minority faith over a majority one and of a land-owning elite over those working the land, but also, for those given to historic resentments, of a conquering race over an oppressed and dispossessed people. In the north of Ireland the earlier 'plantation of Ulster' by Scottish Presbyterians had given a different flavour to things, but while Dissenters still suffered legal and social disabilities those Presbyterians added to the political discontents of the island. An Irish patriotism already present in the eighteenth century could see the relationship between the kingdoms in terms of the triumph of Britannia over Hibernia. The questionable appeal of Westminster's government and Parliament was reflected in concessions to Dublin's own Parliament in 1782, a time when the British-centred definition of nationhood had been challenged and weakened by the successful revolt of the American colonies in securing independence as a republic. But any experiment with an enhanced autonomy for Ireland was short-lived. The impact of the French Revolution (which brought renewed war with France) and the 1798 rebellion of the United Irishmen, militant and largely republican, underlined the precariousness of British control. The Act of Union of 1801 which terminated the Dublin Parliament and brought Ireland under a form of direct rule from Westminster, albeit with some continuing administrative and legislative identity, was inspired by fears of the Irish capacity for dissidence and revolt. Always controversial, more so than the Union of 1707, it amounted to an incorporation of Ireland into a British-dominated United Kingdom where Crown, Parliament and Protestantism defined a nationhood with which much of Ireland's population could barely identify. Whatever its legal status, the United Kingdom as established in 1801 would remain an uncertain focus for national identity, both in Ireland and, to some extent, in Britain where it had little meaning except for Irish purposes. Significantly the term never developed a corresponding adjective, as Britain and the separate countries had done, and has been little used outside legal and diplomatic contexts. Always an artificial construction of constitutional meaning rather than colloquial resonance, the United Kingdom arguably did little to create a nationhood of its own. The future would underline the vulnerability.

The new United Kingdom did, however, possess some integrating influences. One was the Crown itself, now strengthened as a symbol of conservative reaction and national resistance in the aftermath of the French Revolution, the Jacobin challenge and the threat from Napoleon.[4] George III, despite periods of incapacity, gained in popular support and he and his successor could install compatible conservative governments for most of the time until 1830, even delaying Catholic Emancipation for a significant period. Another influence remained the landowning elite, particularly the great aristocracy, much of it owning land in more than one country. Their own security against Jacobinism dictated loyalty to the regime and the nation it represented, as well as close solidarity with the monarchy as two hereditary institutions threatened by radical challenges. Even as Britain was becoming a more bourgeois society, it had rallied in defence of a largely aristocratic and traditional political order. Another influence was the armed forces which recruited heavily from Scotland and Ireland (the navy was sold short by Nelson's 'England expects ...'); they developed loyalty to the Crown as symbol of nation and authority, they fought the French and other foreign foes, expanding in periods of war, and Westminster government was their paymaster. The armed services have perhaps been the most successful embodiments of the United Kingdom, though the army has kept strong regional and national identities for many regiments. The most powerful force for integration was arguably the colonial empire, almost continuously growing in extent and economic importance, an empire that inevitably brought both navy and army into play. The empire represented not just wider dominion and a sense of national success (most of the time) but also commercial and professional opportunity. It offered mobility and settlement to land-hungry emigrants, many from Scotland or Ireland, and operated as a safety valve for pressures within the British Isles. Scotland was a conspicuous beneficiary of empire. The Union of 1707 had brought internal free trade and made Britain the largest free market in Europe. Access to colonies (which Scotland had failed to secure for itself), trade and jobs helped to cement Scotland into the Union and blur the distinction between Scottishness and Britishness. The nature of its economy made some of those factors less valuable to Ireland, but much post-Famine emigration went to the empire (as into Britain itself) where many Irish soldiers and administrators were prominent and the Victorian industrial expansion of the

---

[4] On the 'apotheosis of monarchy, see Linda Colley, *Britons. Forging the Nation 1707-1837* (New Haven & London, 1992), especially Ch. 5, 'Majesty'. Colley sees an enhanced British nationalism as 'an invention forged above all by war', though her emphasis on that identity as substantially 'engineered from above' has been more contentious.

island's north-eastern corner served to integrate its economy with Britain and the empire. After the Famine the decline of subsistence production and the growth of market-orientated agriculture made Ireland a major and profitable supplier of food to the British market. How far these integrative features converted into personal loyalties and conscious identities back home is another matter. Despite its Irish regiments and recruitment, the army remained a controversial element in much of Ireland during the nineteenth century, even as its standing elsewhere in the British Isles improved. What was not in doubt was the symbolic importance of the Crown itself to the purposes of any United Kingdom consciousness. It remained one of the few institutions shared by all the countries comprising that conglomerate even when responsibilities of the Westminster Parliament and government were devolved, as to the Irish Parliament in 1782, to the white-settler dominions from the late nineteenth century or to the Parliament of Northern Ireland in 1922. As the colonial empire moved from administration by chartered companies to direct imperial rule, as happened most dramatically in India after the Mutiny of 1857, the Crown's symbolic importance increased. The centrality of the Crown to any definition of the United Kingdom and its empire was clear and the meaning of these institutions would be bound up together.

Some of these features have remained recognizably the same over the two centuries since the Act of Union of 1801; others have changed dramatically. The position of either element, Crown or United Kingdom, has never been completely static. The challenge from a non-Christian, republican and anti-aristocratic Jacobinism after 1789 helped to lessen the Protestant and anti-Catholic focus of the monarchy and government which needed alliances with Catholic Austria and Catholic Spain in order to restore a Catholic monarchy in France. The long wars with France between 1793 and 1815 confirmed the anti-French significance of the United Kingdom and of the Crown. The war against republican France in the 1790s and then the threat of Napoleonic invasion triggered a loyalist surge, so that George III became a more conspicuous focus for patriotism than the Crown would ever be again in a European war. The barely tuneful 'God Save the King' became accepted as the national anthem. This patriotic loyalism came to be labelled Tory, a revival in a new context of an ancient name with Church-and-King connotations, but 'King-and-Country' had broader appeal. War threw up other patriotic heroes –the younger Pitt as the political 'pilot who weathered the storm', Nelson and Wellington above all as victors in battle. Prestige from victories at arms never accrued mainly to the Crown, though members of the royal family pursued military or naval careers. The final victory at Waterloo in 1815, won under an Anglo-Irish commander and with Prussian assistance, symbolized not just the endurance and success of Anglo-German relationships, the monarchy among them, but also the triumph of a patriotically aroused United Kingdom over France and the victory, Europe-wide, of a conservative legitimacy over both Jacobin republicanism and Napoleonic imperialism.

That moment of victory, however much it would be commemorated in the reconstruction of London as a capital city, proved to be an ephemeral high. The political implications of loyalist patriotism had always been equivocal. George III's long reign (his jubilee had been much celebrated) ended under the regency of his eldest son, a figure conspicuously lacking in familial virtues and the latter-day aura of sanctity his father had gained. Despite George IV's well-orchestrated visits to Dublin in 1821 and to Edinburgh the following year, he lacked the widespread respect his father had accrued, as the Queen Caroline episode of 1820 showed, not least for London itself. But political realities also re-asserted themselves, as wartime loyalism faded and the post-war economy suffered. Even the Tory government had to distance itself from continental monarchies and their autocratic tendencies. Foreign Secretaries Castlereagh and Canning concluded that close association with the imperial monarchies of the Holy Alliance was more than Parliament and British constitutionalism could stomach. A Whig interpretation of national identity was emerging –or re-emerging– to counter-balance the Tory one. In the 1820s Britain was shielding republican revolt in South America from the intervention of European monarchies and in 1830 France's restored Bourbon monarchy was overthrown to considerable approbation from British opinion. In Ireland the Ascendency's control suffered as Daniel O'Connell organized the Catholic tenantry and made himself the hero of a new-style Irish (and now pro-Catholic) patriotism. His ultimate goal was the restoration of an Irish Parliament, but without the republic Irish Jacobinism had favoured. Britain itself, its sense of well-being disturbed by a series of economic shocks, witnessed revivals of both popular radicalism and aristocratic Whiggery, the latter attempting to exploit the former.

George IV was humiliated in his attempt to divorce his Queen in 1820; in 1829 his Tory prime minister, Wellington, forced him, over threats of abdication, to concede Catholic Emancipation for the sake of stability in Ireland. Church-and-King had their limitations. His brother and successor, William IV, suffered public defeats at the hands of the Whigs over parliamentary reform in 1832, over Irish Church reform and in 1835 after he had dismissed his government, the last time a monarch would attempt that. The monarchy was bowing to political realities. In 1841 a telling defeat was inflicted upon the young Queen Victoria, a Whig herself, after she publicly backed her ministry against their Conservative opponents in the general election. The monarchy would never attempt such public partisanship again, though its attempts at more covert political influence continued. It had been forced to accept the leading role of the major party groupings in the House of Commons and the importance of general elections. A long process of 'economical reform' had reduced the influence the Crown and its advisers could wield over elections and the Commons through the exercise of patronage and now the 1832 Reform Act had created a larger and more bourgeois electorate and a revised constituency distribution. Politics reflected the diversity of the United Kingdom and of opinion within it and the Crown was being forced to accept the limitations which its position as the figurehead of that multi-national conglomerate imposed. In the following decades the theory of a monarchy 'above politics' developed, even ahead of the realities.

This waning of the Crown's political strength, above all its ability to choose its own governments, also dictated a modification in its public style. Monarchy and the popular sense of national identity might otherwise have diverged dangerously, as happened with various continental monarchies later. A rethinking of royal strategies was assisted (though not originated) by Albert, the Prince Consort, aided by German confidants who had some sense of the precarious relationship between princely dynasties and public opinion. The Crown's and the royal family's involvements with charitable institutions were extended in both type and number, with a new emphasis on provincial institutions rather than mainly London ones. The arrival of the railways and easier travel helped the development of nationwide activity. The growth of what has been labelled a 'welfare monarchy', one involved with the patronage of good causes, had not fallen back even under George IV and William IV and the significant contributions of queen consorts Charlotte and Adelaide had given the monarchy a role and appeal in areas of social activism dominated by women.[5] Another feature of Albertine monarchy was a withdrawal from overtly partisan involvement, with all its now evident dangers, to concentrate on a more disguised influence behind the scenes. His almost obsessive interventions, particularly in foreign policy, sometimes irritated ministers who saw him as both overweening and pro-German and might not have been easily continued in the decades after his death in 1861. His greatest public success was as the patron of the Great Exhibition of 1851, a nominally internationalist event celebrated with much self-congratulatory British patriotism. The fragmentation of parties between 1846 and 1859 gave the royal couple more opportunities for influence, but the Palace, with Albert ascendant, remained distrusted by many politicians rather than accepted as an unquestioned focus for patriotism. Despite the royal couple's Russophobic enthusiasm for the Crimean War in 1854, it was Henry Temple, Lord Palmerston, their least favourite politician, who emerged as a popular hero with victory in 1856 and who remained the embodiment of patriotic sentiment and consensus politics until his death in 1865. The Crown's pro-German image remained problematic, particularly during the war between the Germanic powers and Denmark over Schleswig-Holstein in 1864 and again in 1870-71 when Prussia defeated France and proclaimed a German empire. The marriage of the Princess Victoria, the Queen's eldest child, to the heir to the Prussian crown had, despite their own liberal views, linked the monarchy with the Bismarckian Germany seen by much British opinion as militaristic, politically authoritarian and diplomatically overbearing. That was one factor, alongside the widowed Victoria's absence from many public duties, in the spasm of republican feeling in Britain in 1871 to which some politicians gave countenance. The republican moment was short-lived – except for a new militant republicanism (Fenianism) in Ireland, largely sustained by Irish-American money – but the episode was a reminder that the

---

[5] On the philanthropic involvements of the royals, see Frank Prochaska, *Royal Bounty. The Making of a Welfare Monarchy* (Yale, New Haven & London, 1995), which argues for the importance of this aspect from the late- eighteenth century onwards. It fed into the development of a 'working monarchy' with the diaries of its active members now dominated by 'public engagements' running into hundreds each year.

Crown's claims to represent nationhood and patriotism were not independent of its standing with society at large.[6]

The next forty years would, though, see a further strengthening of the monarchy's position and popularity and perhaps a peak of its identification with national interests and sentiment. The royal Jubilees of 1887 and 1897, the latter a particularly spectacular and popular celebration of Britain's world empire, with Indian cavalry prominent in London, and the reconquest of the Sudan (nominally an Egyptian province) in 1898 would be the highpoints of this phase. The Crown's general withdrawal from overt political partisanship had allowed Victoria to establish a standing above public politics without the narrowly Tory image of her predecessors. The respectability and familial morality which she and Albert imposed upon their court had a strong appeal to religious and middle-class opinion, including Nonconformity in its various shapes. If this style of 'bourgeois monarchy' resumed the tone of George III's reign, it also anticipated the reigns of two Georges in the following century. The more moralistic elements in public opinion were largely supportive of the monarchy as representative of the best in British society. Walter Bagehot, an influential commentator on the monarchy and the constitution, contrasted what he saw as its political weakness with its public standing as a familial and ceremonial embodiment of the nation's culture. It had, he argued, ceased to be part of the 'efficient' government but embodied the 'dignified' aspects of constitution and state as well as the human interest of family life. That achievement included a Scottish dimension. The development of Balmoral as a royal residence, (journeys there would become the bane of Victoria's ministers, despite the contribution of the new railway system) and Victoria's publication in 1867 of the Albertine kitsch, *Leaves from a Journal of Our Life in the Highlands,* helped to give the monarchy a Scottish and British rather than a narrowly English or Anglo-German identity. Victoria even made clear her preference for the Scottish Kirk over the Church of England as representative of the rational Protestantism with which she identified.

There were other influences that went well beyond Victoria's personal preferences or style. The most significant was the

---

[6] For these 'republican moments' and more sustained republican sentiment, see Frank Prochaska, *The Republic of Britain 1760-2000* (London, 2000).

development of a more self-conscious imperialism than the old colonial system had produced. The late-Victorian empire underwent rapid expansion, partly through the 'scramble for Africa', and challenges from rival imperialist powers like France, Germany and the USA sharpened Britain's response. Friction and rivalry stimulated the assertion of national identity and interests, as had competition and war with France in the previous century. As Britain's territories around the world multiplied and produced an empire on which, in the popular phrase, 'the sun never set', national identity outgrew the British Isles. In the process the Crown had a key symbolic role going beyond religious identity or constitutional systems. In the 1870s the Conservative leader Disraeli had seen the opportunity, with the Liberals now led by the internationalist Gladstone, to link Crown, patriotism and Empire in one identity and to commandeer it for party purposes. The assumption by parliamentary measure in 1876 of the Empress of India title for Victoria (something she herself wanted) reflected his personal enthusiasm for Britain's destiny as an Eastern power but also an attempt to neutralize the tendencies of both Liberalism and mass suffrage. Despite the answering echo of popular 'jingoism' behind Britain's stance against Russia in support of the Ottoman Empire in 1878, the translation of patriotic loyalism into a flamboyant foreign policy had dangers and limitations too, as humiliations in colonial wars and the Conservative electoral defeat in 1880 showed. But Disraeli's administration had helped to establish a new political rhetoric and imagery to be developed, more cautiously, by both military and diplomatic means under his successor as Conservative leader, Salisbury. The new Primrose League, the party's populist rally, would combine patriotism, imperialism and loyalty to the Crown with established-church Christianity and social hierarchy in a political confection with widespread appeal, not least to the more prosperous urban middle-classes. Despite recurrent setbacks, that appeal would retain much of its power until the twentieth-century decolonization that ended the recognizable empire. Its peak in Victoria's Jubilees had been orchestrated by Conservative-dominated governments and had focussed patriotic pride on an imperial identity embodied in the person of the sovereign. To Victoria's head on the coinage had now been added 'Ind.Imp' and she showed personal enthusiasm for the imperial role. Also influential were the emerging white-settler colonies, destinations for emigration, increasingly populous and economically developed, some of them coming to assume 'dominion' (largely self-governing) status within the empire and under the Crown. The first Colonial Conferences were held in London. To the confused and sometimes competing national identities within the United Kingdom had been added an imperial identity with the Crown its centrepiece. Arthur Balfour, Unionist prime minister-in-waiting, proclaimed just after the accession of Edward VII in 1901, 'All the patriotic sentiment which makes such an Empire possible ... resides chiefly in him.' To complement this iconic status, the new King's heir, George, Duke of York, departed on the royal family's first world tour, visiting Australia, South Africa and Canada as well as minor colonies. In 1911, as George V, he would visit India as its Emperor, though the semi-coronation of his spectacular Delhi Durbar hardly checked the growth of nationalist feeling in the sub-continent.

The appeal of an imperial monarchy hardly overrode all domestic problems. Ireland remained the greatest and, despite a mid-Victorian lull, had by the 1880s become more troubling. The emergence of a new nationalistic radicalism was nourished by Irish-American Fenianism which cultivated revolutionary and republican traditions and then by acute agricultural depression which radicalised the tenant-farmer class and worsened relations with the landlords of the Ascendency. By 1885, aided by the secret ballot and a more democratic franchise, the re-formed Irish party had won most of the Irish seats at Westminster and were pressing for Home Rule (a subordinate Irish Parliament in Dublin), though its more radical wing had visions of a fully independent and perhaps republican Ireland. The disestablishment of the Church of Ireland in 1869, the Land Acts that followed, also from Liberal governments, and then the land purchase schemes accepted by both main parties by the late 1880s showed Westminster having to treat Ireland as a political and legislative issue distinct from the rest of the kingdom. However reluctantly, a separate identity was being conceded. Gladstone's conversion to Home Rule in 1886 split the Liberal party and introduced a new division in political life which largely, though not exactly, followed the lines of controversy over empire. On the one hand was a liberal, internationalist position which disliked militarism and realpolitik and which, distrustful of the emotional appeal of jingoist patriotism and imperialism, was increasingly prepared to make concessions to alternative national identities within the United Kingdom and overseas. (By 1892 the Gladstonian Liberals had espoused 'Home Rule all round', a devolutionary concession to Scotland and Wales as well as Ireland.) Against it stood a patriotic, sometimes militaristic and imperialistic, definition of British nationhood which proclaimed the assertion and defence of national interests abroad and maintenance of the unity of the United Kingdom itself as the main tasks of government. The latter position emphasised the Crown as a main symbol and particular focus of loyalty and nationhood. The support was reciprocal; through her last decades Victoria identified herself firmly with patriotism, Unionism and empire, as did her successors.

Though the Gladstonians never accepted the idea of a fully independent, let alone republican, Ireland, they sympathised with the ideal of a transformation of a centralised United Kingdom into a looser federation of countries, with Westminster retaining authority for foreign policy, defence and empire. The empire itself was now producing devolved self-government for white settler colonies; Canada (the proto-type), New Zealand, Australia and South Africa had all assumed dominion status by 1914, though the last only after the military setbacks and divisive politics of the Boer War had taken some of the gloss off imperialistic fervour. Some saw this status as India's future too. Though designed mainly to meet the case of Ireland, this approach found resonance in late-Victorian and Edwardian Wales where the language issue and religious Nonconformity generated some antagonism towards the dominant culture of Westminster, Whitehall and the Anglican Church. An informal 'Welsh party' formed on the Liberal benches in the Commons. Separatism, however mildly conceived, had less appeal in Scotland where the economic benefits of empire still stifled the challenge that Scottishness could mount to Britishness. Scotland contained areas of strong anti-Irish and anti-Catholic sentiment, partly as a reaction against Irish immigration into its cities, and the Liberal split over Home Rule made Unionism a powerful force north of the border. Even so, in 1885 governments of both parties had agreed to establish the position of Secretary of State for Scotland as a sop to any sense of separate identity. (The first holder of the position was the Conservative grandee, the Duke of Richmond and Gordon, holder of both English and Scottish dukedoms and of large estates in both countries.) But the main impact of the threat of a self-governing Ireland was to provoke a Unionist backlash in both England and Scotland which looked to defend the unity of both the British Isles and the empire under the Crown. Ireland itself remained bitterly divided. Perhaps the majority of Home Rulers were not republicans or wanted full independence (Charles Stewart Parnell was a master of ambiguity on such matters), though terrorist-inclined Fenianism was, and when Arthur Griffiths founded Sinn Fein in 1906, initially as a largely cultural movement, it advocated a 'dual monarchy' for Britain and Ireland on the lines of the Austro-Hungarian model. As the local politics of Dublin, the vice-regal capital, came to be dominated increasingly by Home Rulers, Irish Unionism found its strongest support in the north-eastern counties centred on Belfast, a fast-growing, industrialized city of both national and imperial significance. There Scots-Irish ethnicity based on earlier Scottish settlement and Presbyterian religion provided the underpinning for a militant Unionism and a fervent loyalty to the Crown (particularly as distinct from Liberal governments) as a symbol of Union. The working out of these divisions within both Ireland and Britain was a painful one. It forced the reduction, by the 1912 Parliament Act, of the powers of the House of Lords, a bulwark of the old aristocratic constitution, and, with Home Rule nearing the statute book, by 1914 Ireland itself seemed to be on the brink of civil war. The Easter Rising of 1916 and its aftermath established in power in most of the island a nationalism that aimed to sever links with Britain and the Crown. The nationalist leadership compromised with Westminster government to agree the Anglo-Irish Treaty of 1921 establishing south of the border of a now partitioned Ireland an Irish Free State still within the empire and under the Crown. In the 1930s a harder nationalistic policy under Eamon de Valera would transform it into Eire, a wholly independent country (in terms of its own legislation anyway), a republic and outside the empire. Stiffly neutral during the Second World War, Eire disowned partition and asserted a claim to the whole island of Ireland despite the truculent opposition of the new and partly self-governing Northern Ireland. This was a defeat, both symbolic and real, for the United Kingdom as an entity and for its monarchy, but it brought compensatory benefits to both and was never seen as a defeat comparable with the loss of the New England colonies under George III. A troublesome problem was now largely excised from the United Kingdom's politics, its dissident and obstructive MPs removed from the Commons (a benefit to Conservative governments for the future) and the body of republican opinion within the larger polity much reduced. The United Kingdom was redefined even as it was impaired. In the province of Northern Ireland – Ulster' to its Protestant majority– there had been created an entity which, despite some internal divisions, asserted a strong British loyalism, the last bastion of the former Unionist consciousness. For its majority the Crown retained its appeal as a political symbol and focus of identity. Even as the old sectarian divisions dissolved in twentieth-century Britain, they remained part of the structure of Northern Ireland politics. The departure of the Free State was overshadowed in British politics by the effects of the Great War, the serious economic recessions that followed and the threat to the established order from both the Labour Party and militant trade unionism, some of it communist-inspired. For nervous conservatives and the security services from the 1920s the most pressing menace was no longer Fenian terrorism but Russian-inspired communism.

No other issue has seen the Crown involved so centrally as a focus of loyalties and Northern Ireland remains a special case. Even so, by 1914 some of the shine had come off the colonial empire. The Boer War had shown Britain's military limitations, as also the lack of British patriotism and identity among its Boer subjects. The campaign for Imperial Preference (a system of tariffs on imports from outside the empire) had bitterly divided domestic opinion and met with much indifference, even some hostility, from the dominions. It also helped to end an era of Conservative and Unionist government. Between 1910 and 1914 the new King, George V, found increasing difficulties with issues like Irish Home Rule and the powers of the House of Lords and found himself typecast as a pro-Unionist and pro-Conservative monarch. A highly imaginative investiture ceremony for the new Prince of Wales in 1911 (thought up by the Liberal minister, David Lloyd George, formerly a spokesman for Welsh Nonconformity) was intended as a sop to Welsh discontents, but a measure for the disestablishment of the Anglican Church in Wales was passed in 1914, though, like the Home Rule Act, its implementation was then suspended during the war. Already the new century was seeing a weakening of the patriotic loyalism that had peaked in Victoria's later years. The refulgent pageantry of the Carnarvon investiture and the Delhi Durbar notwithstanding, the position of the Crown and the acceptance of a United Kingdom identity were both facing challenges. George strove (unsuccessfully) to present himself as the ultimate 'guardian of the constitution', but of what country and what constitution? King-and-Country had found their limitations.

The twentieth century would witness the monarchy re-shaping itself, necessarily, to suit the coming of full democracy, the shifting relativities of social classes and interest groups within society and the changing extent, status and power of the United Kingdom, both in itself and in the wider world. The Great War that started in 1914 shaped an outcome of the crisis of identities within Ireland and emphasised the relationship of the Crown with a British rather than a United Kingdom identity. The war, the first great anti-German war, also forced the monarchy into a hurried abandonment of its own part-German roots and identity. The patriotic mood damaged the careers of public figures with German associations and persuaded George V to transform his family name of Saxe-Coburg-Gotha into 'the House of Windsor' and to eschew the traditional marriage market for his eldest sons. The uncertainties of that new freedom of choice fed into an abdication crisis. When the Duke of York succeeded as George VI in 1936 his queen, daughter of a Scottish earl, would be the first British native consort of a reigning monarch since the last wife of Henry VIII. After a second war against Germany the chosen husband for his eldest daughter and heir bore the anglicised name Mountbatten (formerly Battenburg) and his German connections were de-emphasised to the advantage of British and Greek ones. The once powerful German associations of the monarchy would become largely buried. In time the marriage partners of the Windsors might not even come from the native aristocracy.

The last years of the Great War had generated another kind of nervousness. Russian Tsardom had never enjoyed popularity in Britain and, when its fall in 1917 led Nicholas II to seek asylum in Britain for his family, George V's personal refusal to afford them refuge –fearful for his own crown's association with a defeated, discredited and unpopular monarchy– in effect condemned them to death at the hands of the Bolsheviks. The war's conclusion also toppled the imperial crowns of Germany and Austria-Hungary. Perhaps monarchy could not be taken for granted. At this point if any figures focussed British patriotism they were David Lloyd George, the Welsh Liberal whose government had overseen victory with the aid of the empire and the French and American republics, and military figures like Douglas Haig. At the same time a successful war was better than a defeat and the soon-instituted annual Armistice commemoration established a widely-observed reminder of the Crown's ceremonial and symbolic role representing the nation. Though communism and other forms of socialism inspired by the Soviet model in Russia added to the critics of monarchy and aristocracy and perhaps to republican sentiments, much of the militancy of the left between the wars focussed on other issues –mass unemployment, trade unionism, the Spanish Civil War, the rise of fascist dictatorships on the continent– rather than the position of a widely-accepted monarchy at home. Full adult democracy could be presented as bringing the working-classes and the unpropertied within a conservatively-defined national polity.

The inter-war period saw not only the arrival of full adult (including female) suffrage but also the rise of the trade union-based Labour Party to become the second party in the political system and to form two minority governments, and growing resistance to British rule in India. At least the Labour Party had strong support in Wales and Scotland (though not Northern Ireland) and did nothing to fragment the British part of the United Kingdom. Its dominance in industrial South Wales helped to still the stirrings of Welsh separatism. But national identities were changing their ideological complexion and required some reshaping of the monarchy's image if it was to continue to embody the nation. The *Almanack de Gotha* style of monarchy, already diminished by the war, would be replaced by something more domesticated and familial – less aristocratic, less militaristic, less imperialistic. The public ceremonials of these years, even George V's Jubilee in 1935 or the coronation of George VI in 1937, scarcely rivalled the bombastic magnificence of the 1897 Jubilee or George V's Delhi Durbar. Parallel to the evolution under Stanley Baldwin of a 'New Conservatism', more bourgeois, domesticated and democratic than its pre-1914 equivalent, there developed a modified style of monarchy. George V, at least in his domestic life, suited this development more than his father would have done or his eldest son would do. It was a reversion to the familial domesticity and moral respectability of the courts of George III and then Victoria and Albert. Arguably the new threat from an atheistic Communism encouraged this style of generalised Christian piety as evinced by the King and Baldwin. As Bagehot had observed earlier, the monarchy as family (even family saga) had a broader popular appeal than the dry doctrines of the constitution. Now it had firmer foundations in the extended electorate, both the middle-classes and the respectable working-classes, while the new female electorate was a consideration behind the emphasis on family life and religious morality. The Christmas radio broadcast by George, begun in 1932 and reaching into homes with a radio (by then nearly all), embodied this style. Admittedly this family-based style of monarchy had its fragilities.[7] When in 1935 the new King, Edward VIII, formerly widely-admired as Prince of Wales, bucked the trend with a dalliance with an American socialite and divorcee, the Prime Minister Baldwin forced him into abdication and replaced him with the better domesticated Duke of York, complete with devoted wife and two children, as George VI. The abdication crisis of 1935-36 showed the monarchy as an institution had survivability, but also how little a particular sovereign, even a popular one, could control the political forces of the day or determine the nature of the nationhood he was required to represent. (Winston Churchill's attempt to rally a King's Party around Edward failed dismally.) The Crown had to be what the nation —or at least its dominant political culture— required it to be. Though monarchy would survive —and Baldwin, for all his brusqueness towards the Palace, intended that— it was left with a sense of crisis, even insecurity, and in a form that could not be entirely of its own choosing.

Two other features of the period pointed in the same direction. The Labour Party, like much of the Liberal Party it supplanted as the main party of the left, did not share the types of nationalistic values identified earlier with Tory-dominated Unionism. The new party was, at best, cool about imperialism and its aristocratic trappings, it was less militaristic and included pacifist elements and it was committed, at least in theory, to a semi-socialist internationalism. The first Labour government of 1924 was a shock to the Palace, though George V coped manfully. The second disintegrated over economic policy in 1931 in circumstances which saw George play a helpful role in the establishment of a Conservative-dominated National Government that split the Labour Party and led to its crushing electoral defeat. There followed a brief spasm of republican sentiment in the Labour rump; its conference, roused by George's 'palace revolution', approved republican resolutions. The danger to the monarchy of such resentments was obvious,

---

[7] The trend towards a popular or 'democratised' monarchy has never been without critics, even among the institution's admirers. David Sinclair, *Two Georges. The Making of the Modern Monarchy* (London, 1988), is a sustained critique of the 'soap opera' image of monarchy which, the author argues, undermines its constitutional purpose and authority.

particularly as the background was one of industrial depression and mass unemployment in some regions of the country. Fears for the Crown's popularity contributed to that first Christmas broadcast in 1932 and perhaps to expressions of sympathy with the unemployed by the Prince of Wales on visits to the depressed areas. They influenced the abdication crisis, not least in Baldwin's preference for an unprovocative and moralistic style of monarchy, but the abdication itself added to the sense of instability and insecurity for the Crown and its advisers. This nervousness fed into the new King's highly public support for Neville Chamberlain after the Munich crisis of 1938 when he was invited onto the balcony of Buckingham Palace before celebrating crowds. What came to be labelled 'appeasement' abroad and domestic piety, respectability and stability at home were what circumstances required, an appropriate though far from heroic stance for the Crown when prevailing opinion did not want another war and when the nation itself was experiencing bitter political divisions.

Another feature of the period was the redefinition of the Empire as the Empire/Commonwealth through the 1931 Statute of Westminster which recognized and formalised the self-governing status of the dominions and retained the Crown as the titular head of this looser form of association with the mother country. The 1935 Government of India Act was an attempt to appease the growing nationalistic mood in India by granting a limited form of self-government and suggesting by implication a future dominion status. (Winston Churchill, now the embodiment of the romantic right within Conservatism, opposed this measure, as he did Baldwin's line over the abdication and Chamberlain's over appeasement.) The imminent end of the Raj and of the wider colonial empire was not intended or envisaged by most of those directly involved –George V remained wedded to his imperial status and was hostile to Indian nationalism– but the way had been opened to a reformulation of the Empire in terms of popular self-government and consent, a liberal and more democratic understanding of imperial association. Though accelerated by the wars of 1939-45, there was already under way a winding down of the imperialism of the century's start. Britain's economic strength, damaged by war and recession, was anyway less capable of the high maintenance of colonial ventures, though the dismemberment of the Ottoman Empire and the new importance of oil supplies did draw it more closely into the politics of the Middle East. With that change to traditional identities would come others to Britain's own sense of nationhood and the role of the Crown.

Though by 1945 Britain and its Empire/Commonwealth had a victory of a sort, one without the problems of identity that had embarrassed the House of Windsor during the previous war, the conflict and its outcome had implications. George VI and his Queen had won approbation by staying (though not normally sleeping) in London during the Blitz and had worked their way back from their support for 'appeasement' in 1938, but the hero and embodiment of British defiance and survival was Winston Churchill, who, like Chamberlain earlier but in very different circumstances, was invited onto the Palace balcony during the victory celebrations of 1945. Ironically the royalist of 1935-6 now overshadowed the monarchy as the personification of patriotism and nationhood. The national mood, perhaps not wholly at one with Churchill's speeches of patriotic defiance in 1940, was not anti-royalist but it did limit and subordinate the representative and symbolic role of the Crown. The Labour Party had joined the wartime coalition, shared the prestige of victory and now won office with a large majority in the general election of 1945. Happily for the monarchy, it had forgotten about republicanism, though political changes like a National Health Service and nationalisation of industries implied an arguably republican notion of common citizenship. Further, Churchill's wartime strategy –a preferred alliance with the republican and anti-imperialist USA and then a forced alliance with the Soviet Union– had uncomfortable implications for the nation and its empire and even for the Crown. The Labour victory and the years of economic and social austerity that followed reduced the trappings allowed to the monarchy. The retreat from the Raj with the hurried and messy withdrawal from the Indian sub-continent in 1947-49 (no more 'Ind.Imp.'), the formal departure of the Irish Republic from association with the United Kingdom and membership of the Commonwealth, and the election of a Nationalist and less pro-British government in South Africa in 1948, the year after a high-profile tour by the King and his family, all pointed in the same direction. British nationhood and the Crown's role within it found themselves in reduced circumstances, even though the coronation of the young Elizabeth II in 1953, with Churchill prime minister again, tried valiantly to emphasise the colonial and Commonwealth dimensions. The 1956 Suez humiliation and the accelerated burst of decolonization, much of it only hastily prepared, that followed

Harold Macmillan's 'wind of change' speech marked a sharp end of imperial pretensions for both Britain and the Crown. A Commonwealth based on the voluntary membership of self-governing countries would continue and the Crown's role as its head (even though many of its member states were republics) would be embraced enthusiastically by Elizabeth, but the status and glamour of both the UK and the Crown were reduced. Though tours of Commonwealth countries (and others) by members of the royal family would multiply, thanks to improved air travel, the two institutions had in effect fallen back upon the British Isles (minus Eire). In this enforced semi-isolation governments had to rely on the USA and the North Atlantic Treaty Organization for military and diplomatic support in the Cold War and some politicians even looked to an association with the European nations that had clubbed together in the Treaty of Rome in 1957. Another consequence of the not-entirely willing end of Empire would be that some of the bonds of shared identity within the United Kingdom would themselves come under strain.

The Cold War being played out from the late 1940s saw the Soviet Union, the wartime ally, re-identified as a national enemy, to the immense benefit of British conservatism politically. At the same time the USSR's hostility towards what remained of western colonialism worked against the latter's survival. Also, serious as the menace from the Soviets was, it was a threat to 'the West' rather than the UK specifically and so hardly rallied patriotic opinion as historic confrontations with Spain, France or Germany had done. The other wartime ally, the United States, showed its own distaste for European colonialism, though it was itself opposed as an imperialist power by the Soviet Union and its sympathisers. The rightward shift in US policy early in the Cold War disguised some of the problems of the American alliance for Britain, but the hostility of Washington to the Suez operation in 1956 undermined it cruelly and ended the career of Anthony Eden, Churchill's anointed successor. The domestic politics of the American republic made it unsympathetic to Britain's remaining imperial pretensions (except when they suited American needs), as to its remaining position in Ireland. The influence and money of Irish-Americans helped to destabilize Ulster from the late 1960s and to encourage anti-British republicanism among the Catholic population there. At the same time Canada moved further into the economic orbit of the USA and the ambitions of an anti-British and republican

Francophone separatism in Quebec revived. Though the impact of those factors was softened for British opinion by the continuing anti-Soviet solidarity of the two countries and by the sometime closeness of their governments, particularly during the Thatcher/Reagan years, and perhaps also by the enthusiasm of American tourists for the monarchy and its trappings, the long-term influence of the United States (and cultural Americanism) was on balance unhelpful for traditional notions of British nationhood.

The USA also gave encouragement to another feature of this period, Britain's association with the Common Market (later the European Economic Community and then the European Union) established by the Treaty of Rome. British governments, dismayed by what seemed to be their country's faltering economic performance and alarmed by the protectionism of the new continental bloc, applied for membership in 1961-62 (part of Macmillan's reconsideration of Britain's world position), 1968 and 1971-72, the final attempt leading to admission. Though the United Kingdom had no problem with European involvements in NATO and the Cold War or with normal trading relationships, the political aspects of the European Community would always be another matter. Edward Heath's insistence on entry at all costs in the early 1970s raised but never answered questions about Britain's own constitution, democratic legitimacy, relationships between the component countries of the UK itself or links with the Commonwealth, particularly the old dominions. Whatever economic benefits might accrue from Britain's membership of the enlarged bloc, the political implications would remain negative for parliamentary sovereignty, for British nationhood and arguably for the Crown's own role. The tendency of the European venture in its journey towards a continental super-state has inevitably been to diminish the independence and scope of nations in membership and even to aggravate their own divisions. Perhaps that aspect has mattered more for the UK, given its long history of independence from continental dictation and of self-government under its own law, than for most other signatories of the Treaty of Rome. Though the UK formally entered the Common Market in January 1973, enduring unease and opposition forced a referendum on continuing membership of the Common Market in 1975, the first all-UK referendum ever held. The 'remain' verdict of that exercise stilled much of the debate and Margaret Thatcher put her weight behind the Single European Act of 1985 which pushed forward the establishment of a single market within the bloc. But further movement towards centralised authority by Brussels, personified by the French Eurocrat Jacques Delors, soon persuaded Thatcher to oppose new encroachments on national sovereignty, notably in her Bruges speech of 1988. A fairly direct line can be traced from that moment on to the 2016 referendum in which the UK electorate voted to leave the European Union. Signposts along the way included Britain's refusal to join the single currency (the 'euro'), its opt-out from various EU developments including the Schengen agreement on population movement, its domestic political problems (though no referendum as yet) with the Maastricht and Lisbon Treaties, the rise of anti-EU parties (the Referendum Party, then the United Kingdom Independence Party and most recently the Brexit Party) and mounting criticism of the EU within the Conservative Party itself. This trend was still only modestly developed when the first version of this piece was published, but the two decades or more since have made it unmistakable. At the time of writing the UK has not yet left the EU, but it seems that the issue and its polemics have changed much of the nature of both parliamentary and mass politics. If the UK does finally exit the continental bloc, it will raise many questions about national policy but also about the definition of nationhood. In all this the Crown has shown discretion in holding itself above the often impassioned debates and the nature of the EU as a republic has been little commented upon; the only issue where the standing of the Crown was raised was membership of the single currency, which would have meant the disappearance of the Queen's head from the coinage and note issue. If Brexit means the continuation of a distinct and distinctive British state, it also implies the continuation of the Crown as symbolic head of that state.

The issue of EU membership has also influenced debates about the internal nature of the United Kingdom, though as only one of several factors. The strengthening of subordinate nationalisms in Scotland (particularly), Wales and Northern Ireland coincided closely with the ending of the colonial empire and its economic dividends, though the post-war decline of old staple industries like coal-mining, iron and steel and shipbuilding, all most important in the further flung parts of the UK, were factors too. The rapid economic decline of once great cities and regions –Glasgow, Dundee, Belfast, South Wales– has fuelled local resentments against Westminster government and fed into new or revived nationalist movements demanding versions of local autonomy. For Scotland the attraction of its own oil revenues from the North Sea and of 'independence within Europe' (albeit a self-contradictory concept) has become particularly potent. The issue of 'devolution' (various versions of the old Home Rule idea) was already current by the 1960s, though effective movement on devolution for Wales and Scotland had to await the 'New Labour' government led by Tony Blair and elected with a large majority in 1997. The Labour Party had a vested interest in keeping Scotland and Wales within the Westminster system and devolution was intended to placate demands for full independence, but within a few years it became clear that there was a strong body of opinion in Scotland for independence, one that soon installed Nationalist administrations in Edinburgh. This pressure forced the coalition government headed by David Cameron to grant a Scottish referendum on independence in 2014, but, although the verdict was for continued membership of the United Kingdom, the outcome of the EU referendum in 2016 (in which England and Wales voted for Brexit but Scotland and Northern Ireland for remaining) kept the independence issue alive. All this leaves the role of monarchy in heading and representing the now endangered state in question too. The extent of republicanism in Northern Ireland is nothing new, but in Scotland the position is less clear. Within Scottish nationalism there seems to be a sizeable republican element, as there had been in the old Scottish Labour Party. In the 2014 referendum on independence the Nationalists committed themselves to a monarchy shared with the rest of the UK, though one more independently defined, if independence were won, as they did also with sterling as a currency, but Cameron's recent indiscretions in revealing the Queen's personal opinions on the independence question will not have helped the monarchist cause among Nationalist activists. If 'independence within Europe' is the eventual outcome for Scotland, it will leave a reduced meaning and role for the Crown there as parliamentary sovereignty withers further, while the possible integration of a destabilized Northern Ireland into the Irish Republic would submerge one of the last bastions of loyalist feeling. A monarchy reduced to England & Wales, as it was before 1603, is not an impossibility.

Behind these problems of nationhood, both real and symbolic, lie another development not widely recognized in political discourse. The last half-century has seen a marked decline in mass commitment to Christianity and also a withering (outside Northern Ireland) of the hostility between its Protestant and Roman Catholic versions. Though Christianity always had its divisions, it acted as one of the bonds of nationhood and of monarchy; Protestantism was, outside much of Ireland, a potent force for cohesion. Though the present Queen continues her loyalty to a generalised Christian piety alongside her role within the Church of England, it is hard to see that any Christian identity can continue to support national institutions as strongly as before. Mass immigration of non-Christian populations has added to the problem. A coronation cannot be far away and, when it comes, it will draw attention to the monarchy's relationship to Christianity and England's established church. Some will just ignore that as a historic curiosity, but others may question it as a constitutional and political anomaly. Scottish nationalism has been perhaps the greatest gainer from confessional atrophy. The dominant Unionism of Scotland in the late-nineteenth and early-twentieth centuries was underpinned by anti-Catholic (and anti-Irish) feeling; both are now minimal, even in Glasgow. A truculent anti-English nationalism has replaced a truculent anti-Irish Protestantism as a favoured form of Scottish identity. The Irish Republic has recently been freeing itself from the heavily Catholic constitution imposed upon it by de Valera (a Catholic bishop in all but name) and that means there is one fewer obstacle to the incorporation of Northern Ireland into the Republic and also a more acceptable Irish model of independence for nationalist Scots to aspire to. The decline of public and popular Christianity is an under-declared factor in political shifts in many European countries, but the United Kingdom in its received form may be one of the main sufferers. It could be too that the end of the Cold War around 1990 and of the threat from a menacing Soviet Union has weakened the bonds of political cohesion across much of Europe and left many countries, including the UK, to fracture over their own internal and national identities.

The monarchy has survived in an attenuated form as the head and formal symbol of an attenuated nationhood. Changes like the end of Empire and the decline of Protestant cohesion have brought into question many of the old identities and loyalties. The features which made the late-Victorian monarchy so successful, within Britain anyway, as the focus of patriotism among both the elites and a wider public are, for the most part, not recoverable. A new 'republican moment' in the 1990s owed as much to those changes as to the marital problems of the House of Windsor. How far the monarchy will suffer further from its newly ambiguous relationship with domestic piety and familial morality remains to be seen, but for the moment it seems to have recovered some of its popularity. The long and dutiful service of Elizabeth II is widely respected and younger generations of the Windsors have added to the familial and celebrity appeal of their house, though events in 2019 have shown again the fragility of that aspect. At the same time the dividend that George V and his successors gained from the replacement of German identity with a resolutely British one may have ended, given the decline of loyalty to Britain and the UK within the component countries.

The late-nineteenth century zenith of the monarchy as the focus of the emotions generated by a self-confident nationhood (Ireland excepted) can be seen as a temporary phenomenon produced by Britain's economic strength, world status and imperial reach. Though the monarchy survives with majority support in its head-of-state role, that state is itself now a cut-down version of what it was and with its extent and identity much in question. Except for a few Crown Colonies, the former Empire survives mainly in the former of the Commonwealth, an association that inspires only modest sentiment in this country and is hardly a significant force in the wider world. (Oddly, though, the Imperial State Crown continues as second-best and the Order of the British Empire as one of the hierarchic elements in an increasingly bizarre honours system.) The monarch remains nominal head-of-state for three of the former dominions, but even that status is under threat, notably in Australia, and may not survive the passing of the present Queen. As far as the as-yet-unresolved issue of the European Union is concerned, the 'sovereignty' being argued over is that of Parliament and the electorate, not of the Crown itself. Within the United Kingdom the positions of both Scotland and Northern Ireland remain uncertain. The latter could be absorbed into the Dublin Republic and Scotland's relationship to the Crown if it gains independence is unclear. The old sense of a providential (and Protestant) dispensation in these isles has largely evaporated. The suggestion by the present Prince of Wales that the Crown's religious identity be dissolved into a generalised 'faith' shows how far the nation has moved from the Protestant Succession. God will no longer save the Queen. Romantic patriots –there are still some– find that phrases like 'the sovereignty of the Crown-in-Parliament' have a diminishing resonance, perhaps because British traditions of self-government are no longer as unusual in the civilised world as they once were and so less valued. The recent growth of 'identity politics' which place personal interests, identities and feelings before any national ones scarcely helps. Indeed those identity politics may themselves fill a vacuum left by the decline of older identities of religion, race and nation (perhaps class too). Some recent holders of the office of prime minister have been viewed as 'presidential', though not always favourably, and compared with formally presidential and republican systems like those of the United States and France. Just as Churchill remains the name most associated with the Second World War, Margaret Thatcher was the heroine of the Falklands War of 1982, an episode that did, to the surprise of many, see some spirited revival of patriotism and national feeling. (The damage done to Tony Blair's standing by the Iraq War of 2003 shows, though, that the Crown is wise to keep itself at a safe distance from such ventures.) Much of the public looks to party politicians to provide both national policy and leadership. In the long term the tension between an effectively republican form of government and a monarchical form of state has diminished the monarchy's capacity to focus and represent, except for ceremonial purposes, such loyalties as are still felt to the nation. Even a Crown 'above politics' brings some dangers. What remains of the royal prerogative is exercised on the advice of the prime minister and so can be brought into the arena of party politics, as it has been in 2019, and made subject to the opinions of the Supreme Court.

The nationhood that the Crown symbolizes and still seeks to represent and how it represents it is thus uncertain. If the future of a sovereign United Kingdom remains contested, the outcomes of present discontents may raise questions about the monarchy itself. Certainly the Crown itself provides little in the way of cement for the United Kingdom, however dutifully the Queen and her family work at their public roles, some with remarkable commitment. The popularity —or perhaps acceptability— of the monarchy hardly amounts to an effective bulwark of the nation over which it presides. The institution was not able to save either (most of) Ireland or the Empire. Nations, nationhood, national identities are always to some extent constructs, created partly by conscious political will and partly by less deliberated and more circumstantial developments. The United Kingdom and its Empire shared both characters. The monarchy has been moulded and remoulded over the centuries; it has had phases (some of them overlapping) of

Protestant defiance, of anti-Jacobin revival, of aristocratic and dynastic assertion, of popular imperialism, of Evangelical or Baldwinian pietism, of philanthropic patronage, of social democracy, of 'welfare monarchy', of a 'working monarchy' and of media-driven celebrity. It has constantly been forced to 'modernize' (to use the familiar euphemism). In all this the institution has been more passive than active, used by others, more the outcome of forces outside itself than fully in control of its own fate. Political weakness and malleability have helped its survival –it has adapted when and because it has had to adapt. That survival has often been celebrated as a marvel in itself and as a model of the continuity of national institutions, but the historian has to distinguish just what has continued from what has not. A continuity that is largely a matter of institutional survival through adaptation gives few clues to future developments. The British monarchy has, except in Ireland, faced few serious challenges to its existence over the past three centuries, despite occasional 'republican moments', and the extent of popular loyalty to it has rarely been put to serious test. It may soon find itself torn between the diminishing loyalties of the United Kingdom and Great Britain and tactical retreat to a narrower, if more secure, identity as the Crown of just England & Wales. It would not be the first moment in its history to combine both defeat and retrenchment.

How The First World War Helped Winston Churchill To Fight the Second World War

Andrew Roberts

The searing experience of the Great War never left its veterans. That was just as true for politicians as for soldiers, and especially true of Winston Churchill, who had been both. In a career full of dramatic reversals of fortune, Churchill had seen the most dramatic of them during the four years between 1914 and 1918. He had gone from being First Lord of the Admiralty –a post he regarded with something approaching worship– to being forced to resign from that post and then voluntarily resigning as Chancellor of the Duchy of Lancaster six months later. He then spent five months commanding a battalion in the trenches of the Western Front, returned to London and the political wilderness, before spending the last sixteen months of the War as a highly successful Minister of Munitions.

For all that the Great War had seen unimaginable pity and loss, swallowing many close friends of Churchill's in its grinding maws, nonetheless one good thing that came from it was that he diligently absorbed its lessons the better to fight the Second World War over two decades later. 'I felt as if I were walking with Destiny,' he wrote about his feelings on becoming Prime Minister in May 1940, 'and that all my past life had been but a preparation for this hour and for this trial.'[1] It was true, and the remarkable way that he learned from both his and others' mistakes in the Great War and put those lessons to invaluable use in the Second World War was an object lesson in statesmanship.

On the outbreak of the Great War in August 1914, Churchill set up the Admiralty War Group, which consisted of himself and the four most senior admirals there. It met daily – sometimes several times a day –to take all the most important strategic decisions. This concentration of power worked well and set out the Royal Navy's most important policies and objectives for the coming conflict. Elsewhere in Whitehall, however, the organization of the war

---

[1] Winston S. Churchill, *The Second World War. Volume One: The Gathering Storm* (London, 1948), p. 525.

under the prime minster, Herbert Henry Asquith, was ludicrously haphazard. Decisions were taken by a few ministers called together *ad hoc* in emergencies, without minutes being taken. Only at the end of November 1914 was a War Council formed, comprising eight members, including Churchill.

From his own experience, therefore, Churchill learned how important it was to take a grip on the organization of the central decision-making bodies, and to keep the numbers involved as small as possible. On 25 February 1942, justifying his reorganization of the government, Churchill told the House of Commons,

> Attention is naturally concentrated upon the War Cabinet, and no doubt comparisons will be made with the War Cabinet of the last war. I have on previous occasions given the reasons why I do not believe that a war cabinet entirely composed of Ministers without Departments is practicable or convenient. In other ways, however, the resemblance is fairly close ... The new War Cabinet consists of seven members, of whom three have no Department.[2]

Churchill did not want his own Cabinet to be judged negatively against the war-winning one of 1918 adding,

> It is now the fashion to speak of the Lloyd George War Cabinet as if it gave universal satisfaction and conducted the war with unerring judgment and unbroken success. On the contrary, complaints were loud and clamant. Immense disasters, such as the slaughter of Passchendaele, the disaster at Caporetto in 1917, the destruction of the Fifth Army after March 21st 1918 -all these and others befell that rightly famous Administration. It made numerous serious mistakes. No-one was more surprised than its members when the end of the War came suddenly in 1918.[3]

The theme that the Germans had collapsed unexpectedly in November 1918 was one that Churchill often returned to in the Second World War, in an attempt to keep morale high, especially

---

[2] Robert Rhodes James, ed., *Winston S. Churchill: His Complete Speeches,* (London and New York, 1974), vol VI p. 6594.
[3] Ibid.

in the otherwise dismal period between the disaster at Dunkirk in May-June 1940 until the victory at El Alamein a full two and a half years later. As he told the Commons on 27 March 1941, for example,

> I remember at the Ministry of Munitions being told that we were running short of this and that, that we were running out of bauxite and steel, and so forth; but we went on, and, in the end, the only thing we ran short of was Huns. One fine morning we went down to our offices to get on with the work of preparing for the campaign of 1919, and found they had all surrendered. We must prepare ourselves for long pilgrimages and voyages, yet relief may reward patient and resolute effort.[4]

In the first days of the Great War Churchill had set up a new Royal Naval Division, an infantry force under the control of the Admiralty rather than the Army, which was repeatedly to distinguish itself in action in many of the bloodiest engagements of the war. It was to provide the template for later units that he brought into being in the Second World War, such as the Special Air Service, Special Boat Service, Commandos and the Parachute Regiment. When he wrote an introduction to the history of the Royal Naval Division in the 1920s, it was clear that he believed the experiment was worth building upon. Churchill's godfathering of the concept of the tank in the Great War also presaged his support for all kinds of new weaponry in the Second World War. The overall success of the tank encouraged him to support the efforts of military inventors such as Sir Percy Hobart in World War Two, who promoted the use of various ingenious variations of the tank for use on the beaches of Normandy, known as 'Hobart's Funnies'.

In December 1916, Churchill suggested to Lloyd George, the new Prime Minister, the idea of using artificial floating harbours to attack the Frisian Islands of Borkum and Sylt in 1917, which were a precursor to the use of the Mulberry Harbours off the Normandy coast in Operation Overlord in June 1944. Similarly, visiting the front line in February 1918, Churchill conceived the idea that he later worked up into a Cabinet memorandum advocating the dropping of 'not five tons but five hundred tons of bombs each night on the cities and manufacturing establishments' of the enemy.[5]

---

[4] Ibid, volume VI, p. 6369.

The war was won before that became technically possible, but the seeds of what was to become the Combined Bomber Offensive of 1943 were clearly already in Churchill's mind.

Only a fortnight after the outbreak of the Great War, on 19 August 1914, Churchill visited the mayors of Calais and Dunkirk to discuss the redoubts they were building there. His personal knowledge of these Channel ports was further enhanced in May 1918 when Field Marshal Sir Douglas Haig gave him the Chateau de Verchocq in the Pas-de-Calais as his headquarters, which he visited often. Knowing the area intimately was to prove invaluable in the Second World War when decisions had to be taken about the defence of Calais and evacuating the British Expeditionary Force from Dunkirk. Churchill later wrote of those decisions as being amongst the hardest he ever had to take, but at least he took them with full experience of the local geography, thanks to his Great War experiences.

On 26 August 1914, Britain's Russian allies captured the code and cypher books from the German light cruiser *Magdeburg* after it ran aground on the Estonian coast. These allowed the expert cryptographers in Room 40 of the Admiralty -the codebreaking operation that Churchill had set up- to start decoding German signals. Churchill did not inform the Cabinet, but kept the secret within the Admiralty War Group. It was Room 40 that intercepted the Zimmerman Telegram that helped bring the United States into the war in April 1917. Long before the Government Code and Cipher School was established at Bletchley Park, therefore, Churchill had appreciated the vital importance of signals intelligence.

On 7 September 1914, the Belgian Government asked for a force of twenty-five thousand men to defend Antwerp against the German Army, which was moving rapidly towards it. 'The Admiralty regard the sustained and effective defence of Antwerp as a matter of high consequence,' Churchill told Asquith, the Secretary for War Lord Kitchener, and the foreign secretary Sir Edward Grey. 'It preserves the life of the Belgian nation: it safeguards a strategic point which, if captured, would be of the utmost menace.'[6] Churchill then himself

---

[5] Winston S. Churchill, *The World Crisis*, (London, 1923), volume IV, p. 146.
[6] Martin Gilbert, ed., *Winston S. Churchill, Companion*, (London, 1977), volume III, Part 1 p. 97.

went to Antwerp to try to prevent the city falling, which it did not do until 10 October. He was much criticized for this personal intervention, and in 1931 he reflected on the whole episode in his essay, *A Second Choice*. 'I ought, for instance, never to have gone to Antwerp,' he wrote. 'I ought to have remained in London … Those who are charged with the direction of supreme affairs must sit on the mountain-tops of control; they must never descend into the valleys of direct physical and personal action.'[7] Yet in going he displayed the same determination to be at the centre of events that he was to show again and again in the Second World War, as he climbed onto rooftops during the London Blitz, tried to watch D-Day from the English Channel, attended Operation Dragoon in a warship, visited the front line in Italy, crossed the Rhine in a landing craft, and so on. Doing so gave him insights into the conflict that he could not get from the mountain-tops.

After the battleship HMS *Audacious* hit a mine off Lough Swilly on 27 October 1914 while carrying out firing practice, Churchill kept the news out of the newspapers, not wanting to advertise that the Grand Fleet was north of Ireland. His belief in trusting the people occasionally had to be tempered by common sense, and in the Second World War there were also several occasions that Churchill similarly ordered press black-outs, such as after the tragic loss of the RMS *Lancastria* with over four thousand lives lost in June 1940, the Bethnal Green tube disaster which cost 173 civilian lives in March 1943, and the Slapton Sands debacle that killed 749 American servicemen in April 1944. It was during the Great War that Churchill learned, as he joked to Stalin in the Second World War, that, 'In wartime, Truth is so precious that she should always be attended by a bodyguard of lies.'[8]

As First Lord of the Admiralty between September 1939 and May 1940, Churchill scarcely made a speech that did not make an allusion to the previous conflict. In his 'House of Many Mansions' speech of 20 January 1940, for example, he told the Commons,

> It must be remembered that in the last war we suffered very grievous losses from mines, and that at the climax more than

---

[7] Winston S. Churchill, *Thoughts and Adventures*, (London, 1932), pp. 11–12.
[8] W. S. Churchill, *The Second World War: Volume Five, The Closing Ring*, (London, 1951), p. 338.

six hundred British vessels were engaged solely upon the task of mine-sweeping. We must remember that. We must always be expecting some bad thing from Germany, but I will venture to say that it is with growing confidence that we await the further developments or variants of their attack.[9]

Similarly, a week later, in his 'Let Us to the Task' speech, he sought to contrast the war situation favourably with that at the opening stages of the Great War, telling MPs,

We have to increase very largely our manufacture of munitions and equipment of all kinds. The immense plants and factories needed can only gradually come into full production. We are of course much further ahead than we were at this time in the last war, and, guided by the experiences of that war, we ought to make far more rapid progress.[10]

As well as being used to boost morale, Churchill employed the Great War in his speeches to explain why Britain was in a much stronger naval position than before, as when on 23 February 1940 in his 'The Navy is Here!' speech, he explained how, 'During the last war we had to keep always ready thirty or forty battleships, with all their attendant squadrons and flotillas, at short notice, in order to light a main battle with the enemy at any time. But now this preoccupation is greatly diminished. The enemy have only two really big ships, and they cannot attempt to form a line of battle.'[11] Churchill employed wartime historical analogies constantly, including ones invoking Sir Francis Drake, Admiral Nelson and his own great ancestor the 1st Duke of Marlborough, but he knew that the most powerful ones would be to the First World War, in which so many Britons had served.

The Great War was pressed into service to help to try to explain the disaster that befell the Navy at 1.30am on 14 October 1939, when the battleship *Royal Oak* was sunk at anchor at Scapa Flow by a U-boat. 'It is still a matter of conjecture how the U-boat penetrated the defences of the harbor,' Churchill explained to a subdued Commons three days later. 'When we consider that during the

---

[9] Rhodes James, ed., *Winston S. Churchill: His Complete Speeches*, volume VI, p. 6182.
[10] Ibid, volume VI, p. 6188.
[11] Ibid, volume VI, p. 6197.

whole course of the last war this anchorage was found to be immune from such attacks, on account of the obstacles imposed by the currents and the net barrages, this entry by a U-boat must be considered as a remarkable exploit of professional skill and daring.'[12]

Churchill's commendation of the U-boat captain was controversial at the time, but wholly typical of him. He had commended the bravery of the Dervishes in his book *The River War* and of the Boers in his maiden speech to parliament in 1900 when the South African War was far from won, and he was later to commend Rommel as a 'a very daring and skilful opponent' during the Desert War.[13] Yet on 7 May 1941, Churchill explained part of Rommel's victories in terms of sheer technological advance in weaponry since 1918. 'In the last war, tanks were built to go three or four miles an hour and to stand up to rifle or machine-gun bullets,' the godfather of the tank told the House of Commons. 'In the interval the process of mechanical science had advanced so much that it became possible to make a tank which could go 15, 20 or 25 miles an hour and stand up to cannon fire. That was a great revolution, by which Hitler has profited.'[14] When Rommel was defeated at the battle of El Alamein, Churchill reminded the Lord Mayor's Luncheon on 10 November 1942, that 'In the last war the way was uphill almost to the end. We met with continual disappointments, and with disasters far more bloody than anything we have experienced so far in this one. But in the end all the oppositions fell together, and all our foes submitted themselves to our will.'[15]

Churchill's appointment before the Great War of the seventy-three-year-old Lord 'Jacky' Fisher, whom he described as 'a veritable volcano of knowledge and of inspiration' as First Sea Lord taught him a lesson he was not to forget in the Second World War.[16] Along with Haig, Admiral Beatty, and Field Marshal Sir William Robertson, Fisher became an over-mighty subject, virtually unsackable by politicians. In the Second World War, by contrast, Churchill always kept his generals and admirals under no illusions about their subordination to the civil power. Similarly in the Great

[12] Ibid, volume VI, p. 6167.
[13] Ibid, volume VI, p. 6558.
[14] Ibid, volume VI, p. 6393.
[15] Ibid, volume VI, p. 6693.
[16] Royal Archives, Windsor, GV/PRIV/GVD/1914.

War, Lord Kitchener, the Secretary for War, could not be removed due to his great popularity, despite the many mistakes he made. In the Second World War, Churchill appointed himself to the key role of Minister of Defence, giving him command over the Service ministers, none of whom he allowed to wield anything like the power that Kitchener had.

Churchill differentiated rigidly between 'the brass-hats' (the military) and 'frock-coats' (the politicians), and thought that all too often in the Great War the former decided on which battles and campaigns were fought where, using their immense authority with the press and public, while the politicians all too often had to accept it. In his war memoirs after the Second World War he cited the fact that after the failure of the naval attack of 18 March 1915 on the Dardanelles Straits, he had been wrong in 'trying to carry out a major and cardinal operation of war from a subordinate position'.[17] As Minister of Defence after May 1940, he would come up against some tough and even domineering Service chiefs -General Alan Brooke, Admiral Andrew Cunningham and Air Marshal Arthur Harris among them- but they knew themselves always to be in a subordinate position, serving at his pleasure.

On the day that Fisher had taken up his post in 1914, the enemy ships *Goeben* and *Breslau* shelled Odessa and Sebastapol in the Black Sea. In reply, Churchill ordered the bombardment of the Turkish Outer Forts of Sedd-el-Bahr and Kum Kale in the Dardanelles, which was duly done on November 4, one day *before* Britain and France declared war on Turkey.[18] To commence hostilities without a formal declaration of war was a serious matter, but Churchill was to do it again on 3 July 1940, when he ordered the shelling of the Vichy French fleet at Oran.

***

'The British people have taken for themselves this motto,' Churchill declared at the Lord Mayor's Banquet at the Guildhall on 9 November 1914, '"Business carried on as usual during alterations on the map of Europe."'[19] his phrase 'Business as usual' was to be

---

[17] W. S. Churchill, *The Second World War, Volume Two: Their Finest Hour*, (London, 1949), p. 15.
[18] Julian Thompson, et al., *Gallipoli*, (London, 2015), p. 3.

employed frequently during the Second World War, when it raised morale by being chalked up on seemingly bombed-out commercial enterprises during the Blitz.

At the first meeting of the War Council on November 25 1914, Churchill floated the idea of the Navy forcing the Dardanelles, sailing through the Sea of Marmara and anchoring off Constantinople (modern day Istanbul), and then threatening either to shell the city into submission or occupy it, or possibly both. The resulting Dardanelles campaign proved central to Churchill's appreciation of war-fighting during the Second World War. Historians will long debate the pros and cons of the campaign, but one participant who approved of it was a 32-year-old Captain (later Major) Clement Attlee of the South Lancashire Regiment, who believed all his life that, as he put it, 'the strategic conception was sound'.[20] On December 20 1915, Attlee was to be the penultimate man to be evacuated from Suvla Bay. He was convinced that the Dardanelles strategy had been a bold and correct one, and, in the view of his biographer John Bew, this 'gave him his lifelong admiration for Churchill as a military strategist which contributed enormously to their working relationship in the Second World War'.[21]

The Dardanelles taught Churchill a great deal that was to stand him in excellent stead during the Second World War. 'A single, prolonged conference, between the Allied chiefs, civil and martial, in January 1915,' he wrote in his history of the conflict, *The World Crisis*, 'might have saved us from inestimable misfortune'.[22] He learned much about his own limitations, never once overruling his Chiefs of Staff when they unanimously rejected his schemes in the Second World War. Churchill also learned that it was often better to cut Allied losses than massively to increase the stakes, as he had done by landing on the Gallipoli Peninsula after the naval defeat in the Dardanelles Straits. So in Norway, Dakar, Greece and elsewhere in the Second World War – and especially with R.A.F. fighter squadrons over France in mid-May 1940 - he vigilantly guarded against what is today called 'mission-creep', and often

[19] Rhodes James, ed., *Winston S. Churchill: His Complete Speeches*, volume III, p. 2340.
[20] John Bew, *Citizen Clem. A Biography of Attlee,* (London, 2016), pp. 13, 86.
[21] Francis Beckett, *Clem Attlee,* (London, 2007), p. 61.
[22] Churchill, *The World Crisis,* volume 2, p. 22.

disengaged without allowing considerations of prestige to suck him into deeper military commitments.

'I would not grudge a hundred thousand men because of the great political effects in the Balkan Peninsula,' Churchill wrote to Fisher in January 1915 of the coming Dardanelles attack, 'but Germany is the foe, and it is bad war to seek cheaper victories and easier antagonists.'[23] Churchill was to follow this important Clausewitzian precept during the Second World War, when he and President Franklin Roosevelt pioneered the Germany First policy, giving the job of punishing Imperial Japan only second priority despite its attack on the United States at Pearl Harbor.

At the time of his expulsion from the Admiralty in May 1915, Churchill wrote, 'I am strongly in favour of a national Government, and no personal claims or interests should stand in its way at the present crisis.' Asquith's ability to form a Coalition Government presaged what Churchill was able to do a quarter of a century later, when Attlee and Churchill's friend, Archie Sinclair, by then leader of the Liberal Party, joined him in his own National Government. On 9 June 1915 he had told Sinclair, then serving in the 2nd Life Guards, 'Between me and [David] L[loyd] G[eorge] *tout est fini*. I want a breath of fresh air.'[24] The crisis had finally allowed him to see through the new Chancellor of the Exchequer, his former friend but in fact secret enemy. 'You are a clever fellow!' he told Lloyd George to his face, 'You have been scheming for this for months, and have left no stone unturned to get what you wanted.'[25] The Dardanelles put iron into Churchill's soul, and it taught him that he could not trust Lloyd George or that there could be such a thing as true friendship at the very top of politics. In the Second World War, Lloyd George supported peace negotiations with Hitler, and Churchill was forced to sack or demote close friends —such as Bob Boothby, Alfred Duff Cooper and Roger Keyes— who had failed in their posts for one reason or another.

Gallipoli also taught Churchill how to behave in a supreme crisis, something he never forgot during the Second World War. It is not true that he suffered from depression, let alone manic depression or

---

[23] Ibid, volume 2, p. 4.

[24] Churchill College, Cambridge, Churchill Archives, THSO 1/1/2.

[25] A. J. P. Taylor, ed., *Lloyd George: A Diary*, (London, 1971), p. 59.

bipolar disorder, but like anyone else he did get depressed when things went disastrously wrong. The strains of the Second World War –when there were plenty of similarly low moments such as the sinkings of HMS *Prince of Wales, Repulse* and *Hood* and the fall of Singapore and Tobruk– saw him emotionally prepared in a way he would not have been had it not been for his devastating experiences over the Dardanelles, during which he had once briefly considered committing suicide.

The failure of the Allies' imaginative plan to turn the Turkish flank at Suvla Bay on the Gallipoli Peninsula in August 1915 was due in large part to Lt-Gen Sir Frederick Stopford's wasting of opportunities that were never to recur. Almost exactly the same thing was to happen at Anzio in January 1944, which gave Churchill a terrible sense of *déja-vu*, though neither failure could be blamed on him. Yet he never sought to escape responsibility for what had happened at Gallipoli, so long as it was fairly distributed. When in the Second World War his leadership was questioned, he always insisted upon votes of no confidence being debated in the House of Commons as soon as possible. 'Criticism is always advantageous,' he joked. 'I have derived continued benefit from criticism at all periods of my life, and I do not remember any time when I was ever short of it.'[26]

Criticism of Churchill came to a head in February 1942 with a confidence motion in parliament, and in the peroration of his speech defending his conduct of the war he went so far as to repeat verbatim the very words that he used on resigning from Asquith's Government on 15 November 1915. 'I apologise for quoting myself,' he told MPs, 'but I have found comfort in reading them because of the occasion, because of what happened then; and because of our own position now. I said: There is no reason to be discouraged about the progress of the war. We are passing through a bad time now, and it will probably be worse before it is better, but that it will be better, if we only endure and persevere, I have no doubt whatever.' Returning to 1942, he then held out the prospect that,

> Germany may be defeated more fatally in the second or third
> year of the war than if the Allied army had entered Berlin in

---

[26] Rhodes James, ed., *Winston S. Churchill: His Complete Speeches,* volume III, p. 2343.

the first. Actually, as we now know, Germany was not defeated until the fifth year of the last war, and we are already far advanced into the third year of this present struggle; but, excepting in this respect, provided that you add Japan to Germany in each case. I find comfort in this passage which comes back to me like an echo from the past, and I commend it respectfully to the consideration of the House.[27]

'I should have made nothing if I had not made mistakes,' Churchill wrote to his wife Clementine soon after resigning in 1915.[28] He had made serious mistakes during the Gallipoli catastrophe –albeit from the best of motives- but the lessons he learnt from them were of immense value a quarter of a century later. General Stopford's dire performance at Suvla Bay joined those of the Boer War generals in a long catalogue of military incompetence he had witnessed personally. One of the reasons that Churchill sacked so many generals in the Second World War was that he had formed a generally low opinion of the caste in his wide experience up to that point.

Churchill's command of a battalion in the trenches of the Western Front in 1916 was also an excellent preparation for his hour and trial a quarter of a century later. It was while he was there that his several near-death experiences convinced him that he was indeed 'walking with destiny', and was being saved for great things. The way that he took Clementine's excellent advice to stay in the trenches and not return to politics prematurely –advice that it broke her heart to give, as it could easily have led to his death– also convinced him about her sound political judgement and make heed her words of warning to him about becoming unbearable to his staff in June 1940.

Above all, his time in the trenches taught him what the men in the front line wanted and needed in order to fight well –in terms of leadership, of course, but also more practically in terms of bread and beer, weaponry and equipment, de-lousing and entertainment, length of sentry duty, the least tiring way to shoulder a rifle, and all

---

[27] Ibid, volume VI, p. 6600.
[28] Mary Soames, ed., *Speaking for Themselves, The Personal Letters of Winston and Clementine*, (London 1999), p. 149.

the other myriad issues that he sent blizzards of memoranda about
to the War Office and other departments in the Second World
War. He had led soldiers into battle and understood their
psychology far better than any of his predecessors as Prime Minister
since he had entered the Commons, all of whom had been civilians
all their lives.

When Churchill visited Haig at General Headquarters, he was
profoundly unimpressed by the way that his Intelligence chiefs
emphasized evidence to support Haig's preconceived theories. 'The
temptation to tell a chief in a great position the things he most likes
to hear is the commonest explanation of mistaken policy,' Churchill
later wrote in *The World Crisis*. 'Thus the outlook of the leader on
whose decisions fateful events depend is usually far more sanguine
than the brutal facts admit.'[29] In the Second World War he
deliberately appointed senior commanders who never told him
what he wanted to hear, indeed some of them seemed to
concentrate on doing the exact opposite. Churchill's refusal to give
into the temptation to employ 'yes-men' but instead to rely on his
own considerable powers of persuasion was not the least of his
attributes.

The need for Total War -the complete harnessing of the power of
the State for victory- became clear to Churchill by 1916.
'Everything in the State ought now to be devised and regulated with
a view to the development and maintenance of our war power at
the absolute maximum for an indefinite period,' he told the
Commons that August.[30] He urged the Government to control food
prices, nationalize merchant shipping, and prevent 'the
accumulation of extortionate profits in the hands of private
individuals'.[31] This speech was his first advocacy of the Total War
measures that were not fully adopted in the First World War, but
generally were by his Government in the Second.[32]

It was not until 26 April 1917 that the Admiralty finally adopted the
convoy system to protect merchant vessels. Churchill had long
argued for a system whereby merchantmen only moved in large

---

[29] Churchill, *The World Crisis, Volume Three,* Part 1, p. 193.
[30] Rhodes James, ed., *Winston S. Churchill: His Complete Speeches,* volume III, p. 2485.
[31] Gilbert, *Winston S. Churchill Companion,* volume III, pp. 801-2.
[32] A. J. P. Taylor, *English History 1914-1945,* (London, 1965), p. 65.

groups protected by warships, regardless of the fact that they would inevitably attract far more attention from U-boats, but he was unable as First Lord to convince the rest of the Admiralty on the issue. 'The astonishing fact is that the politicians were right,' he was later to write, 'and the Admiralty authorities were wrong.'[33] Here, too, Churchill learnt from the Great War, and the convoy system was adopted early on in the Second World War, to good effect.

When Churchill was appointed as Minister of Munitions on 17 July 1917, he was at last able to get to grips with the shells shortage that had, along with Gallipoli and other failures, brought down the Asquith Government the previous December. He mobilised the war economy from a ministry that employed two and a half million workers and was the biggest purchasing business and industrial employer in the world. Having held this post in the Great War gave Churchill a huge advantage when it came to dealing with his Ministers of Supply and Production during the subsequent world war. 'I was Minister of Munitions in July 1918,' he told the House of Commons on 22 January 1941,

> and I am therefore able to measure more or less the intensity of the effort of munitions production which was then going on. I was greatly encouraged to learn some weeks ago that in the sixteenth month of this war we had already surpassed by several hundred thousand workers the number of persons employed in munitions and aircraft production in the forty-eighth month of the last war.[34]

Churchill cited the Great War over economic issues as much as military and industrial ones. The day after Sir Kingsley Wood, the Chancellor of the Exchequer, suddenly died on September 21 1943, Churchill reassured the Commons that, 'Our rate of borrowing is incredibly low, far lower than it was in the last war.'[35] In terms of manpower, Churchill also used the Great War as the template for what he was trying to do in the Second World War, and did so explicitly. On 2 December 1941, for example, he announced that,

---

[33] Churchill, *Thoughts and Adventures*, p. 137.
[34] Rhodes James, ed., *Winston S. Churchill: His Complete Speeches*, volume VI, p. 6337.
[35] Ibid, volume VII, p. 6852.

We have already reached, in the twenty-seventh month of this war, the same employment of women in industry, the Services and the Forces as in the forty-eighth month of the last war. The munition industries in Great Britain have increased in the first two years of this war more rapidly than in four years of the last war. We have a million more men in munitions industries at this moment than we had at the end of the last war.[36]

He made regular references to his time as Minister of Munitions, reminding people of his expertise in the area. In that speech he had to warn Britons that, 'In raising the age of legal obligation from 41 to 51, we bring under review nearly 2,750,000 more men, the vast majority of whom are already in useful employment, but a portion of whom will now where necessary be moved forward into more direct forms of war effort. We may later have to advance another decade; in the last war, we went to 57.'[37] Because it had been done in the Great War, it was considered a justification.

Churchill was only a few miles behind the Allied lines when the Germans launched their massive Ludendorff Offensive along the Western Front on 21 March 21 1918, in the hope of finally breaking through and winning the war before American troops started to arrive in France in large numbers. Churchill would reminisce about the Spring Offensive for years afterwards. It left him with a profound respect for the German capacity for fighting even while seemingly exhausted, and helps explain why he was less surprised than others when the Germans launched their massive Ardennes Offensive counter-attack in December 1944 popularly known as 'The Battle of the Bulge'.

On 30 March 1918, Churchill discussed the strategic situation with Georges Clemenceau, the Prime Minister of France. 'The old man is very gracious to me and talks in the most confidential way,' he told his wife Clementine.[38] 'He is an extraordinary character. His spirit and energy indomitable.' Churchill was particularly impressed when Clemenceau told him, 'I will fight in front of Paris; I will fight in Paris; I will fight behind Paris.'[39] Echoes of this speech

---

[36] Ibid, volume VI, p. 6517.
[37] Ibid, volume VI, p. 6518.
[38] Soames, *Speaking for Themselves*, p. 206.
[39] James Muller, ed., *Winston Churchill: Great Contemporaries*, London, 1937, p. 300.

can be heard in Churchill's exhortation to the British people of 4 June 1940 to fight on the beaches, landing-grounds, hills and streets.

In Churchill's great morale-boosting speeches of 1940 and 1941, his references to the Great War were almost constant. In his 'Finest Hour' speech of 18 June 1940 he thrice used the phrase 'the last war'. In his 'War of the Unknown Warriors' speech of 14 July 1940 he tried to contrast the state of preparedness for invasion favourably with the situation in 1914-18. 'Never before in the last war -or in this- have we had in this Island an Army comparable in quality, equipment or numbers to that which stands here on guard tonight. We have a million and a half men in the British Army under arms tonight, and every week of June and July has seen their organization, their defenses and their striking power advance by leaps and bounds.'[40]

Similarly, in his 'Never in the Field of Human Conflict' speech of 20 August 1940, Churchill referred regularly to the earlier conflict, saying,

> It is also useful to compare the first year of this second war against German aggression with its forerunner a quarter of a century ago. Although this war is in fact only a continuation of the last, very great differences in its character are apparent. In the last war millions of men fought by hurling enormous masses of steel at one another. 'Men and shells' was the cry, and prodigious slaughter was the consequence. In this war nothing of this kind has yet appeared. It is a conflict of strategy, of organization, of technical apparatus, of science, mechanics and morale. The British casualties in the first twelve months of the Great War amounted to 365,000. In this war, I am thankful to say, British killed, wounded, prisoners and missing, including civilians, do not exceed 92,000, and of these a large proportion are alive as prisoners of war. Looking more widely around, one may say that throughout all Europe, for one man killed or wounded in the first year perhaps five were killed or wounded in 1914-15. The slaughter is only a small fraction, but the consequences to the belligerents have been even more deadly. We have seen great countries with

---

[40] Rhodes James, ed., *Winston S. Churchill: His Complete Speeches,* volume VI, p. 6249.

powerful armies dashed out of coherent existence in a few weeks.[41]

Churchill's opposition to the Great War policy of, as he put it, 'chewing on barbed wire' on the Western Front, was well known, and had been underlined in his passages on the Somme Offensive in his book *The World Crisis*. The realisation that the Second World War was not likely to produce the deaths of British Commonwealth troops on anything like the scale as in the previous war was a great comfort to him and his listeners. He went into further detail on 8 October 1940, when he told the Commons how 22,000 tons of explosives had been dropped on Great Britain since the beginning of the war, and that a few days earlier, 251 tons were dropped on London in a single night,

> that is to say, only a few tons less than the total dropped on the whole country throughout the last war. Now, we know exactly what our casualties have been. On that particular Thursday night 180 persons were killed in London as a result of 251 tons of bombs. That is to say, it took one ton of bombs to kill three-quarters of a person. We know, of course, exactly the ratio of loss in the last war, because all the facts were ascertained after it was over. In that war the small bombs of early patterns which were used killed ten persons for every ton discharged in the built-up areas. Therefore, the deadliness of the attack in this war appears to be only one-thirteenth of that of 1914-18. Let us say "less than one-tenth," so as to be on the safe side. That is, the mortality is less than one-tenth of the mortality attaching to the German bombing attacks in the last war. This is a very remarkable fact ... What is the explanation? There can only be one, namely, the vastly improved methods of shelter which have been adopted. In the last war there were hardly any air-raid shelters, and very few basements had been strengthened.[42]

To modern ears, the almost matter-of-fact way that Churchill set out the very differing ratios of bomb-tonnage to civilian deaths might sound clinical, but at the time there was much comfort to be taken from them.

---

[41] Ibid, volume VI, p. 6261.
[42] Ibid, volume VI, p. 6286.

Churchill had lost many friends in the Somme Offensive, and his thoughts turned to that 'lost generation' on 29 November 1944, when he told the House of Commons to

> Remember we have a missing generation, we must never forget that -the flower of the past, lost in the great battles of the last war. There ought to be another generation in between these young men and us older figures who are soon, haply, to pass from the scene. There ought to be another generation of men, with their flashing lights and leading figures. We must do all we can to try to fill the gap, and, as I say, there is no safer thing to do than to run risks in youth.[43]

The ghosts of friends like Raymond Asquith, Edward Horner, Neil Primrose and Patrick Shaw-Stewart stayed with Churchill through the following conflict. Yet in the Great War, despite the terrible losses, the Asquith and Lloyd George Governments were not held to account in the way that Churchill's constantly was in the Second World War, when there were two confidence motions in 1942 alone. On 10 June 1941 Churchill said of the Fall of Greece that,

> I never remember in the last war, in those great battles which cost something like 40,000, 50,000 or 70,000 men -I am talking of battles of a single day in which sometimes there were very grave errors made- that they were often made the subject of the arraignment of the Government in the House of Commons.[44]

***

In Churchill's 'Give Us the Tools' speech of 9 February 1941, on the eve of the passing of the Lend-Lease Bill in the US Congress, he used the Great War once again as a balm for the sorely-pressed British people. 'It seems now to be certain that the Government and people of the United States intend to supply us with all that is necessary for victory,' he correctly predicted. 'In the last war the United States sent two million men across the Atlantic. But this is not a war of vast armies, firing immense masses of shells at one

---

[43] Ibid, volume VII, p. 7041.
[44] Ibid, volume VI, p. 6417.

another. We do not need the gallant armies which are forming throughout the American Union. We do not need them this year, nor next year; nor any year that I can foresee. But we do need most urgently an immense and continuous supply of war materials and technical apparatus of all kinds.'[45] On reaching the second anniversary of his premiership on 10 May 1940, he summed up the overall situation, asking, 'As in the last war, so in this, we are moving through many reverses and defeats to complete and final victory. We have only to endure and to persevere, to conquer.'[46]

In a speech celebrating the Fourth of July in 1918, Churchill propounded a message that was to become central to his thinking during the Second World War. 'Deep in the hearts of the people of these islands,' he said,

> in the hearts of those who, in the language of the Declaration of Independence, are styled "our British brethren," lay the desire to be truly reconciled before all men and all history with their kindred across the Atlantic Ocean, to blot out the reproaches and redeem the blunders of a bygone age, to dwell once more in spirit with them, to stand once more in battle at their side, to create once more a union of hearts, to write once more a history in common.[47]

The Churchill of the Harvard Speech of September 1943 in the Second World War -in which he went so far as to offer something approaching a common Anglo-American citizenship- was thus already evident during the Great War a quarter of a century earlier.

'A complete agreement about forward steps has been reached between the two Governments,' Churchill reported to the Commons in June 1943. 'There has been no trace of differences, such as occurred in the last war, inevitably on account of the forces at work, between the politicians and the military men.'[48] Of the Combined Chiefs of Staff Committee he said in his Harvard speech, 'This is a wonderful system. There was nothing like it in the last war. There never has been anything like it between two allies.'[49]

---

[45] Ibid, volume VI, pp. 6348-49.
[46] Ibid, volume VI, p. 6630.
[47] Ibid, volume I, p. 2615.
[48] Ibid, volume VI, p. 6787.

***

In Churchill's speech of 25 June 1941 on the Battle of the Atlantic, he employed the phrase 'the last war' no fewer than twelve times. The shipping losses suffered as the result of U-boat action worried him more than anything else in the whole Second World War. 'I went through as a Minister some of the worst periods of the U-boat attack in the last war,' he told the Commons. 'I have studied the conditions long and carefully, and have thought often about them in the intervening years. Nothing that happened then, nothing that we imagined in the interval, however alarming it seemed at the time, was comparable to the dangers and difficulties which now beset us.'[50] Here at least, the Great War was no longer a guide, because, as he told the Commons on 23 April 1942, 'The figures for the last two months on the American coast, plus those in the Indian and Pacific Oceans from the Japanese attacks, constitute totals of monthly losses which are most alarming and formidable and comparable to the worst I have witnessed either in the last war or in this.'[51] Insofar as anything interfered with Churchill's sleep during the war, it was the shipping losses incurred after the Germans had introduced a fourth rotor to their Enigma machines in January 1942, plunging their Shark naval code into gobbledegook at the Government Code and Cypher School at Bletchley Park. It was not until the end of the year that the genius cryptanalysts there were able to break back in.

***

In an extraordinary memorandum of April 1918, Churchill had suggested that Britain should try to persuade the Bolshevik leaders V.I. Lenin and Leon Trotsky to re-enter the Great War after the Bolsheviks had signed a peace treaty with Germany at Brest-Litovsk in March. 'Let us never forget that Lenin and Trotsky are fighting with ropes around their necks,' he argued. 'Show them any real chance of consolidating their power ... and they would be non-human not to embrace it.'[52] The offer was not made, but it is possible to see in Churchill's expansive would-be gesture a

---

[49] Ibid, volume VI, p. 6825.

[50] Ibid, volume VI, p. 6433.

[51] Ibid, volume VI, p. 6622.

[52] Martin Gilbert, *Churchill: A Life*, (London, 1991), pp. 389-90.

precursor of the instantaneous offer of alliance with Stalin after Hitler invaded the Soviet Union.

The Red Army's resilience on the Eastern Front drew Churchill's praise, and as early as 9 September 1941 he was drawing on the Great War to underline his arguments. 'The magnificent resistance of the Russian Armies and the skillful manner in which their vast front is being withdrawn in the teeth of Nazi invasion make it certain that Hitler's hopes of a short war with Russia will be dispelled,' Churchill said. 'Already in three months he has lost more German blood than was shed in any single year of the last war.[53] In November 1942, by which time the Germans were surrounded in Stalingrad, he further stated that, 'It is evident however that Russia is at least three times as strong a living organism as she was in the last war. The idea that Russia could withstand the whole of the German Army in the last war was never for a moment entertained. Then she had only a small fraction of the German power to meet, but now she has the whole weight of it.'[54]

After the success of Operation Overlord in June 1944, Churchill was keen to emphasise that the central assumption of the Great War –that the attacker always suffered far higher losses than the defender– no longer applied. On 2 August he recalled that since D-Day, with General Bradley clearing the Cherbourg Peninsula and General Dempsey occupying the area around Caen, 'We have inflicted losses on the enemy which are about double those we have suffered ourselves. It is remarkable considering we were the challengers, and unusual compared with the experiences of the last war.'[55]

As victory finally came, Churchill's thoughts turned to how best to mark it, and once again the Great War formed his template. On V-E Day –8 May 1945– he told the Speaker of the House of Commons,

> I recollect well at the end of the last war, more than a quarter of a century ago, that the House, when it heard the long list of the surrender terms, the armistice terms, which had been

---

[53] Rhodes James, ed., *Winston S. Churchill: His Complete Speeches,* volume VI, p. 6487.
[54] Ibid, volume VI, p. 6699.
[55] Ibid, volume VII, p. 6973.

imposed upon the Germans, did not feel inclined for debate or business, but desired to offer thanks to Almighty God, to the Great Power which seems to shape and design the fortunes of nations and the destiny of man; and I therefore beg, Sir, with your permission to move: That this House do now attend at the Church of St. Margaret, Westminster, to give humble and reverent thanks to Almighty God for our deliverance from the threat of German domination. This is the identical Motion which was moved in former times.

Again and again, in matters great and small, World War One was a constant lesson for Winston Churchill for how to fight World War Two, the steepest learning curve of his life up to May 1940. In both triumph and disaster, it proved the perfect preparation for this hour and his trial. 'We have had *no end of a lesson*,' wrote one of Churchill's favourite poets, Rudyard Kipling, of the Boer War, adding, 'It will do us *no end* of good.' The same could be said of Churchill's and the British Empire's experiences –good as well as bad- between 1914 and 1918.

Jeremy Black - Publications

England in the Age of Austen (2021)
England in the Age of Dickens (2021)
Strategy: A Global History (2020)
Tank Warfare (2020)
A Brief History of Portugal (2020)
A Brief History of the Mediterranean (2020)
History of the Twentieth Century (2020)
England in the Age of Shakespeare (2019)
Charting the Past. The Historical Worlds of Eighteenth-Century England (2019)
A Brief History of Spain (2019)
War and its Causes (2019)
The English Press, a History (2019)
The World at War, 1914-45 (2019)
History of Europe (2019)
Spain. A Concise History (2019)
Imperial Legacies. The British Empire Around the World (2019)
The English Press. A History (2019)
A History of the World (2018)
Introduction to Global Military History, 3rd edition (2018)
Exeter's University. A History (2018)
War and its Causes (2018)
English Nationalism. A Short History (2018)
A Brief History of Italy (2018)
Forts: an illustrated history (2018)
Fortifications and Siegecraft: Defense and Attack through the Ages (2018)
The Geographies of an Imperial Power: Britain 1688-1815 (2018)
Mapping Shakespeare: An Exploration of Shakespeare's worlds through maps (2018)
(with Ian Crofton) The Little Book of Big History: The Story of the Universe, Human Civilization, and Everything in Between (2018)
Fortifications and Siegecraft: Defense and Attack through the Ages (2018)
English Nationalism: A Short History (2018)
A Brief History of Italy (2018)
Land Warfare Since 1850: A Global History of Boots on the Ground (2018)
Forts: An illustrated history of building for defence (2018)
Exeter's University: A History (2018)
A History of the World: From Prehistory to the 21st Century (2018)

A History of Britain: 1945 to Brexit (2017)
Plotting Power: Strategy in the Eighteenth Century (2017)
The World of James Bond (2017)
Air Power: A Global History (2016)
The Holocaust: History and Memory (2016)
Insurgency and Counterinsurgency (2016)
(ed.) The Tory World: Deep History and the Tory Theme in British
Foreign Policy, 1679-2014 (2015)
The Cold War (2015)
The City on the Hill: A Life of the University of Exeter (2015)
Rethinking World War Two: The Conflict and its Legacy (2015)
War in Europe (2015)
The Atlantic Slave Trade in World History (2015)
Metropolis: Mapping the City (2015)
A Short History of Britain (2015)
Other Pasts, Different Presents, Alternative Futures (2015)
Clio's Battles: Historiography in Practice (2015)
Geopolitics and the Quest for Dominance (2015)
The British Empire (2015)
A Century of Conflict (2014)
Politics and Foreign Policy in the Age of George I, 1714-1727 (2014)
British Politics and Foreign Policy, 1727-44 (2014)
The Power of Knowledge: How Information and Technology Made the
Modern World (2013)
London: A History (2013)
War in the Eighteenth-Century World (2013)
War and Technology (2013)
Introduction to Global Military History: 1775 to the Present Day (2012)
A History of the British Isles (3rd edn) (2012)
Avoiding Armageddon: From the Great War to the Fall of France, 1918-
40 (2012)
War and the Cultural Turn (2012)
Slavery (2011)
Fighting for America (2011)
Debating Foreign Policy in Eighteenth-Century Britain (2011)
The Great War and the Making of the Modern World (2011)
War in the World 1450-1600 (2011)
Crisis of Empire (2010)
A History of Diplomacy (2010)
Waterloo (2010)
War: A Short History (2010)
Naval Power (2009)
Geopolitics (2009
London. A History (2009)

The War of 1812 in the Age of Napoleon (2009)
War in the Nineteenth Century (2009)
The Politics of World War Two (2009)
War Since 1990 (2009)
Europe Since 1990 (2009)
Ideas for the Universities (2009)
Defence: Policy Issues for a New Government (2009)
Great Powers and the Quest for Hegemony. The World Order Since 1500 (2008)
What if? Counterfactualism and the Problem of History (2008)
The Curse of History (2008)
The Holocaust (2008)
Crisis of Empire. Anglo-American Relations in the Eighteenth Century (2008)
The Second World War (2007)
George II (2007)
A Short History of Britain (2007)
European Warfare in a Global Context, 1660-1815 (2007)
Revolutions in the Western World 1775-1825 (2006)
The Age of Total War 1860-1945 (2006)
The European Question and the National Interest (2006)
The Dotted Red Line. Is the British Military Overstretched? (2006)
George III: America's Last King (2006)
Altered States: America Since the 1960s (2006)
The Slave Trade (2006)
War in European History, 1494-1660 (2006)
Using History (2005)
Introduction to Global Military History (2005)
Continental Commitment. Britain, Hanover and Interventionism 1714-1793 (2005)
A Subject for Taste. Culture in Eighteenth-Century England (2005)
Parliament and Foreign Policy in the Eighteenth Century (2004)
The British Seaborne Empire (2004)
Rethinking Military History (2004)
Britain Since the Seventies (2004)
Kings, Nobles and Commoners. States and Societies in Early Modern Europe (2004)
War and the New Disorder in the 21st Century (2004)
The Hanoverians. The History of a Dynasty (2004)
War. An Illustrated History (2003)
Georgian Devon (2003)
World War Two. A Military History (2003)
Italy and the Grand Tour (2003)
Visions of the World: A History of Maps (2003)

France and the Grand Tour (2003)
America as a Military Power 1775-1865 (2003)
The World in the Twentieth Century (2003)
European International Relations 1648-1815 (2003)
The World in the Twentieth Century (2002)
America as a Military Power 1775-1882 (2002)
European Warfare 1494-1660 (2002)
War in the New Century (2001)
Western Warfare 1775-1882 (2001)
Western Warfare 1882-1975 (2001)
Europe and the World 1650-1830 (2001)
Walpole in Power (2001)
The Politics of James Bond: from Fleming's Novels to the Big Screen (2001)
British Diplomats and Diplomacy 1688-1800 (2001)
The English Press 1621-1861 (2001)
Eighteenth-Century Britain 1688-1783 (2001)
The Making of Modern Britain. The Age of Empire to the New Millennium (2001)
War. Past, Present and Future (2000)
A New History of Wales (2000)
Europe in the Eighteenth Century (1990; 2nd edn., 2000)
Modern British History since 1900 (2000)
A New History of England (2000)
Historical Atlas of Britain. The End of the Middle Ages to the Georgian Era (2000)
From Louis XIV to Napoleon. The Fate of a Great Power (1999)
Britain as a Military Power, 1688-1815 (1999)
Why Wars Happen (1998)
War and the World 1450-2000 (1998)
Maps and History (1997)
Maps and Politics (1997)
America or Europe. British Foreign Policy 1739-63 (1997)
History of the British Isles (1996)
Illustrated History of Eighteenth Century Britain (1996)
Warfare Renaissance to Revolution 1492-1792 (1996)
British Foreign Policy in an Age of Revolution (1994)
Convergence or Divergence? Britain and the Continent (1994)
European Warfare, 1660-1815 (1994)
The Politics of Britain 1688-1800 (1993)
History of England (1993)
The British Abroad: The Grand Tour in the Eighteenth Century (1992)
Pitt the Elder (1992)
A System of Ambition? British Foreign Policy 1660-1793 (1991)

A Military Revolution? Military Change and European Society 1550-1800 (1991)

War for America. The Fight for Independence 1775-1783 (1991)

Robert Walpole and the Nature of Politics in Early-Eighteenth Century Britain (1990)

Culloden and the '45 (1990)

The Rise of the European Powers 1679-1793 (1990)

The English Press in the Eighteenth Century (1987)

The Collapse of the Anglo-French Alliance 1727-31 (1987)

Natural and Necessary Enemies: Anglo-French Relations in the Eighteenth Century (1986)

The British and the Grand Tour (1985)

British Foreign Policy in the Age of Walpole (1985)

THE OLD STABLES PRESS

The Old Stables Press
2020